J. COLLIS

THE WIDER WORKS OF
JONATHAN LARSON

OUTER OBSCURITY PUBLICATIONS

Print ISBN: 978-3-00-059113-6
Digital ISBN: 978-3-00-059112-9
Registered with the Deutsche Nationalbibliothek.
Contact: bohodaysbook@gmail.com
An Outer Obscurity Book.

Contents

Introduction

The Event of the Century
The quintessential social adventure
We can not afford to let you
miss your debut...

—**Superbia**

RENT changed the world. Seen by millions of theatre- and film-goers worldwide, Jonathan Larson's magnum opus spoke to a new generation of musical theatre fans, bringing them back to what was widely perceived as a flagging art form. A modern, rock-influenced take on Giacomo Puccini's 1896 opera *La Bohéme*, *RENT* told the story of artists in New York's East Village living amidst the onslaught of HIV. The piece wrapped Larson's romantic ideals in Generation-X-friendly skepticism, reaching across society from post-Reaganite urban Baby Boomers to closeted Midwestern teenagers. The show's messages of love, acceptance, and struggling for self-truth in a crumbling, rapidly-changing world proved irresistible, even as the show became a period piece due to advances in medicine and New York's rapid, ongoing gentrification. The only thing the press and public loved more than *RENT* itself was the tragic story surrounding its creator, Jonathan Larson, and his death on the morning of the show's first public performance.

But Jonathan Larson was more than just *RENT* and its seven-year development. He was also more than the combined sum of his creative output, comprising over 300 songs and a dozen shows. An actor trained on a steady diet of Brecht and modern classics, Larson the composer believed in theatre's power to send a message, be political, and - despite mainstream Broadway's best efforts - remain musically relevant. Mentored by none other than legendary composer Stephen Sondheim, Larson concentrated on composing music full-time, working at New York City's Moondance Diner to pay the bills.

Larson's work also extended past *RENT*, but it remained secret, something only in-the-know types were informed about. The show's original cast performed a benefit concert in 1997, wherein they sang songs from other Larson works. In the days before *tick, tick... BOOM!* opened off-Broadway, this was the most in-depth look anybody in fandom had at Larson's wider catalogue: yes, there were songs from *tick* and early versions of *RENT*, but also beautiful children's songs, an angry biblical number, and two tunes from the mythical *Superbia*. The Library of Congress held a subsequent concert in 2006 to celebrate Larson's papers and recordings entering the archives, premiering additionally unearthed material.

While tales of the frustrated composer staying up through all hours of the night at his keyboard are true, they are also not the entire story: Jonathan Larson did not live or work in a creative bubble. In reality, he worked extensively with up-and-coming, trendy, and established practitioners in the New York theatre scene, creating a diverse catalogue and working in a changing world where gentrification brought skyrocketing costs to theatre production, leading to creative knock-on effects still facing new work today.

But Larson was also more than even his combined, prolific creative output. While he was known for leaving parties to go home and fix songs, he would also charm the ladies, attend New York's most exclusive nightclub, and obsessively follow the New York Mets. He was the man who called his friends in the middle of the day to play Frisbee, sent cards on every possible occasion, and hosted generous holiday meals. An awkward introvert who wanted to be a star. A self-confident composer who knew how good his work was - and how terrified he was of never being able to make a living from it. A broke waiter who produced some of the most advanced demo recordings of his day. A ladies' man who became one of the gay community's most important straight allies in the 1990s, as his work spread a message of tolerance around the world. A man who composed fun, catchy songs but rarely listened to music for pleasure as an adult. A performer who wanted to be Billy Joel but wrote lyrics like Harry Chapin. A driven creative who took as few shifts as possible to focus on his music, turning poverty into creativity: a simple 4th of July party meant a hand-coloured collage for an invitation, and Larson's annual Peasant Feast pot-luck meals at Christmas were the season's highlight for all attending. A passionate progressive who would be endlessly disappointed that *RENT* could still cause controversy after so many years.

To understand *RENT*'s role in Larson's canon, his complete output first needs to be established and examined - a task previously undertaken for archival purposes but not in the public discourse. Despite the squalor of his apartment, with its broken heaters, grimy walls, and bathtub in the kitchen, Larson kept a remarkably complete collection of his creations, which he stuffed into folders, old mailing envelopes, and any cassette holder he could find. In the aftermath of Larson's death, the expectation among his friends was that a flood of his past work would see rapid release, bringing 17 years of hard graft to light and telling the world what they already knew: Jonathan Larson was not a one-hit wonder.

Instead, *RENT* exploded across the theatre, spawning obsessive fans and becoming an insatiable beast with the media. Attempts were made to bring Larson's work forward, but fame and fortune were unable to change a key fact: all this material was written by somebody's son, somebody's brother, and somebody's friend. *RENT*'s overnight success left little time for private grief.

Even after years of poring over his notes, talking to those closest to him, and burying oneself in his output, it is difficult to grasp Jonathan Larson as a person, rather than a Rachel-Whiteread-esque casting around his presence: the shape is there, but the form is hollow.1 Jonathan Larson was more than just his work, but his work is the most tangible part of him which remains.

That said, readers should not approach Larson's canon under false pretences: not everything is a work of genius meriting extensive discussion. The most minor of works, such as short pieces written for *Rolling Stone* founder Jann Wenner's home videos and a spec script written (and not picked up) for *The Wonder Years*, will not be covered here. But despite some pieces not showing Larson at his best or most creatively consistent, very little of his output is less than interesting, and hidden gems abound. This book's goal is to bring the diversity of Larson's work to light. Areas outside the author's qualifications (such as the composer's passion for and interaction with the dance community) are mostly left for those with an appropriate background to pursue.

Likewise, this book is not just about Jonathan Larson but also the people around him. For over 20 years, Larson's image has been of a man in solitude, trying to write the great American musical. But in addition to his major projects - *Superbia, tick, tick... BOOM!*, and *RENT* - Larson also wrote music for friends, built connections, and worked with some of New York's most interesting

---

1. Rachel Whiteread is a Turner Award-winning sculpture artist who rose to prominence for her focus on inverse-spaces, from the space under a bed to an entire Victorian house.

theatre companies. Most of this output, however, has remained consigned to archive since Larson's death. In uncovering these works, the book tracks Larson's professional growth from a headstrong college student in 1979 to his growth under the tutelage of Stephen Sondheim, through his passing in 1996.

This book is also not a tabloid tell-all. Specific details on his personal life and relationships are left out in order to respect the privacy of all involved.

This is, however, the first volume to probe Larson's vast output in depth. The Larson Estate hired veteran archivist Amy Asch to catalogue Larson's work in 1998, but her volume serves more to index rather than analyse the collection. Likewise, the major publications on *RENT* touch on Larson's early writings and composition merely as stepping stones, rather than individual projects worthy of extended study. For a Tony and Pulitzer Prize-winning author, the idea that 85% of his creations would go unexplored is mind-boggling.

At the same time, the work required to do them justice is anything but minimal. Surprises waited in every archive folder and across hundreds of hours of tape. Every time a chapter seemed finished, a new question arose, and another person needed to be interviewed. The result, currently sitting in your hands, represents over six years of work stuffed around the needs of freelancing and a full-time office job. Paying the rent had to come before researching *RENT*.

As each of Larson's projects has its own character and style, so too does every chapter. Readers should feel free to skip around as they see fit, as each chapter is designed to both stand alone in addressing a specific work (or set of works) while also coming together to tell an overarching biography. While the story is presented in a roughly chronological fashion, the layout is arranged so that each of Larson's tent pole shows - *Superbia, tick, tick... BOOM!,* and *RENT -* is mirrored by its contemporary side projects.

Chapter One begins with Larson's time at Adelphi University, where he learned acting and wrote for student productions, finding his style in the university's quarterly cabarets. Larson continued working in this style for his collaborative work from 1983 through 1991, including his return to Adelphi as a contributing alumnus and his external projects with various classmates.

Chapter Two is an updated version of the author's article 'Static on a Screen,' which covers Larson's attempt to musicalise *1984* and its evolution into *Superbia.* In addition to integrating new interviews, the chapter also includes material previously excluded for space limitations, making it the definitive version of the text.

Chapter Three looks at Larson's side projects from the end of the *Superbia* era to the start of his serious work on *RENT,* namely his creation for an aborted National Lampoon revue, his work with Naked Angels theatre company, and the five-composer musical *Sacred Cows.* It should be noted here that the *Cows* section is a revised and expanded version of the author's article on the subject for playbill.com and again, depreciates previous editions (including that in the *Sacred Cows* album liner notes) as incomplete.

Chapter Four shows Larson starting to diverge from overtly political to character-driven work as he struggled with his one-man show, *tick, tick... BOOM! tick* is primarily known through the rearranged version which premiered in 2001, and this chapter looks at the show's origins before contrasting Larson's original with the published edition.

Chapters Five and Six cover Larson's remaining collaborations from the 1990s. Chapter Five is a brief look at his material for youth audiences, namely the children's video *Away We Go* and theatre-in-education revue *Blocks -* material straddling both sides of the stylistic divide between character and theme. On the other hand, *J. P. Morgan Saves the Nation* (Chapter Six) – Larson's sole high-profile collaborative musical - is pure politics and shows numerous similarities to a popular show which opened 20 years later.

It seems obvious to say that Chapter Seven is about *RENT*, but the author almost left the show out on principle. So much has already been written about *RENT* and its impact that it seemed there was little left to say about a work so intertwined with Laron's death - especially when writing about his life. However, it quickly became clear that a book focused on Larson's work before *RENT* would ultimately be a book about how he reached and composed it, making the subject unavoidable. Chapter Seven therefore goes through *RENT*'s development history and Larson's maturation as a writer, bound together with input from those who were on the ground in the show's early years.

The epilogue tells the story of 1999's abandoned *1/2 MT House* project, the first attempt to bring Larson's back catalogue to the stage.

Appendix A covers Larson's smaller musical side projects, namely his dance scores for the Brenda Daniels Dance Company and standalone pop songs. Some of these pieces have extended backstories; others were just fun to write about.

Appendix B is a bonus for *RENT* fans; a series of side stories and analyses which were too long to keep with the main narrative, such as a breakdown comparing scenes in *RENT* to *La Bohème,* an overview of at noteworthy material lost in revision, and summaries of Larson's backstories for the major characters.

Appendix C features detailed synopses for major revisions of *Superbia, tick, tick... BOOM!*, *J.P. Morgan Saves the Nation,* and *RENT.* Even people who were involved in these shows routinely got timelines and editions mixed up, and there should be no shame in flipping (or clicking) to the back for a refresh, especially when Larson had a tendency to restructure his major shows at some point in development.

Virtually all of the research in this book comes from primary sources, with an overwhelming focus on the Jonathan Larson Collection at the Library of Congress. In addition to Larson's papers and recordings, the author reached out to as many direct collaborators and participants in his projects as possible in an attempt to allow previously-unheard voices to contribute their own perspectives to the story. Over 80% of those approached agreed to participate in the project, resulting in approximately 100 interviews being conducted with just over 60 of Larson's contemporaries. New interviews are referred to in the present, journalistic tense ('She remembers'), whereas interviews taken from books, videos, etc. are referred to in the past tense ('At the service, he said'). For previously existing material, such as interviews from the 1997 *RENT* collector's book, CD liner notes, or memorial speeches, standard citations are provided. Any interviews or quotes without citations are from personal communications with the quoted subject, an attempt to keep the footnotes under control. All theatrical definitions come from the English edition of Patrice Pavis' *Dictionary of Theatre* and are cited accordingly.

Regarding archival citations: material from the Jonathan Larson collection at the Library of Congress is cited either by box and folder or by MAVIS (digital audio file reference) number. Pages for handwritten and printed material in the archive are not always available, as the numbering was inconsistently added by Library staff. In some additional cases, material was kept in a notebook, rather than loose-leaf paper, and these materials were left unnumbered. Cited numbers including an 'H' are handwritten numbers added by the Library of Congress.

Audio files are kept by the Library as one file per tape side/reel/

DAT, and metadata is often incomplete or missing in the system: Larson was not always the best at labelling his tapes beyond what made sense to him, and tape labels were often not transcribed for the digitised audio. Likewise, performers are frequently uncredited even when metadata exists, depending on what material Larson kept from the recording sessions (and even these often contain only first names). Larson was entirely reliant upon his computer for annotating sheet music, making any pre-1989 recordings vital to appreciate his musical output. For a researcher with no training in music theory and unable to carry a tune, the post-1989 recordings were just as necessary.

At the time of writing, no video material was held in the Larson Collection, and all videos referenced in this text are courtesy of Victoria Leacock Hoffman's private collection. As the book entered late-stage revisions, Leacock Hoffman's videos began their journey through the Library's ingest process and will be available for future researchers to reference, though not in time to rearrange the citations here.

With shows like *Next to Normal* and *Hamilton* capturing audiences and continuing Larson's dreams, the theatre has started catching up to Jonathan Larson. Now it's time to catch up with *him*.

Chapter One

From Here On In...
Student and Early Projects (1979-1991)

Am I human?
If I'm pricked, do I bleed?
I've got all the guilt
And more money than I need

—**Prostate of the Union**

The Beginning

JONATHAN LARSON WAS born on 4 February 1960, and grew up in White Plains, NY. Raised by his parents, Allan and Nanette, Larson's upbringing was standard and suburban. Older sister Julie Larson McCollum remembers her brother's childhood thusly:

> Growing up, [he was] always doing creative things. When we had to do book reports, he'd say 'I'd like to make a movie' and use our dad's Super 8 camera. He was always creative [but] horrible at sports, which was tough for him. In third grade or something, he wrote a play for his class. He was absolutely a wonderful presence on stage. He was the

king of White Plains High School['s] theatre. He was goofy and funny and we were intensely close.

In high school, he would always be at the piano, and everyone called him 'Piano Man.' He played a lot of Billy Joel, and that was his crutch - he'd sit at the piano at a party and just play. He only had a couple years of formal piano lessons because he didn't want to be stuck playing classical music, but he could listen to something and just play it with passion - not with accuracy but with absolute passion. He and I would spend lots of time listening to Broadway musicals and reading the backs of [the records].

We had what I consider a *Leave it to Beaver* childhood in the suburbs but [lived] only a half hour outside of [New York City], so we would go into the city and see the Rockettes, and go to the [Metropolitan Museum of Art], and see Broadway shows on special occasions, but basically, we'd be hanging out with friends and riding our bikes and creating our own fun. He played the trumpet and then tuba in the [school] orchestra. We really had a very nice childhood.

Upon completing high school, Larson attended Adelphi University in Garden City, NY, on a four-year acting scholarship. According to Nick Petron, one of Larson's professors and now head of Adelphi's theatre department, Larson received the scholarship not only for his acting skills but also for these very 'Piano Man' qualities: at his audition, Larson sat in front of a piano and took requests from the other auditionees, keeping spirits high amongst the group. The staff recognised the young performer's charisma, tipping the odds in his favour.

Man of 1000 Faces

In 1973, charismatic department chair Jacques Burdick rebuilt Adelphi University's theatre department following a four-year sabbatical at Yale Drama School. Burdick, forced to return or lose his tenure, had taken to Yale's practice-driven methodologies - as devised by his own mentor, theatrical radicalist Robert Brustein - and struck a deal that, upon his return, he could implement a similar structure built on repertory producing at Adelphi:[1]

"[Burdick] was a big influence on us," recollects Larson's fellow student and collaborator Dan Kagan. "He was sort of a bully and sort of a baby. We all sat at his feet. He had so much knowledge and [was] so much above what we were capable of knowing at that point, and he never babied us in any way. Even if we didn't get it, he just wanted us to hear what he had to say."

Todd Robinson, Larson's on-and-off roommate at Adelphi and beyond, remembered Burdick as "a consummate intellectual. Beyond that was a true mentor. Intimidating at times, wildly brilliant. He taught you principles to live by: you think he's teaching you about theatre, but really he's teaching you about life, and those lessons are powerful metaphors and onions that are never

---

1. Patrice Pavis defines 'repertory' as "the classics, contemporary creations, and everything that a director deems useful for drawing up a quality program structured over several years." (308) Historically, theatre companies would hire actors to fill stock character types and build a season around the company's talents, with shows rotating on and off the schedule every few days or weeks. New cast members in repertory companies would work their way up from ensemble to supporting or leading roles over years, making a single theatre their professional home. Opera companies still follow this model, as do companies such as the National Theatre in London, GRIPS Theater in Berlin, Germany, and the Takarazuka Revue in Japan.

fully peeled. He could be intense and critical and 100% human."
Robinson's younger sister Traci, who began studying theatre at
Adelphi a year later, agrees: "They said 'if there's anything that you
can do in this world and be happy doing it, then do it, because it's
the only thing you'll ever want to do.' They said it to my brother
the year before; they said it to everybody. It set you off on a trajectory of what you wanted to do - or not to do."

In addition to teaching theatrical history and practice, Burdick
also taught his students to approach their craft philosophically.
Burdick's 1974 book on the subject, *Theater*, begins with his own
definition of the form:

> THE UNWRITTEN HISTORY of theater is the
> history of mankind, for in its essentials that set of
> human actions which the ancient Greeks formal-
> ized as *theater* belongs to no single race, age, or cul-
> ture. It is, rather, an act of language, one by which
> the dangerous phenomenal world is safely imitated
> and celebrated. This act, lying as it does at the very
> heart of ritual, has been common to all men - albeit
> in varying degrees - since man was created.[2]

In discussing the Greek origins of modern theatre, Burdick
introduced his students to the idea of *kefi*, which he described
in *Theater* as "spontaneous good humor" (presumably referring
to both mood and the laugh-inducing sort).[3] In a letter, read by
Adelphi alumnus Nancy Mansbach at Larson's memorial service,
Burdick explained further: "It has no true equivalent in our culture, but it means a quality of existence, a kind of generous grace,
that if it is present, the simplest food becomes a feast, a hole in

---

2. Jacques Burdick, *Theater* (New York: Newsweek Books, 1974), 7.

3. Ibid., 8.

the wall becomes the Ritz. *Kefi* became something special for us."[4] After graduating, Larson kept a note with the word '*kefi*' tacked up on a board by his desk.

Burdick also shared an early impression of Larson in the same letter:

> I had said to his class, "Theatre is a type of mistress: 7-15 years of making the rounds, finding an agent, no work you like, too little money, poor food, poor clothes. You're never through paying your dues. If you're not sure you can put up with that, get out now." After class, Jonathan came up to me with that wide-eyed look he always had when he was serious. He just said, "I don't have a choice. I don't know what all those things mean, but I'll do them. I'll pay my dues." I can't remember any other beginning actor with such self-confidence.[5]

In addition to Burdick and Petron, Larson made numerous friends in the theatre programme and stuck with many of them for the rest of his life. Among them, he became particularly close to Victoria Leacock, a freshman during his senior year.[6] The two dated for a while before Larson's graduation, and she remained his close friend and champion after.

---

4. Jonathan Larson Memorial Service. Video. 3 Feb 1996. Privately held by Victoria Leacock Hoffman, Washington, D.C.

5. Ibid.

6. I use 'Victoria Leacock' if her maiden name was used in an interview or a specific historical reference. Interviews conducted during this book's production refer to her using her current name, 'Victoria Leacock Hoffman.'

Lay Your Hands-On On Me

"We learned by doing", recalls Larson's classmate, David Glenn Armstrong. "We had a show on almost every week. There were four main stage shows, four cabarets, and 20-25 shows in the studio." "We were all well-rounded," remembers Alicia Stone, another of Larson's university colleagues. "Everyone learned all aspects of the theatre at Adelphi and how everybody worked together as a team."

Despite putting up so many shows, Adelphi University had no house acting style. Whereas most conservatories offer programmes focusing on classical acting, method acting (placing oneself inside the scene by becoming the character), or other acting types, each of Adelphi's staff had their own preferences and would teach their classes and direct productions as they saw fit: "It was very Uta Hagen [basing acting on personal experience] and Fourth Wall [acting realistically, as though there were no audience], definitely no method," remembers Armstrong. The main influence, he says, was Burdick, who focused on Brechtian acting: "It was very presentational - say the words and get out of the way."[7]

Setting Adelphi's department apart from other acting and conservatory programmes was its focus on an all-inclusive immersion. When not acting, students would work technical positions, make costumes, write, stage manage, paint sets, or work other jobs behind the scenes to feed the constant churn of new shows. During summer, most students would continue working backstage on the school's summer productions, which were performed by professional actors. While the programme focused on producing well-rounded practitioners, students would also be encouraged to pursue their specialties and build upon their talents, including the musical Larson. According to Petron, "he had this actual spark,

---

7. Pavis defines Brechtian acting as one which "favours audience participation, mainly through the demonstrative ('showing') nature of the acting." (39)

and he wanted to do this thing - badly - and he did. He was always driving himself."

At the same time, Burdick and the staff made sure not to let anybody become too precious: for example, musical or classically-focused actors would be intentionally excluded from relevant productions, nor would senior year status guarantee leading roles. Likewise, harsh comments from the staff were in no short supply. Students would be flatly judged on appearances and habits - whether it be to lose weight or butch up - as though their professors were demonic incarnations of casting agents. "They didn't hold anything back," remembers Traci Robinson. "What they said to me was, 'don't let your looks get you where you might go.'"

Todd Robinson was Larson's roommate for a year and a half and remembers starting in the department:

> I was a transfer student, [so] I was a year ahead
> of Jonathan, but because of how the department
> worked at that time, you had to go through their
> boot camp. I had to catch up, and would graduate
> on time, but I was put in with Jonathan's class. I
> met [him] on the first day of school and he was
> very musical, right from the beginning. There was
> this grand piano in the rehearsal studio, and from
> day one, he was on there, banging away on Billy
> Joel and Elton John. I walked up to him, and I
> made some remark about Barry Manilow, because
> Barry Manilow was a piano player and he had
> that crossover musical theatre vibe going on, and
> Jonathan looked at me like I had six heads. I had
> just invoked the name of Satan. It was hilarious. I
> didn't realise how uncool [that] was.

The following winter, Larson wrote a letter to Stephen

Sondheim, even then acknowledged as one of the great composers in musical theatre. Sondheim replied with a kind - albeit generic - response, which was enough to send Larson leaping for joy. Says Robinson:

> I thought Jonathan's head was going to explode. He'd already read the letter and was like, "Sit down, sit down, you have to listen to this!" He read me the letter from Steven Sondheim, which was nothing more than an encouraging note, but he would not let me touch the letter. He would let me look at it. He'd be happy to read it to me. But he would not let me physically touch the letter.

To Days of Inspiration

In the autumn of 1979, Larson's sophomore year, Burdick approached him about scoring a new musical for that year's freshman workshop: an adaptation of Spanish poet Juan Ruiz's medieval narratives titled *El Libro del Buen Amor*.[8] According to Larson's sister, Julie, being asked to score *El Libro* validated Larson's burgeoning sense of self as a composer, and he threw himself into the project.

The cast were less thrilled: the freshman workshop was centred on the performers mocking themselves in front of a paying audience. As Traci Robinson remembers: "I was this young, sweet, innocent ingénue virgin, and [Burdick] cast me as the town harlot. You had to do whatever they said, [which was] what you were not comfortable doing."

In a proposal for *El Libro*, Burdick described the show as: "Presented in the style of COMEDIA DEL ARTE by a troupe of

---

8. Ruiz is the creator of legendary lover Don Juan.

seven performers. Three are principals, and the other four who [play all of the others (sic) roles. This keeping in style with Comedia del Arte, [...] it should be clear that they are serving as players and should be applauded for their skills."[9] In practice, however, the cast proved to be much larger, and the show was expanded to accommodate 14 performers, with three principals and three members of 'The Tuna,' a group of onstage troubadours narrating and playing supporting characters, plus eight more actors in the ensemble.

Musically, *El Libro del Buen Amor* is built upon Spanish folk music such as flamenco, which forced Larson to work to form. While songs such as 'Don't Slander Love' and 'Wandering Students Song' veer towards the sound of 1970s Broadway, the score never strays too far from the medieval and Renaissance traditions at its core. Jauntier than *Man of La Mancha*, *El Libro*'s musical fusion never quite comes together, but recordings reveal the composer's potential nonetheless.

The show meant enough to Larson that he kept his composition notebook from the production, which he used as a journal rather than for the music paper its sheets contained. In his early entries, Larson commented on vocal exercises and the professional difficulties of working as a music director with friends and fellow students. Later, Larson vented his frustration with finding the music in his head and scrambling to make deadline: "Prepare everything for Sunday. Read something!!! Get another angle. Work!!!"[10] Two days later, and nine days to opening, Larson replied to himself: "I am far ahead of the game. I have the majority of my songs written."[11] He continued to outline ideas for the remaining numbers (Burdick was yet to provide the lyrics), and Larson

---

9. Jacques Burdick. *El Libro del Buen Amor* (Synopsis). Box 7, Folder 1, Jonathan Larson Papers, Music Division, Library of Congress, Washington, D.C.

10. Ibid. Underlines in original

11. Ibid.

stopped journaling before production week. Following its run at Adelphi, *El Libro del Buen Amor* would be revised and performed in 1985 at the University of Missouri.

Larson's second show, *The Steak Tartare Caper*, was performed in April 1981. "He wanted to do something set in Chicago in the 1940's," says Petron, who wrote the script and most of the lyrics: "His father had spent some time there, and while he wasn't that fond of Nick and Nora Charles, I liked them." Featuring music by Larson and additional lyrics by Dan Kagan, *Steak Tartare* brought various American mystery heroes (e.g. Nancy Drew and the aforementioned Charles siblings) together to solve a crime. Set at the end of the Great Depression, the score is reminiscent of Kander & Ebb's *Chicago*, with hefty tributes to early jazz and swing.[12]

Unfortunately, Larson did not keep the script from *Steak Tartare*, making it difficult to judge the work as a whole or to see a clearer influence on his later work. As with *El Libro*, Larson was working in a confined genre, and being tapped by his mentors would have been a boost to his spirit, but the work lacks the flourishes (fugues, rapid counterpoint, popular influences) which would ultimately define his style. For that, Larson would need to turn to Adelphi's quarterly student cabarets.

Life is a Cabaret

Adelphi's cabarets - instituted when Jacques Burdick took over the theatre department - were (and remain) based in the Germanic tradition of *kabarett*: a style of hastily composed shows packed with contemporary political targets, music, and a rowdy atmosphere full of heady, yet shocking, humour.[13] In the 1960s, TV shows such as

---

12. The finale, 'Crime Don't Pay,' cribbed its piano riff from *The Music Man*'s 'Marian the Librarian'.

13. Pavis ignores *kabarett* in his dictionary, merely listing it as one of many

That Was the Week That Was brought the form to the small screen, but the form always thrived best on the stage where, today, groups like the Capitol Steps in Washington, DC continue the tradition.[14]

Nick Petron remembers how he got involved: "I met Jacques at a cabaret workshop up in New Haven, at [Yale] Drama School one summer, and when I was back down here finishing my Master's, Jacques called and said 'I want you to take over the cabaret programme.' It was all [his], though. He taught us about Brecht and what cabaret really was." For Larson - an actor with a musical flourish - these quarterly events were a way for him to spread his wings and find a musical voice: one based equally on the contemporary music in his record collection and the theatrical traditions he adored.

The cabarets also taught Larson how to work fast. While some pre-existing material could be integrated into a show, an Adelphi cabaret was typically written during the first half of the two-week

---

forms of "agit-prop" (short for agitation and propaganda) theatre. (16) Pavis notes that agit-prop is "clearly a leftist ideology, with its criticism of bourgeois domination, initiation to Marxism, and attempts to promote a socialist or communist society. The main contradiction of this critical movement is that it is sometimes at the service of a certain political line trying to prevail (as in Germany)." (16-17) and dismisses it as "proclaim[ing] its desire for immediate action by defining itself as "agitory play rather than theatre" and "the text is only one means among many of stirring political awareness, and it is relayed by gestural and stage effects that are intended to be as clear and direct as possible - hence its attraction to the circus, pantomime, buffoonery and cabaret." (17)

Curiously, Burdick skips over *kabarett* in his own book, though this may be due to lack of space and the fact that *Theater* was meant to be a mainstream survey, rather than an academic guide.

14. *That Was the Week That Was* had separate editions in both the United States and United Kingdom. The former is now remembered mostly for its songs by satirical songwriter Tom Lehrer. Larson's copy of Lehrer's sheet music collection *Too Many Songs by Tom Lehrer* is held with his papers at the Library of Congress.

Petron considers National Lampoon's 1973 stage show *Lemmings* to be a pinnacle of the genre, and the cast recording was - and still is - frequently used in lectures at Adelphi.

rehearsal period and revised during the second, with questionable songs and skits jettisoned and replacement material hastily hammered out. "It was a lot like *Saturday Night Live*," remembers Armstrong, who became Larson's lyricist and collaborator on 1981's *Sacrimmoralinority* (pronounced 'sacrim-moral-inority'). "Nick [Petron] and 10-15 kids would get together and do the thing. A lot of it was random and poorly done." "The sketches," recall Petron, "were almost always based on improv, based on the newspaper from the last two weeks. [...] Often, there was no real script."

Students would be (and still are) selected to write and perform the cabarets on a semesterly basis: a class was taught on the subject, students submitted proposals, and Petron selected the best offer. Occasionally, alumni would come back to contribute their own ideas if student submissions were lacking, though this has since fallen out of practice.

Recordings from Larson's era reflect the rushed nature of the cabaret productions: the cast often sang off-key, sped through material, and performed as brashly - and loudly - as possible. However, the audience lapped it up; for them, cabaret wasn't a play, but a party. Says Armstrong:

> The cabarets were set up in the University Center's cafeteria, and the shows would be performed on Friday and Saturday at 8 and 10. As soon as the cafeteria closed at 6, they'd move in platforms and maybe a drop or a flat, have maybe six lights on two poles, and some really bad [microphones]. The cast wouldn't have a chance to get on stage until 10 minutes before the first performance on Friday, so nobody knew where the lights would be. It was always a rowdy crowd as well - there was beer for sale, and the drinking age back then was 18, so you

had a pretty drunken audience who came in knowing they'd see something controversial. Everybody
also expected the late show to be raunchier, especially on Saturday, where the 10 o'clock show was
anything goes. There was a lot of 'who can top
who' coming from stressed actors, but it was also
the production we all wanted to do because it was
where we could blow off steam.

Petron also remembers the rambunctious audiences: "When
they got quiet because they got nailed, they got *nailed*, and they
were weeping and crying out, and then when the song was over,
there'd be four, five, six seconds of silence."

The rushed nature, combined with Larson's burgeoning (and
at the time limited) musical skills and abilities are reflected in the
remaining material: very little survives of these shows past a poster,
audio tapes of the songs, and typewritten paperwork with handwritten chords as a guide. "Jonathan never wrote anything down in
those days," remembers Armstrong. "He could barely read music
then, let alone write it. He'd write out some chords and play it dif-
ferently every time, always making it better."

Mixed in with Larson's papers from *El Libro* is a handout
from Jacques Burdick, dated March 1982, from a class on 'Radical
Theatre Techniques.' Reasserting the master's dominance of the
cabaret form, Burdick states:

> No one understood better than Bert [sic] Brecht
> the true function of songs in a production. He had
> not only grown up in Cabarets and knew their
> style perfectly, he had the same disdain for con-
> ventional middle class theatre that Meyerhold had
> in addition to some very deeply held convictions

about using the theatre to instruct and incite the audience.[15]

This approach melded with Larson's own upbringing. Julie Larson McCollum explains the family's own political background:

My parents weren't particularly active politically when we were growing up, but they had been in the 1950s. We were always made aware of what was going on in our world - it was the [1970s], and I was very involved in politics. I was a [political science] and history major, but I worked for George McGovern, then got very involved in other local politics, so discussions at our table always [involved] events of the day. Jon wasn't expressly political until after college when he was living in the city and AIDS became the scourge that it did. No one was talking about it, and he was watching friends die right and left, but we were a family who were always aware. Beyond Broadway musicals, we'd listen to a lot of singers like Pete Seeger, Paul Robeson, and folk songs. Songs of work and struggle were the background of our childhood, so he was always aware of things political, and issues of the day, but it wasn't at the forefront until post-college.

Larson's first written contribution to the Adelphi cabaret programme came in the form of two songs for the Fall 1980 show, a spoof of the mega-hit book and TV miniseries *Shogun*. "We sent up everything about [Japanese] culture," remembers co-author Nick Petron, "and another student, David Stewart, did all the music, but Jonathan wrote these two songs which were just fantastic."[16] 'O Yoseru' is a love song disguised as a language lesson between the leads, and one can see early signs of Larson's *1984* score in the mournful 'The Letter Home.'

On his next cabaret, April 1980's *Herstory* (or *Little Miss Muffet Spat on her Tuffet*), Larson took over all composing duties and could finally cut loose, beginning his quest to modernise the musical. As with *Steak Tartare,* the skits for *Herstory* were written by Nicholas Petron with Larson's classmates Dan Kagan and Melody Cooper contributing additional lyrics. Focused on women's issues, *Herstory* looked at such topics as sexism ("All we want is liberty, fertility, equality"), women's health, and body issues.[17]

Like most of the Adelphi cabarets, the songs are a mixed bag of parodies (Roger Miller's 'King of the Road' became 'Queen of the Home,' about the annoyances of a housewife's life) and original tunes. The majority of songs, such as the counterpointed, Jacques Brel-inspired waltz, 'The Same' show Larson advancing technically as a composer over *El Libro del Buen Amor* but are ultimately forgettable, quick work put together to get the show on stage with no thought of an afterlife.[18]

As would become standard with Larson's cabaret work, two songs were notable exceptions. 'Menopause,' with lyrics by Dan Kagan, would be a favourite for both men throughout the 1980s.

---

16. Not to be confused with music producer and pop star Dave Stewart from The Eurythmics.

17. Nick Petron (Lyrics) & Jonathan Larson (Music). *Herstory*. Box 8, Folder 9, Jonathan Larson Papers, Music Division, Library of Congress, Washington, D.C.

Unfortunately, Larson only kept the lyric sheets for *Herstory*'s original songs and the recording is likewise only of the music.

18. Jacques Brel was a Belgian singer-songwriter who rose to prominence in the 1960s with his songs of lost love and war. A revue built upon his translated song book, *Jacques Brel is Alive and Well and Living in Paris* is credited as starting modern off-Broadway.

A loud, thrashing, punk-inspired tribute to The Change and The Waitresses boasting the line, "My uterus is about to fall out."[19] Larson chose the subject, and Kagan had a fascination with list songs. The duo created a list of terms related to the subject, and it progressed from there. The song was repurposed in Kagan's later play *Martin on the Inside*, along with 'The Same.'

The other highlight, 'Money is Power (The Lesson),' is an upbeat tune with a cynical message from Nick Petron: getting ahead and finding success means selling out in pursuit of the almighty dollar. As the hippies abandoned their idealism at the end of the 1970s and their younger siblings joined the rising ranks of the dawning yuppie revolution, the song's lyrics ("And I ain't rebelling / 'cuz I have the things that money can buy / the limousine and the cocaine high") were almost prescient in predicting the age of excess.[20] Worth noting for its incredibly catchy hook alone, the song is Larson's first encounter with a theme he'd repeatedly return to in his work.

Immorally Moral

Compared to the standard Adelphi production cycle, Larson's second full-length cabaret - *Sacrimmoralinority* - was blessed with the most valuable asset in theatre: time. Burdick assigned Larson to work with David Glenn Armstrong, and the pair secured their autumn production slot at the end of the spring 1981 semester, giving them the entire summer to write and refine the show. "We wanted to do a true Brechtian cabaret," recalls Armstrong. "We

19. Dan Kagan (Lyrics) & Jonathan Larson (Music). Menopause. Box 37, Folder 1, Jonathan Larson Papers, Music Division, Library of Congress, Washington, D.C.

20. Nick Petron (Lyrics) & Jonathan Larson (Music). Money Is Power (The Lesson). Box 8, Folder 9, Jonathan Larson Papers, Music Division, Library of Congress, Washington, D.C.

picked the theme and built it around the issues." In a written statement from 1983, Armstrong noted: "My personal interest in the Moral Majority is a result of living for 14 years in Lynchburg, Virginia - the national headquarters of the Moral Majority and Jerry Falwell."[21]

Sacrimmoralinority: An Immoral Musical on the Moral Majority ran for its weekend in October 1981 at Adelphi. Featuring music by Larson (who borrowed his idol's name and billed himself as "Joe Sondheim") and book, lyrics, direction, and choreography by Armstrong, *Sacrimmoralinority* aimed to hit where it hurt. Performed almost entirely in song, the show targeted all the major right-wing players at the end of Jimmy Carter's and beginning of Ronald Reagan's presidencies, refusing to pull punches.

The opening, 'Saved/We're the New Christian Right,' combines a jaunty patter song on the evils of society ("Truman Capote, coat hanger killers, marijuana, Proctor & Gamble") with a march proclaiming, "We're the New Christian Right! We're new! We're Christian! And we're right!"[22] The song not only merged things Larson loved musically - fugues and patter - but Armstrong structured the groups to each sing words with a different number of syllables, hitting different beats in the final round. 'Saved' also includes the first mention of "bisexuals, trisexuals," a phrase Larson would rehouse in *RENT*.

While the first half waved jaunty middle fingers at religious conservatism, *Sacrimmoralinority* took a darker turn in its second half. 'Abortion' is an uncomfortable ballad interrupted with a loud,

---

21. David G. Armstrong. Letter to Producers re: Saved! Privately held by David G. Armstrong, New York, NY. Page 2.

22. David G. Armstrong (Lyrics) & Jonathan Larson (Music). *Saved! An Immoral Musical on the MORAL MAJORITY.* Privately held by David G. Armstrong, New York, NY. 4.

Neither Larson nor Armstrong saved the script from *Sacrimmoralinority* in its original form, but the line is present in all recordings.

thrashing chorus about a woman whose husband sends money to televangelists and refuses to let her terminate a post-rape pregnancy, despite already having multiple children. 'When I Grow Up (E.R.A.)' is similarly disturbing - as a young girl wistfully sings of her longing to be just like her mother: trapped in the kitchen, rather than out in the dangers of the wider world:[23]

> I'll only live for my husband
>
> All I can give, I'll give to him
>
> He will rule me to the utmost
>
> So I can be his loving slave.[24]

Sacrimmoralinority's cornerstone, however, was a 15-minute segment on anti-gay crusader Anita Bryant. Structured like The Who's 'A Quick One While He's Away,' 'Anita' used quick scenes and short musical phrases, blending original tunes with multiple parodies of Andrew Lloyd and Tim Rice's new hit, *Evita*, to dramatise Bryant's actions to see a gay rights law rescinded in Florida. The miniature bio-musical is equally tacky and hilarious, and reminds the audience that while Anita won her battle, she lost her marriage (and role as a moral crusader) as a result.

Wrapping up *Sacrimmoralinority* is the finale, a reprise of 'We're the New Christian Right,' but this time using fear and the power of imagery to strike the audience with its unsubtle point: as the song climaxes, the cast change the sole set piece - a Christian cross - into a swastika, and the song is counterpointed with the German national anthem.

---

23. The E.R.A., or Equal Rights Amendment, was written to enshrine protection against sexual discrimination in the United States constitution, but the bill failed to pass in enough state legislatures to become law.

24. David G. Armstrong (Lyrics) & Jonathan Larson (Music). *Saved! An Immoral Musical on the MORAL MAJORITY.* Privately held by David G. Armstrong, New York, NY. 23. As before, this song made the conversion from *Sacrimmoralinority* to *Saved!* unchanged.

The audience (and Jacques Burdick) loved it, even if the students were less enthralled about being asked to not smoke during the show. The Dean of Studies, Bill Foster, attended with his wife and sent congratulations to Larson and Armstrong: "We were talking, as we came out, about the pleasure of seeing students do positive and creative things displaying and using their talents."[25] Larson and Armstrong quickly filmed the show in a rehearsal room in black and white for the university's archive.

For transgender activist and cabaret legend Justin Vivian Bond, then a freshman at Adelphi, the show was a life-changer:

> The first show I ever saw in college that I thought was good was [Sacrimmoralinority]. I thought it was really beautiful, and it was political and smart, and it was the first time I ever saw something that was like "that's what I want to do! I want to do theatre that says something. I want to do work that [speaks] to my generation!" I had grown up on old movies and thought they were beautiful, but I also thought you could make something contemporary that was beautiful, that you didn't have to live in the past, that you could take what was best about theatre and making something relevant, and he did that."[26]

Over the end of their winter break in January 1982, Larson and Armstrong remounted *Sacrimmoralinority* on the university's main stage, filming it for broadcast on Manhattan Cable. Speaking to Larson archivist Amy Asch in 1999, Armstrong claimed the

25. Bill Foster. Letter to David G. Armstrong re: Sacrimmoralinority. Privately held by David G. Armstrong, New York, NY. Lack of commas in original.

26. Vicky's Larson Evening, Tape #3. Video. February 1996. Privately held by Victoria Leacock Hoffman, Washington, D.C.

revisions made along the way, as well as the endless recording session (the cameras kept rolling until everybody was happy with a take) stripped the show of its urgency and punch.[27] While most of the show remained the same, additional material was written for the 'Anita' segment, which put it over the top into being preachy rather than biting.

While the recording never saw transmission, Larson and Armstrong would rework their material again, giving it an update in the winter of 1983 and mounting it as a showcase off-off-Broadway under the name Saved![28] This version featured six actors, including Larson's new summer stock colleagues Scott Burkell and Joe Aiello, as well as Toni Wilen, who would bow out after a week to play The Mistress in the first US tour of Evita. Bambi Jones, who appeared in the Adelphi edition, stepped in as her replacement.[29]

Saved!'s best new material came in a trio of running gags about school prayer, 'Moment of Silence'. Each version looks at what students think about during a post-Pledge-of-Allegiance prayer moment, none of which is what their parents hoped for. One wants to go to the bathroom, another student thinks her colleague is a religious freak (while he fantasises about having sex with her), and a third pair of students pray for the moment to be abolished.

27. Amy Asch (Typed) & David G. Armstrong (Handwritten revisions). Sacrimmoralinority/Saved! (Notes), January & June 1999. Privately held by David G. Armstrong, New York, NY. 3.

28. According to Armstrong, the name change was a request from the producer, who believed nobody would attend a show whose name they couldn't pronounce.

29. Jones has since become a go-to performer for productions of Dan Goggin's series of Nunsense musicals.

Where is the Dream?

Shortly before Larson's graduation in April 1982, classmate Maggie Lally took the helm on the quarterly cabaret. Lally, who now teaches and researches radical theatre techniques and cabaret at her alma mater, won the bid and began writing original material, in addition to accepting submissions from other students.

Her show, *American Scream* (subtitled *The Great American Letdown*), took inspiration from Studs Terkel's 1980 interview anthology *American Dreams: Lost and Found* and looked at success (or a lack thereof) from multiple perspectives. Like *Sacrimmoralinority*, *Scream* was mostly sung-through, but unlike *Sacrim*, it was written in the standard rehearsal period and benefitted instead from spreading the writing across multiple lyricists, allowing Larson to flex his musical wings and work across genres.

American Scream opened with a 10-minute medley, wherein the entire cast of characters asked where - and whose - is the American Dream:

Seek, find, don't waste time, it's not far away

Keep your feet moving forward

Don't get lazy, wake up, think!

Go searching for what you dream![30]

The chorus - a repetition of "What is your American Dream?" (and subsequent variations) - is driving and invasive, as the song hops between eight characters, including a Jewish-American Princess,[31] a disillusioned elderly woman, and racist punks.

---

30. *American Scream* (Performance & Rehearsals). Apr. 1982. MAVIS 186127-3-1/2/3. Jonathan Larson Recordings, Recorded Sound Division, Library of Congress, Washington, D.C.

31. Larson would rework the chorus from this segment, the 'JAP Rap,' into 1991's *Rap Mitzvah*, co-written with Ben Stiller for the opening night party for William Finn's *Falsettos* on Broadway.

Each subject takes on a different musical style (e.g. a Princess Di-wannabe has a Gilbert-&-Sullivan-inspired segment), keeping the number from feeling too long.

For classmate Alicia Stone - a theatre student in the year behind Larson's - working with him on *American Scream* was a crash course in songwriting:

> I was the [Assistant Stage Manager] on [*American Scream*] and also taking a history class on how art influenced society and politics, as well as the inverse. It was a super-creative time, and I was always writing and reading a lot of Brecht. I wrote the beginning of some lyrics and brought them to Maggie [Lally]. She read it and handed it off to Jonathan. He looked it over, and they decided they could use it. He started on it, asked for a bridge, explained what he'd need, and different things would come forth as a result.

The song in question, 'Atarii Videoland,' was *American Scream*'s apex: an ethereal satire of early '80s arcade culture. "[Arcade games were] a means of escape for people," recalls Stone, "and it had a way of controlling their energies. There was an arcade on campus next to the bookstore, and there'd be lots of young guys - it was mostly guys - playing the games."

For Stone, the games were a double-edged sword, tied up in the masculinity of the scene, a view reflected in her lyrics:

> Decide who lives or dies
>
> So what if it's a lie?
>
> You're a king
>
> You are a man

In Videoland[32]

To the young, politically-charged lyricist, such an outlet helped contain some of the anger on campus, but also became a distraction from more serious foci of campus life, not least of which the threat to the university itself amidst funding cuts: "We were trying to raise awareness, to reflect issues in society."

Post-Graduate Studies

By the time he graduated from Adelphi in 1982, Larson had scored two musicals and three cabarets, returning in 1984, 1985, and 1987 to score another musical, *Pageantry*, and three more cabarets. This was a tremendous output for such a short period, especially when these four works were written alongside Larson's adaptation of *1984*, the first drafts for *Superbia*, and music for six songs as part of his collaboration on *Mowgli*.[33]

Pageantry, which saw Larson reuniting with David Glenn Armstrong, is set at a county beauty pageant in 1950s Iowa. The participants cross a spectrum of types - the overachiever, the underage Junior Miss champion tired of being treated like a child, and the reluctant daughter - hosted by an embittered ex-pageant winner desperate to revisit her glory days after a divorce left her a single mother in an unforgiving era. Again, Armstrong had a personal connection to the material: "I grew up in Iowa, and the fact that we'd had a Miss Universe from our county was a big deal. People talked about it, everybody remembered it."

In musical tone and style, *Pageantry* is similar to William Finn's

---

32. Alicia Stone (Lyrics) & Jonathan Larson (Music). *Atarii Videoland*. Box 8, Folder 9, Jonathan Larson Papers, Music Division, Library of Congress, Washington, D.C.

33. *1984* and *Superbia* are discussed in Chapter Two; *Mowgli* in Chapter Five on Larson's youth/family projects.

more recent *25th Annual Putnam County Spelling Bee*, loaded with bouncy tunes sung by miserable youths, while the beauty pageant concept later reached Broadway in Howard Ashman and Marvin Hamlisch's *Smile*.

Having been invited back by the school, Larson and Armstrong were in a position to make some requests: they wanted to do a book musical despite writing for the quarterly cabaret slot, and needed an all-female cast. As such, they asked to hold auditions versus being assigned their students. "It was a very different setup from usual," remembers Armstrong.

Lasting only a svelte 60 minutes, *Pageantry* ran for two nights in November 1984. Beth Flynn led the cast as hostess Velma Wilma Rill and subsequently became one of Larson's go-to performers through the 1980s, appearing in readings of *Superbia* and other productions.

Amongst all of his cabaret collaborators, however, Larson kept the most material from his three collaborations with Michael Lindsay: *One Big Happy Family, Prostate of the Union,* and *Emote Control.* "Michael had more of a bite about his stuff," remembers Petron, "but Jonathan loved where he went with [it], so they got along very well in terms of collaboration."

The pair first met in 1981, with Larson on the judging panel for the next year's scholarship auditions. Lindsay, three years younger than Larson, received the same four-year scholarship as his senior, and the two became friends over the rest of Larson's senior year, remaining in regular contact until Larson's death.

One Big Happy Family, written and performed in April 1985 at Adelphi (the spring semester of Lindsay's senior year) and again at a New York City nightclub that October, focused its skits on the continuing rise of the religious right and its consumerist impact on 1980s America. Following the opening number (lyrically reminiscent of Tom Lehrer's 'National Brotherhood Week'), the show began with a series of skits about televangelism and the contemporary boom in religious broadcasting. Charitable fundraising (and society's increasing resistance to it) was also skewered viciously in 'Ethiopian Humor,' where starving Africans were mocked on television while a pair of gluttonous Americans cracked jokes of their own.

One Big Happy Family also featured a young student named Clinton Leupp - now known professionally as drag legend Miss Coco Peru. "I knew I was never going to be an actor that was taken seriously," remembers Peru, "but I was able to play roles where the audiences were coming to see me and my humour and what I brought to it. Part of what was wonderful at Adelphi for me - besides dealing with my sexuality - was the cabaret shows. I realise now, that was the world I wanted to exist in as a performer."

Peru also lived in the same dorm as Michael Lindsay: "I looked up to him [so much]," recalls Peru.

> Just having his acceptance and him thinking I was funny? That meant the world to me. I had seen some of [Larson's] other shows. He had already graduated by the time I was [a student], and we only knew him as someone who came back to do these shows with us. I'd seen [*Pageantry*], and it was just so funny, and I remember loving the music. Jonathan tried to teach me to sing harmony, and for the life of me, I could never get it. He never lost his patience with me. He was just a super sweet guy, and would laugh about it.

Peru also remembers:

> My mom came to see [*Family*] with her church
> friends, and we were doing a song called
> 'Homosexual Rag,' where for the last line of the
> song, we all turned around and stuck our butts out
> at the audience and went "Pack Fudge!" The audi-
> ence roared, and after the show, my mother's girl-
> friends were asking her, "What does 'pack fudge'
> mean?" And my mother was like "Oh, you know
> gays, they love making things, and they love to
> make chocolate and give it to each other." That was
> my mother's cover-up. I was still very closeted, and
> I remember feeling 'There's so much gay material,'
> and it was because I was so afraid of addressing
> that within myself. I couldn't cope with it at the
> time.

Larson brought Michael Lindsay back to Adelphi in February 1987 to write *Prostate of the Union* (subtitled *The Evils of Ronald Reagan's America*), a controversial choice on Larson's behalf: Lindsay was considered *persona non grata* on campus, having been quite a wild child as a student and was only allowed back upon Larson's request. To Lindsay's relief, the show was a hit. *Prostate* focused on yuppification, a tongue-in-cheek look the subject Bret Easton Ellis would satirically redefine in *American Psycho*. Musically, the show is easily the best of the Larson-Lindsay collaborations, minus the cringe-worthy opener, 'Words,' a vaudevillian number mocking the audience:

> Now we've got you thinking
>
> Isn't thinking fun?
>
> Judging by your faces
>
> it is rarely done.[34]

---

34. Michael Lindsay (Lyrics) & Jonathan Larson (Music). 'Opening (aka

The musical strengths begin with 'Emotional Fallout of Success,' a Tears-for-Fears-inspired introspection on making it in business only to find an empty emotional core.[35]'Will' takes on racism in a slow, gnawing number which begins bleak and transitions into a hopeful protest song. The highest emotional point comes during 'Falling Apart,' a ballad bemoaning the state of urban living and the US in general:

> On Wall Street
>
> On my street
>
> Plaster and paste
>
> In the White House
>
> In the poor house
>
> Going to waste[36]

The Finale turns downbeat again, but with a sign of hope:

> Looks like we've been fooled again
>
> Welcome to the lion's den

Words)' in *Prostate of the Union*. Box 9, Folder 5, Jonathan Larson Papers, Music Division, Library of Congress, Washington, D.C.

The text is printed as "It's rarely ever done," but both Larson's solo recording of the song and the Adelphi performance recording feature the revised line quoted above. The change was most likely made to improve the text's scansion. The song is also listed in Larson's papers as both 'Opening' and 'Words.' I went with the latter for the sake of clarity.

Scansion itself is an aspect of music where stressed syllables of a word come on the downbeat, such as the first and third beats in 4/4 time.

35. Tears for Fears were a popular British band in the 1980s, known for riding the genre borders between new romanticism, new wave, and synth pop. The songs 'Everybody Wants to Rule the World' and 'Mad World' are the best known representations of their sound.

36. Michael Lindsay (Lyrics) & Jonathan Larson (Music). 'Falling Apart' in *Prostate of the Union*. Box 9, Folder 5, Jonathan Larson Papers, Music Division, Library of Congress, Washington, D.C.

Tomorrow looks a lot like yesterday

[…] Raise a glass and raise a fist and say

What the hell's going on?[37]

In true Brechtian tradition, the goal is to rouse the audience to action, addressing the viewers directly to remind them that societal issues exist beyond the stage.

Prostate's top song, however, is 'Valentine's Day,' one of Larson's favourite compositions and a solo contribution to the show (the other songs were Larson music/Lindsay lyrics). "He swore it would be a big hit," reminisces Victoria Leacock Hoffman. "He loved that song." Larson's notes on the chord sheet describe it musically as "Phil Spector Wall of Sound / Girl Groups, etc."[38] A rocking tune, 'Valentine's Day' is sung by a sexual assault victim turned S&M enthusiast. The idea, according to Lindsay, came from the show's timing: it was performed on Friday, February 13th and Valentine's Day 1987. Skits tied into the song, with a series of disappointed lovers being unable to attain their partners and reacting in increasingly harmful ways, primarily towards themselves.

Larson stuck with the song, making it part of his personal repertoire. Featuring a catchy chorus ("Draw a little heart / Draw a little arrow / Draw a little blood"[39]), the disparity between the upbeat tune and vicious lyrics makes it hard to resist, and it is one of the few songs from outside Larson's major shows to see a commercial release.[40] In addition to its cabaret origins, Larson considered using

---

37. Michael Lindsay (Lyrics) & Jonathan Larson (Music). 'Finale' in *Prostate of the Union*. Box 36, Folder 9, Jonathan Larson Papers, Music Division, Library of Congress, Washington, D.C.

38. Jonathan Larson. 'Valentine's Day' in *Prostate of the Union*. Box 9, Folder 5, Jonathan Larson Papers, Music Division, Library of Congress, D.C.

39. Ibid.

40. A slightly altered version, changed from first to third person perspective

'Valentine's Day' for an abandoned project in 1991 before working it into *RENT*. In this version, Mimi tells her backstory during one of Maureen's performances. Larson rewrote the song again in early 1994 as a failed attempt to rekindle Roger's passions at the start of the second act. In this later version, the bridge and third verse shift from seduction to revealing the character's pain:

> All the others loved to make me cry
>
> You want to save me from myself?
>
> Good luck, you're the first one to try
>
> (Roger (walks out): Goodbye)
>
> I love you 'cuz you try...
>
> You see, the truth is, I'm desperate for true love
>
> Not once a year chocolate cherries, bloody and red
>
> I was praying that it would be you, love,
>
> To show me before I drove you out of my bed...[41]

Ultimately, Larson dropped the song from *RENT* before the October 1994 workshop production, but friends swear he would have eventually found a home for it somewhere.

Like its songs, the skits in *Prostate* took on a darker tone than the ones in *One Big Happy Family*, questioning President Ronald Reagan's leadership, mocking an asbestos discovery on the Adelphi campus and skewering the scare tactics used in covering crack cocaine ("When I did Crack, I fucked his grandmother!" [...] "When I did Crack, I got to appear on the Oprah Winfrey show.")[42]

---

and sung by the composer with unknown accompaniment, is on the *Jonathan Sings Larson* CD from PS Classics.

41. Jonathan Larson. *RENT* (July 1994 Draft). Box 14, Folder 1, Jonathan Larson Papers, Music Division, Library of Congress, Washington, D.C., 73-74.

42. Michael Lindsay. 'Crack' in *Prostate of the Union*. Box 9, Folder 5, Jonathan Larson Papers, Music Division, Library of Congress, Washington, D.C.

Prostate also boasted one of Adelphi Cabaret's most controversial posters, featuring a drawing of President Reagan with the state of Florida as his penis. "One of my student loan jobs [at Adelphi] was in the library," says Coco Peru, "and there was this woman there and we got along really well. The show was coming up, and I was very excited about it [...] but she thought the poster was so disrespectful that she ripped it off the wall and threw it in the garbage. We weren't friends after that." Nick Petron also remembers most of the posters vanishing, only to be found hanging in various students' dorm rooms.

Returning for one last show in October 1987, Larson and Lindsay wrote *Emote Control* (subtitled '*or Sofa Q. Spuds*'), driven by their dislike and distrust of television.[43] While Larson expressed serious interest in new media outlets like MTV and pieces like Apple's *1984* commercial, he worried about television's ability to shape and control society. His obsession with this question was also running at its peak as he worked on a massive overhaul of *Superbia*, wherein humanity is controlled by a never-ending stream of watching - or appearing on - reality television. While Larson had largely mitigated his cynical outlook in *Superbia*'s early drafts, his personal frustration was rising to the forefront, and working on *Emote Control* allowed him to expand on the theme and try out new material.

On Lindsay's side, *Emote Control*'s skits involved crossing *Sesame Street* with sensationalism over surrogate parents, home shopping (wherein the hosts sell a literal 'piece of shit' to customers with ulterior motives for hopping on the phone), and sleazy talk shows. A separate trio of skits looked at how parties changed over the previous 20 years, from purely socialising to taking a break and gathering over *Saturday Night Live*, and finally to an entire group channel-surfing and barely talking, ultimately deciding to

---

43. Read it out loud.

set up a camera and watch themselves watching the screen.[44] If *Prostate of the Union* was a condemnation of American society at large, *Emote Control* looked at the average home and its withdrawal from social responsibility.

Musically, *Emote Control* is lighter and goofier than *Prostate of the Union*. The opening title song is bouncy and jangling, asking the audience if they've succumbed to the screen. The next song, 'I Am the Very Model of a Modern Couch Potato', is a Gilbert & Sullivan parody which Larson, says Lindsay, rejected until it reached perfection: "It wasn't enough just to do the parody, it had to be *better*."

'People Meters' features a hypnotic riff and lyrics about the invasion of ratings and demographics, the data masters deducing a person's sexual preferences through their taste in sports. 'Another Rainy Saturday' takes heavy musical influence from punk band My Bloody Valentine, as a hyperactive girl violently parades through the endless cast of toy tie-in cartoons flooding American airwaves post-advertising deregulation:

Strawberry Shortcake filled with dread

Didn't use a condom giving GI Joe Head.[45]

The finale, 'Television Babylon,' suggests what humanity will become if it remains enslaved to the screen: unable to connect, read, or move.

In addition to its original material, Larson used *Emote Control* to try out a new song from *Superbia*, a haunting ballad called 'I Won't Close My Eyes'. The audience responded positively, and

---

44. Needless to say, the skit predated YouTube 'Reaction' videos by over 25 years.

45. Michael Lindsay (Lyrics) & Jonathan Larson (Music). 'Another Rainy Saturday' in *Emote Control*. Box 4, Folder 3, Jonathan Larson Papers, Music Division, Library of Congress, Washington, D.C.

even in rehearsal, it was clear that Larson was on to something. In *Emote Control*, the song would be rough, raw, and a sign of Larson's ability to subsume the popular form.[46] In *Superbia*, the song reached perfection.

Alumni Associated

1987 also saw Larson reuniting with Alicia Stone, this time to compose four songs for her one-woman show *Bubble Gum*. The show follows Judy, a working-class English girl who lucked into a gimmick when she accidentally popped her gum in her hair just before a concert. Her friends, the blue-collar Rockanne, hardcore middle-class feminist Suzanna, yuppie Hillary, and fashionista Marta, have all followed separate paths.[47] While Rockanne struggles to contact Judy to reunite her with a hospitalised relative, Suzanna and Marta have risen in the world as a performance artist and fashion designer, respectively, and embrace the materialistic 1980s life. Despite Judy's attempts to engage in serious conversation, both are more interested in the juicy (and planted) tabloid stories about her private life. Judy and Rockanne reunite, but the former is left changed by the experience, submitting to her agent's wishes and giving truth to the gossip.

Stone wrote *Bubble Gum* while continuing her acting studies after graduation. The final project for students at her acting studio - to create a one-person show - often led to frustration: "It was meant to be something to market yourself," recalls Stone, "and a lot of people did adaptations and ended up unable to get the underlying rights. I saw that and said 'no way' - I was going to write something original." Having enjoyed working with Larson at

---

46. 'I Won't Close My Eyes' and its role in *Superbia* are discussed in further detail in the next chapter.

47. Stone renamed the 'Hillary' character 'Kimberly' in post-2003 rewrites to avoid drawing parallels to Hillary Clinton.

Adelphi, Stone approached him about writing music and turned to David Glenn Armstrong to direct: "We never got to work together at Adelphi, and I always wanted to do something with him."

As the show's monologues became a story, Larson and Stone rehearsed the music. One day, in Larson's kitchen, Stone was fretting over the show's name. The two kept coming back to the use of bubble gum as a prop, and Larson suggested it be the title. And so it stuck, endowing the show with a short, catchy, and layered title, *Bubble Gum,* conjuring images of pink femininity, saccharine artificiality, Judy's hair, empty calories, and teen-targeted pop music.

Stone remembers the collaboration process as productive and positive: "It was a really great relationship. We didn't have disagreements often, but when we did, we still trusted and respected each other. We were able to say, 'Yeah, that works.'" One example is the show's first song, 'Life Is (What a Freak)'. At first, Stone was surprised about Larson's choice to score her downer about an unmarried pregnant girl with an upbeat girl-group melody, but came to appreciate the juxtaposition. The final song, 'Look at You (Judy's Song),' came together out of improvisation: "I didn't know how to end the song. Jonathan said 'Just sing, and I'll play something,' and it just worked."

Stone workshopped *Bubble Gum* at Adelphi and the now-defunct Theatre 22 in the spring of 1987, but as the 1980s drew to a close, Stone's career took a turn from political theatre into actual law and politics:

> I was working for an entertainment attorney part-time in New York while trying to make it as an actress, but wasn't finding the acting work satisfying - the only thing I was getting offered was ditz roles. I needed to do something more fulfilling. In law, I was able to try and affect change like I

had in my writing, by being a steward for people
and the planet, and try to bring some awareness to
what was going on. There are a lot of similarities
between law and art.

In 1986, cabaret collaborator Dan Kagan wrote *Martin on the
Inside,* a dying AIDS patient's reflection on his life and love, as
part of his MFA in playwriting at Brandeis University in Boston.
Needing songs for a feminist chanteuse, Kagan asked Larson if he
could borrow a couple of their prior tunes, co-opting 'I Wish I
Could Say' from *The Steak Tartare Caper* as well as 'Menopause'
and 'The Same' from *Herstory.* Larson visited Kagan at Brandeis
and taught the songs to the cast. Kagan would continue writing
politically charged pieces, remembering "[Jacques Burdick] used
to tell me he was waiting for me to write a better play than [Caryl
Churchill's] *Cloud 9* - that was the perfect play to him."

Larson and Kagan also began working on a musical adaption of
Nikolai Erdman's play *The Suicide* in 1987, getting as far as outlining the songs and writing an opening scene before calling it quits.
Larson was focused on *Superbia* and wary of getting too involved
in writing an adaptation after failing to secure the rights for *1984.*
Kagan also felt unsure of his own abilities to do the text justice,
especially in the face of Larson's rapid progress as a composer.

The two continued to intersect and diverge personally and
professionally, reuniting with Maggie Lally in 1990 for the latter's
cabarets at the New York Repertory Theatre, and one of Larson's
final compositions would be scoring the song 'I Told My Mother I
Hate Her,' the first-act closer in Kagan's play of the same name. "It
was many years after we'd been in school," remembers Kagan, "but
there would still be this push and pull, and Jonathan would change
lyrics, and it would upset me, but he was always kinda right. I was
so proud of those songs we wrote - I still love them."

Two of Lally's aforementioned cabarets contained new Larson-penned material. For October 1990's *Bonfire of the Insanities*, Larson wrote a new song about post-*A-Chorus-Line* New York with Dan Kagan and also presented a trio of songs from *tick, tick... BOOM!*, then in early development.[48] In spring 1991, Lally tapped Larson to handle general musical arrangements and write a new song for her latest work, *Skirting the Issues.*

Larson's song for *Issues*, 'White Male World,' is imposing, in-your-face, and brutal. The rhythm line pulses and the keys thud as choruses of men and women deliver a driving list of yuppie middle-class accoutrements:

> Stay-Free, Yeast-X, Estée Lauder,
>
> Revlon, Calvin Klein's Obsession
>
> Advil, Ultra-Brite, No-Nonsense,
>
> Diamonds are forever[49]

The song continues as the participants debate between following a health fad ("Salad Bar / No, Candy Bar") and yuppie mating rituals ("Husband hunting / Binge and purge"), proclaiming at the end of each stanza that "It's just another day in a White Male World."[50] The bridge, however, takes a darker turn and reveals the undercurrent beneath the commercially bland and benign:

> Let's cut down a jungle
>
> Let's go start a war

---

48. No tape appears to exist of this song, and no lyrics are in the Larson collection, but Larson's digital composition MIDI was saved amongst his digital files. The piece opens with a clearly rock-inspired segment in line with the compositions for *tick, tick... BOOM!* and segues back and forth with bits of 'One Singular Sensation' from *A Chorus Line.*

49. Jonathan Larson. 'White Male World,' stored as "White Male songs" (Microsoft Word Document). Contained within disk35.img. Jonathan Larson Papers, Music Division, Library of Congress, Washington, D.C.

50. Ibid.

Let's go rape a co-ed

What a lovely thing to do[51]

Obviously, Larson was not above using shock to get a message across - the Adelphi cabarets were a firing line of ideas where subtlety failed to carry the calibre necessary to hit a drunken audience with the message. Offence, however, was guaranteed to hold attention through a mixture of disbelief and fascination. Listening to 'White Male World' almost 25 years after its premiere, the bluntness of its language highlights how far society has come.

While the New York Repertory shows were Larson's final cabaret compositions, his refined ability to work quickly and engage with political and challenging material would work to his advantage when working on *J.P. Morgan Saves the Nation* in 1995 and, of course, *RENT*.

Bringing it Together

Looking at Larson's earliest work some 25-30 years later, it is tempting to write off certain aspects as being of their era - as anything reliant upon cultural references tends to be - while simultaneously being shocked by the thematic timelessness in much of the work. For example, technology may have moved on since 'Atarii Videoland' was first penned, but its theme of focusing anger and motivation into empty entertainment versus actual issues remains current. One need only look at the outrage generated on social media over minor scandals in television, video games, or niche entertainment versus large-scale political and economic actions to realise the average American will put up with a great deal of abuse until it affects his entertainment. The level of hatred caused during 2014's GamerGate fiasco, wherein large numbers of hardcore video-game fans targeted women in the industry and gaming press as

51. Ibid.

outsiders needing to be purged, also reflects how much people can dedicate themselves to politicising their hobby. If someone wants to teach Americans about history or social issues, the only way to get it across is in a flashy, entertaining way.

What Larson learned at Adelphi, though, was that theatre could educate and inspire action, that while entertaining an audience was vital to basic engagement, good productions could (and *should*) convey something vital and relevant, and that engaging with the audience meant reaching hearts *and* minds. These early works, born of Brechtian and *kabarett* traditions by an immature talent, see Larson at his most overtly political, working with collaborators for whom delivering the message required overcoming limits in performance and staging - or their own capacities as writers.

The cost, however, was that Larson worked with material too rough for the conservative business of commercial theatre, and he would need to learn how to moderate his Brechtian tendencies through characters and subtext - something he received little instruction on at Adelphi or from his earliest collaborators, no matter how established a group they would later become. Larson had, however, learned the basics of working with others and how to take a back seat when brought on board for a specific task, and his confidence increased as the Adelphi system allowed his talents to grow.

For the actor/musician-turned-composer, however, words would quickly begin getting in the way, as a musical does not live on music alone.

Chapter Two

Static on a Screen[1]
1984 & Superbia

I worship you
I'm your vessel
Show some mercy and drain
All this life from me
TV

— **Superbia**[2]

FTER GRADUATING FROM Adelphi in 1987, Larson began writing his first full-length musical, taking him on a creative journey spanning nine years, from 1982 through 1991, ultimately ending with a fascinating, original, and un-produced book musical called *Superbia*. While *Superbia's* tortured development process is often referenced when discussing *RENT*, little consideration has been given to *Superbia* itself in

---

1. This chapter was originally published in *Studies in Musical Theatre*, (6:2): 2012, 213-226. As mentioned in the introduction, I have added new material to this edition.

2. *Superbia 1989 DAT Demo*. MAVIS 187228-3-1. Jonathan Larson Recordings, Recorded Sound Division, Library of Congress, Washington, D.C.

This recording uses a slightly modified lyric to any of the scripts.

terms of its themes, narrative, and musical voice, despite its well-deserved place as the third major work in Larson's canon. With the show unfinished, it is perhaps impossible to completely answer the question, 'What is *Superbia*?'

Based on what exists, *Superbia* would have been Larson's most intellectually engaging show, one that has both gained thematic relevance and retained its unique sound after 25 years in obscurity. While initially written as a light-hearted satire of 1980s conspicuous consumption, using traditional musical theatre forms, *Superbia* ultimately took a darker turn, increasingly reflecting upon Larson's political opinions, pessimism about the growing influence of television and technology on daily life, and anger over the show's lack of a production. Musically, *Superbia* achieved Larson's goal of merging popular song form with theatrical needs to an even more successful degree than *RENT*.

Superbia was also undoubtedly ahead of its time - but what does that expression actually mean? In most instances, the phrase is used to describe a work that is not initially appreciated but gains appreciation at a later point. The alternative definition is used to reflect upon a piece or concept that actually predicts or fits in with a trend in the future - a step or two past 'being ahead of the curve.' *Superbia* is a flat-out example of the latter definition and, as this chapter hopes to prove, one of the former, as well.

In light of the author's pedigree and the quality of the work itself, it is rather surprising that *Superbia* has never seen production, given the publicity a run would be afforded as the long-lost Larson. That said, the show's reputation for its troubled book and 1980s pop score offer a counterbalance from the potential producer's perspective, in addition to the science-fiction setting's staging demands. Nevertheless, *Superbia* is an inherently theatrical work that belongs on a stage, with many of its previously demanding tech requirements now standard in smaller-scale productions, and its themes, alien in the 1980s, remain just as, if not more, relevant.[3]

1984

Larson's first attempt to take Broadway by storm led him to write a musical adaptation of George Orwell's *1984*. He worked quickly, writing most of the show in autumn 1982, after settling in New York City, with the goal of opening the show on Broadway in 1984 itself. Retaining a lawyer and sending the script to several leading creatives in the field, Larson opened communication with the Orwell Estate, but failed to secure the rights due to an upcoming film. Dismayed, he heeded the advice he received in a letter from Jacques Burdick: "Take all you've done and write your own book[.]"[4]

While *1984* never made it past this initial development, it laid *Superbia*'s foundation. In a drafted letter to esteemed producer Hal Prince, Larson wrote: "I do not consider myself to be a writer. I am an actor who composes musicals."[5] Indeed, while *1984* had some questionable moments (described below), the adaptation was successful in fulfilling Larson's goal to "adapt Orwell's wordy novel into action in musical theatre terms," and his decision to have the lead, Winston Smith, speak into a video camera instead of writing

---

3. Sadly, *Superbia* has remained just as relevant since this chapter's initial publication in *Studies in Musical Theatre* Issue 6:2 from Intellect Books in 2012.

4. Jacques Burdick. Letter to Jonathan Larson. Box 1, Folder 10, Jonathan Larson Papers, Music Division, Library of Congress, Washington, D.C.

In this case, Burdick is referring to the book of a musical, aka the non-sung part (which is known as the libretto).

5. Jonathan Larson. Letter to Hal Prince. Box 1, Folder 10, Jonathan Larson Papers, Music Division, Library of Congress, Washington, D.C., 1.

Prince did respond to the letter, but the response has been lost.

a journal allowed Larson to retain the character's inner monologues in a method more suitable for a visual format.[6]

To give an idea of how much Larson condensed Orwell's masterpiece, the 1983 draft for *1984* is a mere 60 typewritten pages across two acts, with Larson's demo tape running approximately 45 minutes. The script focuses on the novel's key scenes, such as Winston meeting fellow rebel Julia and his torture in Room 101, but relies upon the visuals to flesh out details. Larson even went so far as to create basic stage designs, framing the proscenium arch with the outline of a two-way Telescreen, maintaining the Thought Police's constant presence without requiring additional actors onstage. Such material demonstrates Larson's penchant for thinking on a macro- vs. micro-scale: throughout his career, Larson always kept a full staging of his shows in mind, even as he struggled with committing them to paper.

Musically, songs such as 'The Brotherhood,' 'SOS,' and the show's Epilogue (which compared Orwell's world to real life in the early 1980s) show a vibrant composer finding his voice, but the remainder of the score is highly problematic: The Prologue - a 15-minute sequence of short scenes - quickly becomes laden down with repetitive music and exposition. Similarly, the comedic songs, 'A Pint Ain't a Pint' and 'It Could Be Worse' are a mush of dated jokes and bland 1940s pub song pastiche. In 1995, Larson admitted in an interview that "it was a good thing we didn't [get the rights] because it was not a very good show. But it was my first real attempt to write a big show."[7]

Actor and composer Scott Burkell sang on the demo tapes for *1984* and reminisced at the composer's memorial service about

---

6. Ibid., 1-2

7. John Istel. "'I Have Something to Say': An interview with Jonathan Larson," *American Theater*, Jul/Aug 1996, 14.

performing one song alongside Broadway actress Marin Mazzie as part of the trio's club act, J. Glitz:[8]

> [It was] called 'After the Revolution.' It was actu-
> ally really good. [...] [When] Jon started writing
> *Superbia*, the song showed up again, only this time
> it was called 'Ever After.' It went through a number
> of changes, big lyric changes. I'm actually surprised
> he didn't put it in *RENT* somewhere; it seemed to
> be the song that just would not go away. But the
> first lyrics for the song that he wrote were so sweet
> and optimistic and a little awkward and romantic
> and just a little bit goofy, and I think they'll always
> remind me of [him].[9]

The score's problems are only exacerbated on tape. Recorded in Larson's living room, *1984* was intended to have a mixture of traditional and electronic orchestrations, but the recording shows little of such potential except on 'The Brotherhood,' which was backed by a Casio synthesiser patch instead of a 'standard' piano setting.[10] While Larson declared his pop influences in the letter to Hal Prince, *1984*'s score is traditional musical theatre, not pop.[11] It quickly became clear to Larson that his music would not be served by the traditional piano/vocal recordings used by most composers, and if he wanted the music in his head to reach producers' ears, his methods would need to change.

---

8. J. Glitz is discussed in Appendix A.

9. Jonathan Larson Memorial Service. Video. 3 Feb 1996. Privately held by Victoria Leacock Hoffman, Washington, D.C.

10. *1984 Demo*. MAVIS 186111-3-1. Jonathan Larson Recordings, Recorded Sound Division, Library of Congress, Washington, D.C.

11. Jonathon Larson. Letter to Hal Prince. Box 1, Folder 10, Jonathan Larson Papers, Music Division, Library of Congress, Washington, D.C., 3-4

Let's All Sing A Jingo

According to Larson's then-flatmate, Jonathan Burkhart, *Superbia* was born in late 1984 at New York's legendary nightclub Area, where Burkhart worked with his sister. A high-concept venue where celebrities rubbed shoulders with the wildest of New York's bohemian artists and style royalty, Area quickly became one of the hottest spots in town, with thousands of people queuing (and often failing) to make it past the club's infamous bouncers. Inside, a surreal world of ever-changing thematic art installations awaited visitors, with the club's interior gutted and rebuilt every six weeks.[12] On this night in particular, Larson envisioned the venue as a space satellite, where the 'coolest of the cool' were blasted away from New York's grime, and *Superbia*'s world was born.

Todd Robinson remembers accompanying Larson to a night at Area:

> It was like descending into Dante's *Inferno*. I'd never seen anything like it. First of all, it was packed. Second, it was like going into a maze. You couldn't have gotten your bearings. If there had been a fire, you would have died. I can't believe they allowed a club in that space. It was pre-rave, but it had that kind of feeling. It put you out of your body a little bit. People were undone there, you dropped your social mores.

Superbia, as initially drafted, is set in 2064 and tells the story of Josh Out #177583962, the last man with true feelings and emotions on Outland (a plastic, suburban Planet Earth). A failed inventor, Josh stumbles upon an old music box and believes it capable of restoring emotions. Rejected by his family in favour of

---

12. Particularly memorable themes included science fiction, suburbia, and the colour red.

watching the Media Transmitter (MT), Josh seeks solace with the box in the one area of the planet with actual nature and meets Elizabeth In #319, whom he persuades to try it out. The two hit it off, and Elizabeth offers to sneak Josh into Incity, where the upper classes live their lives on camera selling Shapes (useless, disposable hunks of plastic) to the Outs, so that he can play the music box on MT for all Superbia (comprising Incity and Outland) to hear. Interfering are Studd Starr - the top celebrity and Elizabeth's programmed mate - and Roi, a mysterious In woman. After Roi gets Josh high and sleeps with him on the air, he is increasingly drawn into the Incity lifestyle. It is ultimately up to Elizabeth to bring Josh back to his senses, whereafter he confronts the evil Master Babble Articulator (MBA) and saves humanity from destruction.

While the underlying nature of Ins, Outs, Shapes, the MT, and limits on human emotions were established early on, the details took time to solidify. As 1985 progressed, Larson outlined the initial draft that would serve as the basis for *Superbia* v1.[13] Outlining his themes, Larson's message remained through *Superbia's* entire development: "Come to your senses! Media desensitizes people - Without your senses you are not an individual."[14] Larson also imagined the show as a futuristic fairy tale combining aspects of *Cinderella* and *The Emperor's New Clothes*.[15]

A core aspect of Larson's vision was the detail of Incity life: Ins lived their entire lives on camera in a never-ending series of reality TV programmes and Shape commercials. Like the Outs, the

---

13. *Superbia* underwent massive reworking during its development, including a complete overhaul in late 1987. Following Asch's model in the Larson catalogue, I refer to all drafts through September 1987 as *Superbia* v1 and November 1987 on as *Superbia* v2.

14. Jonathan Larson. Handwritten Notes. Box 22, Folder 3. Jonathan Larson Papers, Music Division, Library of Congress, Washington, D.C., 71H.

15. Jonathan Larson. Handwritten Notes. Box 22, Folder 5, Jonathan Larson Papers, Music Division, Library of Congress, Washington, D.C., 25H.

Ins also had their emotions limited from birth and were required to obey daily programmes (e.g. 'Appear at Gate Nine at 7:00, fall in love with so and so') written by the MBA and the Prods, Incity's upper crust. While reality TV as we know it was still seven years away, Larson had predicted the invention of a celebrity class famous not for the membership's talent or ability, but for partying on screen.[16]

In November and December 1985, Larson was invited to present songs from *Superbia* to composers at the ASCAP Musical Theatre Workshop, beginning a six-year trek through an arduous process of workshops and readings. Actress Marin Mazzie recalls those days:

> Nobody knew what they were doing. Jon would put together a reading and we'd show up and do it. No one had any of this "Oh, we're doing this for [someone]..." It was like "Oh, great. We made a demo and someone will listen to it." It was not as romantic as people think it was.

The initial ASCAP session began with optimism. Two songs were presented, the first being a repurposed - but not rewritten - 'After the Revolution.' The second, 'Face Value,' was a punchy satire of club bouncers and was well received, with feedback given by Stephen Sondheim and Charles Strouse.[17] Larson presented two more songs in December ('Eye On Her/Mr. Hammerstein II' and 'Sextet') to a panel featuring playwright Peter Stone (*1776*), composer Nancy Ford (*Shelter*), and theatrical jack-of-all-trades Tony Tanner. Sondheim, Tanner, and Ford expressed enthusiasm for Larson's ambition and desire to write in a new style (albeit one they felt was undermined by the show's more traditional songs), but

---

16. MTV's *The Real World*, which first aired in 1992, is the earliest identifiable US reality TV series in the current model.

17. Strouse is the composer of such musicals as *Annie* and *Bye Bye Birdie*.

Stone and Strouse countered with extensive criticism regarding the script's internal rules, complexity, and the perceived weakness of its political message.[18]

One audience member caught on to Larson's message more than the panel, seeing the excerpts not "in the anti-utopian Aldous Huxley sense of a logical extension of current trends but [as] a very broad satire of the world that exists" and spoke of trend-hoppers he knew "who need this show."[19] At the end of the panel, Larson wondered aloud if he was "limiting [the] intended audience by generation [...] trying to aim the piece at people between the ages of 22 and 40."[20] Unfortunately, Larson's recording of the session ran out of tape at this point, and any further discussion is lost.

In April 1986, Larson presented the first hour of the show for a panel of Dramatist Guild members, including ASCAP panelists Stephen Sondheim and Peter Stone as well as Martin Charnin (*Annie*), John Kander (*Cabaret*), and Stephen Schwartz (*Godspell*). Sondheim called the piece 'new and terrific' and praised how the content matched the style, but found it too traditionally formed as a musical and suggested it would benefit by deviating from established norms - or being written for television or film instead of the stage.[21] Stone and Charnin went for the book's jugular, targeting the lack of overt politics, the first act's length, and the balance of action. Despite the criticism, Larson was thrilled to have his work seen and was establishing himself as an up-and-coming talent. Larson also took the feedback from these sessions to heart, and

---

18. *Superbia* ASCAP Readings 4 Nov and 16 Dec 1985. MAVIS 186412-3-1/2. Jonathan Larson Recordings, Recorded Sound Division, Library of Congress, Washington, D.C.

19. Ibid.

20. Ibid.

21. *Superbia* Dramatist's Guild Reading. MAVIS 186452-3-1/2/3. Jonathan Larson Recordings, Recorded Sound Division, Library of Congress, Washington, D.C.

revisions directly reflected comments from the panelists. For example, working from Charnin's comments, Larson would rewrite Josh's original 'I want' song, 'One of These Days' (wherein he wants everyone to have feelings like him), into 'Too Cold To Care,' whereby he expresses his failed desires to be numb like everybody else.[22]

Andrea Wolper, who played Jennifer Out #177583962 in various readings, feels the problems were inherent to the story Larson wanted to tell:

> [Y]ou have only two redeemable characters, and everyone else is pretty much a cartoon… and that's the point of the story! Naming a character Studd Star is a shorthand way of telling us something about the character, but it's also pretty unsophisticated and entirely one-dimensional. Which is the point of the show, right? Rampant consumerism, out of control technology (maybe even fascism) have the potential to reduce us to one-dimensional beings.

Along the way, Larson continued taking his friends into the studio and recording demo tapes. "Jonathan loved all the synths," remembered Scott Burkell, "and he preferred being in the studio [to recording at home]. That was when he came into his own as a composer and believed in himself."

---

22. Ibid.

Larson would tweak the song again for *Superbia* v2, having Josh declare his plan to abandon all emotion and party through humanity's impending destruction.

1985 is 2064

Amongst Larson's papers for *Superbia* is a 1984 New York Times article by Norman Lear entitled 'Bottom Linemanship'. In the article, Lear argues that television production and the creative industries as a whole are driven by numerical success: what gets made is what sells and earns Nielsen ratings, not necessarily quality programming.[23] Larson saw this number-focused mentality as harmful to not just the arts, but humanity as a whole. By ensuring the rules of *Superbia* always benefitted a status quo along a financial bottom line, Larson established a society wherein emotional thinking breaks the rationality which upholds the peace. Using a strictly delineated class system, *Superbia*'s working class has been replaced by robots. By ensuring that Shapes fall apart, a planned economy guarantees the Outs maintain steady Shape businesses, living repetitive lives driven by the MT. The Ins, allowed enough freedom to know what's going on within their level of society, take vacations and do as they please in their rare moments off camera. The Prods provide scripts to the Ins and fulfil the wishes of the MBA (itself a humanoid computer) at the top. As all humans are literally kept numb by consuming electricity ('plugging in' or 'singajing'), a political uprising is nigh on impossible and the wheels of commerce are kept safely in motion.

Larson also wished to set his world apart from the current day with language. The influence of *1984*'s Newspeak remained in Larson's mind and, with the rise of personal computing and consumer technology in the '80s, a new vocabulary of industrial language and terms began entering colloquial English. Larson attempted to stay on top of such developments, changing from "tape" to "disc" as the revisions passed and including exclamations

---

23. Norman Lear. "Bottom Linemanship," *New York Times*, 20 May 1984, Clipping held in Box 26, Folder 3, Jonathan Larson Papers, Music Division, Library of Congress, Washington, D.C.

such as "Digital!" ("Great!").[24] In notes from January 1988, Larson defined his Superbiage as "[an] attempt to simplify language[.] The basic idea rules are to generally make words refer to Shapes or numbers, subliminally reinforcing the ideas of consumerism and contentrification."[25] From *Superbia*'s fourth draft onward, a glossary of terms was included at the end of every script. While the earliest drafts used the glossary to define the world as much as the lingo (e.g. expanding upon basic concepts such as "In" and "Shape"), later versions would focus on the varying amounts of in-world language in the scripts.

The Superbian mental condition also brought its own linguistic problems. In v1, Larson used the term 'desensitized' to describe the limitation of feelings and emotions, causing everyone to act "like they're in a Kellogg's Corn Flakes commercial."[26] Following feedback from the Dramatists Guild panel, Larson defined the condition further and questioned the terminology to use in a world where people *are* sensitive to certain issues. Ultimately, Larson used 'contentrification' for v2, whereby Superbians are assigned a 'role' by the MBA and programmed accordingly at birth (e.g. Josh's sister Jennifer is contentrified as a brat). The term also has a smart double meaning: the characters are both content with their situations and loaded like a computer with content to run through.

24. Jonathan Larson. *Superbia* (June 1988 Draft) (w/ Sound Cues). Box 25, Folder 8, Jonathan Larson Papers, Music Division, Library of Congress, Washington, D.C.

25. Jonathan Larson. Handwritten Note. Box 26, Folder 4, Jonathan Larson Papers, Music Division, Library of Congress, Washington, D.C., 5H.

26. *Superbia* ASCAP Readings 4 Nov and 16 Dec 1985. MAVIS 186412-3-1/2. Jonathan Larson Recordings, Recorded Sound Division, Library of Congress, Washington, D.C.

1989 is 2064

Following its initial creative burst of revisions, workshops, and feedback sessions, *Superbia* remained in an endless cycle of development. While the show reflected Larson's technological cynicism in a theatrically romantic setting, the show always ended on a positive note: Josh defeats the MBA using the power of emotion and unleashing his music box on society, offering hope and a chance at a simpler, more human life. By late 1987, though, Larson began questioning himself. Composing (but possibly not sending) a letter to Sondheim: "I've always assumed that Josh would win - but I'm not sure anymore."[27] Larson also discarded the music box concept, leading to further self-doubt: "Sometimes I think that I'm just missing the heart of things. I'm afraid that I'm not thinking fundamentally. How can I sharpen this? CAN I??"[28]

Following the overhaul into *Superbia* v2, Elizabeth is now an Out, and she is due to enter an MBA-arranged marriage with Josh. However, Josh rejects Elizabeth when his family chooses to get high and watch MT after an alert that all humans are to become victims at the end of the weekend. Deciding to forsake his humanity, Josh gives Elizabeth a rose as a parting gift and leaves for Incity, encountering Studd Starr en route and only making it past the bouncer due to a seemingly-chance encounter with Roi. Elizabeth has an emotional awakening and pursues Josh, only to be spurned when the pair are reunited. Josh reflects on his guilt after having wild, drug-fuelled sex with Roi on the air, and Elizabeth hides from Studd after he attempts to force her into a man-woman-droid

---

27. Jonathan Larson. Draft Letter to Stephen Sondheim. Box 30, Folder 8, Jonathan Larson Papers, Music Division, Library of Congress, Washington, D.C. U.

The letter is dated January 1987, but is with papers from and refers to events in late 1987 and early 1988 - the copy in the archive was likely not sent due to this typing error.

28. Ibid.

threesome. As Josh continues succumbing to the Incity lifestyle, Elizabeth's feelings blossom. After one last attempt to reconnect with Josh, Elizabeth is sent to the Outer Obscurity prison satellite, and Studd denounces Josh on the air shortly thereafter. On Outer Obscurity, Elizabeth has a nightmare during the MBA's speech on humanity's upcoming Delimbination - the planned removal of mankind's arms, legs, and torsos in exchange for climate controlled cubicles and a 36" colour MT for each head. Josh is deposited in Elizabeth's cell, but fails to awaken before she declares her love for a broken MT and electrocutes herself. Josh is left devastated.

The show first took on a darker tone in the November 1987 draft. Having won the Richard Rodgers Development Grant at the end of that year, Larson wrote to Sondheim in January 1988, expressing his gratitude: "This news couldn't have arrived at a better time, as I've just completed my revision."[29] In this version, the MBA's attempt to pursue the bottom line is taken to its furthest extreme: using a set of stolen nuclear weapons, Outland will be eliminated and the MBA itself will exterminate Incity before exploring outer space with an army of clones as the self-proclaimed higher species. Promoted to the populace as the media event of the century, humanity is expected to accept its destruction with an almost comical blasé as the MT blares the news:

> The countdown continues for the Final Act Event
> which occurs tomorrow night
>
> 29-60s remain before you're vaporized in the hot, white light
>
> In other news...[30]

The money Larson won with the Rodgers grant funded a

29. Ibid.

30. Jonathan Larson. *Superbia* (Nov. 1987 Draft). Box 25, Folder 4, Jonathan Larson Papers, Music Division, Library of Congress, Washington, D.C. I-8-57.

reading in December 1988 at Playwrights Horizon in New York, where Larson was able to get into a rehearsal room, and make revisions, with the further possibly of winning a further grant for a full-on workshop production never far from his mind. Larson described his feelings in a monologue for *tick, tick…BOOM!*, venting his anger at not being able to use a non-union cast (including the friends he wrote many of the songs for), have proper staging, or hire an actual rock band:

> Jonathan finally convinces Andy that the rap song won't work without a drum - so he's allowed a taped accompaniment for that one song.[31] The house rocks - Until Andy hurdles three rows of seats screaming, "JONATHAN - WE CAN'T USE IT!! IT STICKS OUT LIKE A SORE THUMB! IT SOUNDS LIKE ANOTHER SHOW!" "YEAH. […] IT SOUNDS LIKE MY SHOW."[32]

Listening to a recording of the Playwrights reading, it's easy to see why Larson was so upset: the cast was comprised of traditional musical theatre performers who sounded disassociated from the book and sang Larson's pop-rock score as if it were Gershwin. With only a single piano as accompaniment, the score lost its standout synthesizer sound, though some numbers like new addition 'LCD Readout' held up. While Sondheim attended his pupil's production, he left following the first act.

Convinced that he could do a better job himself, Larson teamed up with longtime friend and stalwart Victoria Leacock to

---

31. 'Andy' is inspired by Ira Weitzman, then-director of Musical Theatre at Playwrights Horizon, and a champion of Larson's work despite their disagreements on this production.

32. Jonathan Larson. *tick, tick… BOOM!*, stored as "!93 TIXK TEXT" (Microsoft Word File). Contained within disk8.img. Jonathan Larson Papers, Music Division, Library of Congress, Washington, D.C.

present *Superbia* "like it oughta be" in concert at the Village Gate "using a live band - and actors who sing rock."[33] The concert, starring Larson's friend and future Broadway star Roger Bart as Josh and future *RENT* cast member and Naked Angel Timothy Britten Parker as gaudy agent Tim Pursent, would be performed to 400 people. It would also be one of only two times *Superbia* was performed with a full band.[34]

While *Superbia*'s plot solidified once Larson set things in place in late 1987, it is necessary to know the backstory in order to appreciate why Larson made such a radical tonal shift. Area closed that year, and Larson likely doubted whether or not his audience was moving on from the parallels he was building in his show. Likewise, some of Larson's closest associates - including life-long friend Matthew O'Grady and Jonathan Burkhart - found steady jobs in their fields, leading an impoverished Larson to feel everyone around him was moving on.

In other words, the shift to a darker tone in *Superbia* is a metatextual reflection of Larson's real-life state-of-mind, wherein he projected his frustrations on the characters. While obliterating humanity (or reducing it to a state of permanent suffering) is easy to dismiss as an angry writer's revenge fantasy, certain revisions take on a more personal tone. The demo tape for the song 'Gettim' While He's Hot' reveals Larson singing a cynical, business-jargon list song about buying and selling a person - Josh/Larson himself. The song ends with Studd Starr revealing Josh's true identity

33. Jonathan Larson & Victoria Leacock. Invitation to *Superbia* Concert. Box 28, Folder 7, Jonathan Larson Papers, Music Division, Library of Congress, Washington, D.C., 70H.

The Village Gate was a nightclub in Greenwich Village known both as a popular concert venue and for kicking off the 1960s Off-Broadway renaissance by housing *Jacques Brel Is Alive and Well and Living in Paris* in its second, smaller room. The venue closed in 1994, but was reopened in 2008 as (Le) Poisson Rouge.

34. The other being a 1991 reading at the Public Theatre in New York. Most readings were done with backing tapes.

as an Out and Tim Pursent promoting the safe, skyrocketing Studd instead.

In January 1991, Larson submitted *Superbia* and his follow-up, *tick, tick... BOOM!* to the Buxton Opera House's 'Quest for New Musicals' competition in the United Kingdom. *Superbia* was particularly well received and made the shortlist for selection.[35] However, Larson was unhappy with the contract for further consideration: the festival would hold exclusive production rights to the shows through mid-1992 and, even then, could guarantee at most a workshop. The festival also held right of first refusal on full productions thereafter, limiting Larson's ability to pitch his show in New York. When the Public Theater expressed interest in a new reading of *Superbia*, Larson withdrew his entry and took a gamble at home. In years of working on the show, pulling it from the UK may have been the biggest mistake Larson could have made.

To say the 1991 *Superbia* reading at the Public was disastrous would be a misnomer. The show was well-cast and played with a full band, and the actual performance may have gone fine.[36] However, the show was performed under less-than-ideal circumstances. Fellow composer Paul Scott Goodman played rock singer Mick Knife, and remembered the performance accordingly:

> We got to the Public Theater on the day of this reading, and everyone's hyped up and ready to go, and the guy from the [office] comes out and says "Oh, Jon, it's great you're here. Everybody's really looking forward to the musical, but we're having the Christmas party today. We forgot to tell you." Jon's like "Yeah, when does it start?" "It starts at

35. Chris Grady. Letter to Jonathan Larson (28 October 1991). Box 39, Folder 4, Jonathan Larson Papers, Music Division, Library of Congress, Washington, D.C.

36. Curiously, no recordings of this reading exist.

the intermission of your show..." I recognised that expression on Jonathan's face. It was wh'at I'd describe as barely concealed hurt, which quickly transferred to "Fuck you!" which I liked. And I liked him for that.[37]

A Cracked Lens on the Future

While Larson's overhaul ultimately streamlined *Superbia*'s plot and made it vastly more approachable than before, the script still needed reworking. According to Sondheim, "*Superbia* was simply unsolvable[.] I became convinced that the book could not be fixed."[38] Unfortunately, Sondheim does not recall his exact reasons for making that statement, but suggests "it had to do with the plot." Based on Sondheim's own guiding principles in his book *Finishing the Hat* (content dictates form, less is more, and God is in the details), it is the latter which plagues *Superbia*'s script, especially in *Superbia* v2.[39]

First and foremost, Larson never wrote a satisfying ending. Even in early drafts where the ending is tonally and theatrically appropriate (Josh confronts the MBA, wins, and opens the music box on the air), every draft featured new changes: some cartoonish, others seeing Josh turning the MBA's reliance on numbers against

---

37. 1998 Jonathan Larson Performing Arts Foundation Awards Ceremony. Video. February 1998. Privately held by Victoria Leacock Hoffman, Washington, D.C.

Goodman also recalled at another memorial evening that there were maybe 25 people in the audience at the start of the show and at most ten after the interval.

38. Barry Singer. *Ever After, The Last Years of Musical Theater and Beyond.* (New York: Applause Theatre & Cinema Books, 2004), 41.

39. Stephen Sondheim. *Finishing the Hat: Collected Lyrics (1954-1981) with Attendant Comments, Principles, Heresies, Grudges, Whines and Anecdotes.* (New York: Alfred A. Knopf, 2010), xv.

it - sometimes with Elizabeth's help, sometimes with a small group. As Larson was preparing to transition the show from v1 to v2, ambiguity began to settle in as Josh was shown puzzling over whether to use the box or not as the lights faded out. Once Larson abandoned the music box plot, the ending immediately took a darker tone. In most editions of v2, Josh is trapped on Outer Obscurity with the elderly, exiled celebrity Mick Knife, confronted by Elizabeth's death and the resurgence of his own emotions as Delimbination begins.

In this author's opinion, the most satisfying ending for v2 comes from the June 1988 draft, wherein Josh, following Elizabeth's suicide, returns to Incity to confront the MBA but, incapable of successfully arguing humanity's case, is unable to save it from nuclear devastation, and the MBA escapes. While the scene can be seen as preachy (the MBA lectures Josh on humanity's failings and the evolutionary link between the contentrified humans and computer-on-computer societies), it rings theatrically and emotionally true: the man who discarded his love and emotions to party away the end of humanity is the last one left to see the results.

Surprisingly, *Superbia* never had a proper musical 'finale': while some versions involved Josh and Elisabeth singing down the MBA with lines from classic musicals and reprising 'Ever After,' about hopes for a simpler life, there was never a true, unique song to end the show in v1. Likewise, v2 went between a dialogue-only ending and a chant of 'Love Has No Bottom Line,' similar to the end of 'Let the Sun Shine In' from *Hair*, which, based on the 1989 Village Gate recording, was less effective. Instead, Larson made his 11 o'clock number the musical crux of the second act, placing the power in his heroine's hands.[40] Both 'Come to Your Senses' (v1) and 'I Won't Close My Eyes' (v2) are memorable, intense

---

40. An '11 o'clock Number' is a song (usually a ballad) towards the end of a musical which puts things in place for the finale. In *RENT*, it is 'What You Own'.

moments worthy of carrying the show to its climax, and both are difficult to follow up musically without a tonally dissonant production number.

Larson also struggled to keep his timelines in order. While the duration of events in v1 was a non-issue (there was no conflict other than whether or not Josh would get the box on the air), v2 relies on the underlying threat of humanity facing extinction at the hands of the MBA. The question then arises of how much time is needed to allow Josh to go through his own personal story at a realistic pace while always remembering the time is ticking. In the June and August 1988 drafts, the action is mapped out on the scene list over a period of 48 hours, with Larson detailing the timeline in the list of scenes.[41] Subsequent versions shorten this time to 36 hours, heightening urgency but undermining the sheer volume of events and time skips implied in Josh and Elizabeth's stories.

A Sound Unlike Any Other

When asked if he composed *Superbia*'s score on a piano during a presentation, Larson replied: "It was written on a keyboard - on a synthesiser."[42] As synthpop, New Wave, and studio-glossed rock exploded across the pop charts, Larson couldn't have picked a better time to be composing a show for a new generation. The inherent theatricality of 1980s pop, with its layered synths and intense drum machines merged with progressive rock's complexity, meant that pop music was finding new ways to build upon the

---

41. Jonathan Larson. *Superbia* (Aug 1988 Draft), Box 27, Folder 1, Jonathan Larson Papers, Music Division, Library of Congress, Washington, D.C.

Jonathan Larson. *Superbia* (June 1988 Draft), Box 25, Folder 8, Jonathan Larson Papers, Music Division, Library of Congress, Washington, D.C.

42. *Superbia* Dramatist's Guild Reading. MAVIS 186452-3-1/2/3. Jonathan Larson Recordings, Recorded Sound Division, Library of Congress, Washington, D.C.

history of three-minute songs, and *Superbia* capitalised beautifully upon the decade's hit styles.

Initially, the score blended sounds of new wave and synthpop with traditionalist showtunes. Some tracks, like 'Tapecopy #001 (Superbia)' are clearly theatrical while using syncopated synths and vocal triplets to create a driving, robotic sound.[43] Others, such as 'Eye on Her/Mr. Hammerstein II' and 'Doin' It on the Air' play on traditional Broadway and vaudevillian structures with an electronic tint, while 'Turn the Key' is a duet full of catchy pop hooks and layered keyboards.

These early songs - about two-thirds of which would remain in the show's second incarnation - were composed on a 50 key Casio keyboard and deserve the attention Larson began to receive from the industry. By the late 1980s, Larson was composing on a full Yamaha DX7 and arranging his work digitally, allowing for a fuller, more advanced sound in the studio. This expansion also allowed Larson the ability to import custom synth patches into his home keyboard, often designed by recording engineer and programmer Steve Skinner, who created the echoing, crystalline piano-bell hybrid used in 'LCD Readout'. Larson began working with Skinner in 1984 on his score for *Mowgli*, and remained loyal to him throughout his entire career.[44] At the start of *Superbia*, Skinner was working on a pre-MIDI system. By the end, Larson could play keyboards directly into a Macintosh and arrange an entire orchestra on the computer.

Larson's demos were appropriately stellar, using digital renders and overdubbed vocals plus extensive post-production to showcase

---

43. Triplets are a musical pattern wherein three evenly-spaced notes are presented across single beats in the measure. If a song is in 4/4 time, the beats are 1-2-3-4. A triplet would be annotated as 1-a-b-c-3-4.

44. *Mowgli* is discussed in Chapter Six. Skinner's further reflections on working with Larson are included in Chapter Seven and Appendices A and B.

his ideas. Comparing the 1989 demo to one from mid-1986 shows just how far Larson advanced both as a composer and in his collaborations with Skinner. While some songs ('Incity,' 'Sextet') used the same backing tracks, the new songs are more complex and radio friendly: 'Uncomfortable' uses extensive stereo panning on its electric percussion and bursts from the speakers, while Elizabeth's other big songs, 'Pale Blue Square' and 'I Won't Close My Eyes,' are commercially viable pop ballads with an '80s MTV sensibility.

The live arrangements created for the 1989 Village Gate concert are notably edgier and bring the later editions' rock influences to the forefront. Confined to two keyboards, electric guitar, electric bass, and actual drums, the score was laid out to be played fast and hard, adding a new level of viciousness to tracks like the New-Wave-inspired 'Face Value' (already sharpened satirically in the later drafts' darker context) and furthering the MBA and MT's menace in 'Sextet' while highlighting the tenderness in Elizabeth's section.

Larson also wasn't above paying homage to the day's hits and built upon familiar riffs in his songs. Early arrangements for 'One of These Days/Too Cold to Care' feature an ending hook similar to the theme from the television show *The Greatest American Hero*; 'Uncomfortable' uses a vocal nod to The Police's 'Don't Stand So Close To Me' and eschews a bass part a la Prince's 'When Doves Cry.' More esoterically, 'Sextet's arrangements show an influence from early synth musician Jean Michel Jarre.

A core number in the show, 'Let's All Sing,' is a biting satire of 'We Are the World,' complete with over-the-top Bob Dylan and Bruce Springsteen impersonations. As friend and 1987 workshop cast member Michael Lindsay remembers, "He wanted it to be the most annoying song ever." Larson had attended the 'We Are the World' launch party at Area in 1985, and his hatred for the song was well known amongst his friends. According to Burkhart, Larson felt using music to unite people for a worthy cause was

a solid idea, but was wary of the organisation's overhead costs and felt more could be done. Likewise, he believed the song itself was cloying and repetitive, brainwashing America with its 'buy a record, save the world' mentality. Believing he could do one better, 'Let's All Sing' sarcastically sells world peace to the viewer through a course of self-electrocution leading to eternal indifference.

2017 is 2064

What ultimately scuppered *Superbia*'s chances, though, were the production demands and technological limitations of non-mega-musical budgets in the 1980s. For example, Larson's v1 design notes call for conveyor belts, neon outlines, projections, and a moving gate to frame off portions of the stage, yet also ask for a 'new minimalist aesthetic.'[45] While the design demands would ease off in v2, the notes still called for a polished stage and fully tracked and suspended scenery, giving the idea of full automation and floating action - a nightmare to implement or even maintain through a single performance, let alone an extended run.

Larson's costuming ideas were equally demanding, calling for futuristic designs across his class system, from true minimalism for the Outs to full-on exotic club-wear for the Ins going above and beyond what the trendsetters and club kids at Area and Limelight were making and wearing. Combined with a cast requiring 18 performers and a minimum of five costumes each to handle necessary scene and ensemble changes, the fiscal demands immediately went above and beyond what an off-Broadway production could support.[46]

---

45. Jonathan Larson. *Superbia* (May 1987 Draft), Box 25, Folder 1, Jonathan Larson Papers, Music Division, Library of Congress, Washington, D.C.

46. 'Off-Broadway' refers to New York theatres which seat 100-499 people. 'Broadway' refers to 500+ seat venues that are also members of various professional organisations.

The final trouble at the time was the high-end sound require-
ment. Larson's design notes stated flat-out in 1989 that the sound
was equally - if not more - important than any other aspect of the
production, calling for a rock concert-type setup, letting the music
hold its own against the cast while maintaining the clarity necessary to ensure his lyrics were heard. Interviewed for the *New York
Times* on the eve of his death in 1996, Larson himself admitted,
"I'm only as good as my sound board operator," and knew how
demanding his work was for those trained on an entirely different
paradigm of sound design.[47] Given the few rock-inspired musicals to reach Broadway by the start of *Superbia's* development (or
through the end of it), sound designers capable of filling this need
and board operators capable of ensuring consistency would have
been rare finds.

Thankfully, technology has mitigated this issue to a large
extent: while many complain about the ongoing move to isolate
and move musicians away from traditional pit or on-stage appearances, *Superbia's* score all but demands such an arrangement, being
composed entirely on synthesiser with electronic instruments in
mind. While musical purists may find such a setup revolting, it is
now possible to play *Superbia* using Larson and Skinner's original
arrangements and maintain full control over the entire score, opening the door to cinematic design via surround implementation,
seamless integration with drum machines, loops, and samples, and
digital soundboards allowing everything to stay clear at safe decibel
levels without losing the band's vibrancy and presence.

That said, the question remains as to whether or not *Superbia*
would be best realised on the stage or, given its unique demands,
in an alternative form such as cinema or (ironically) television.
Larson himself investigated the possibility, adapting the show into

---

47. Steve Nelson. Liner notes to *Jonathan Sings Larson*. PS Classics, CD,
2007. 2.

a film script in 1991, though only as a writing exercise: the 'screen-play' features minimal world expansion and often belies his lack of screenwriting experience. An attempt was made in the mid-2000s to create an animated adaptation, but the project fell through in pre-production and a screenplay was never finalised for this edition. Despite not being a 1:1 parallel, many elements of *Superbia* v1's storyline can be seen in the 2008 film *Wall-E*: an outsider in a world of junk finds emotion in a musical and meets a girl from the utopia above. The two outsiders find love in a plastic, lazy world controlled by a supercomputer micromanaging a TV-numbed humanity's existence.

When work was undertaken on the animated adaption, a great deal of time was spent simply coming to terms with the material: characters who worked on stage suddenly needed additional depth and backstory, the plot needed fleshing out, and various songs, such as Josh's soliloquy, 'LCD Readout' - wherein he sits awake in bed reflecting on his actions - would have been difficult, if not impossible, to film effectively, yet work within the theatre. As such, the resultant film would have required the extensive level of restructuring demonstrated in the *Hedwig and the Angry Inch* film versus a more traditional stage-to-screen translation.

Thematically, Larson could not have predicted how quickly the world he envisioned would come to fruition. People can cut themselves off completely from outside social interaction while still living what resembles a productive life. It is now possible to work from home, be paid electronically, order all necessities online for delivery, and deal with friends and family solely through social media and text-based communication. The internet allows us to buy, stream, or pirate any entertainment we could ever want, and home A/V systems keep getting bigger and better. An entire class of celebrity has been born not off of talent, but by screaming at their housemates, while advertising is constant and embedded in

American culture to the point that it is inescapable in any setting - even the theatre, where sponsors and donors often get a plug before the performance. Meanwhile, our media addiction may not have reached the state it has in the show, but it is rare to see anybody not within consistent reach of some form of media-capable device.

With all of this access also comes the hyper-focusing of content and worldviews. The politicisation of cable TV news and the internet's opt-in nature means one can ignore all contrasting viewpoints, if not any events outside of one's direct sphere of personal and hobby-based foci.[48] While technology has allowed us to reach out to people more easily and across greater distances than ever before, it has also brought with it the ability to shut ourselves in and ignore anything unpleasant.

Larson also failed to predict the impact the internet would have on popular culture. While he saw going online as providing a way for Big Brother to invade his computer, the internet has tied us even more to our screens, making it possible to watch TV everywhere and endlessly demanding our attention with a constant stream of instant content. While social media has proven capable of great good, such as Twitter's use as a check-in point during the 2011 earthquake and tsunami in Japan, it also fills our lives with a constant feed of minimal importance and, increasingly, negativity and abuse. French sociologist Jacques Bourdieu addresses the value of time in discussion in his book *On Television*: "[w]hen you use up precious time to say banal things, to the extent that they cover up precious things, these banalities become in fact very important."[49]

Bourdieu's statements on banality are reflected throughout *Superbia*: Across all of Larson's drafts, the drafts, Josh's family

---

48. British documentarian Adam Curtis discusses this theme and its role in politics in his 2016 film *HyperNormalisation*.

49. Pierre Bordieu, Priscilla Ferguson, trans., *On Television*, (New York: W. W. Norton and Co. Inc., 1998), 18.

endlessly watch the *This Nite* show in the evening and the *Last Nite* show in the morning and afternoon, catching endless reruns of parties and Shape adverts on an ever-increasing number of channels. The Ins live and die by their ratings and ability to improvise witty dialogue, obsessed with winning a Face Award or creating the ideal product to cross-market with a new celebrity, case in point: Josh winds up advertising laser razors after a laser-based incident during Roi's seduction. By the early 2010s, even the American 'educational' networks had been given over to reality-based programming about large families and home repair, and British viewers are faced with similar dross. While calling television a wasteland is nothing new, Larson's attack was prescient in its extremity.

One of These Days

By looking at the increasing importance of media during a period of excess, Larson created a piece satirising his own era, while also serving as a warning for a future now coming to fruition. With the deregulation of television advertising in 1984, the American viewing public was introduced to product placement, the infomercial, and a generation raised on 24-minute cartoon toy commercials, creating a society with a desire to consume like never before. As advertising minutes per hour of programming continue to increase and low-intellect reality television spreads, the American population finds itself becoming the nation of Outland, kept placid by the kilowatts of media and social networking while a new class of Ins ride the airwaves. While the internet and video on demand have changed the way people consume media and brought a revolution in the scope of material available, it has also driven demand to watch large event shows in order to participate in online discussions immediately following (and even during) broadcast. As such, the integration of the internet and television creates a falsely active experience, keeping the viewer even more plugged in than before.

Unfortunately, as with Richard O'Brien's 1981 film *Shock Treatment*, which also predicted reality TV years before its inception, Larson wrote a show too far ahead of the curve for his audiences to keep up. Given that theatregoers in the mid-1980s were not even guaranteed to own VCRs, let alone follow the new computer-based jargon, audiences would almost certainly have been more confused by the wording than the play's deeper messages. With reality shows now a staple of broadcasting, the idea of Incity and a class of drugged up z-listers selling products to stoned viewers is far less alien to a modern audience. As such, *Superbia* is ripe for reinvestigation, its message of warning and its intellectual undertones just as (if not more) valid than when first written.

To Larson, love and emotions were more important than the stock market or housing prices. He believed that by putting a number on every aspect of our existence, we were diminishing our humanity rather than embellishing or improving it. As cynicism reigns in modern entertainment (either through sarcasm, 'hipster irony,' or by adjusting material to appeal to Bottom Line test audiences), works with genuine emotion are becoming welcome once again. While *Superbia* is not entirely free of the cynical plague, the author's intentions and words are genuine.

Creatively, *Superbia* is an exciting and musically radiant, albeit flawed, show which is not only a product of its era, capturing the urgency and vibrancy of 1980s music, but also a universal one, reminding us that people are more important than programmes and profits. Bringing the show to production would require careful revision in order to clean up the timeline and terminology, as well as to reinforce Larson's message and creative choices. Additionally, with two distinct yet overlapping versions of the material, the producer would be required to decide between the first edition's more light-hearted satire or the latter's streamlined edge, or make an attempt to combine both in a satisfying way. A conceptualist above

all else, Larson knew his message needed to make it through the show intact despite his difficulty in committing it to the page. In the right space, *Superbia* could still be a show capable of immersing an audience in its futuristic world, even with a small budget, so long as it is joined with big creativity. No matter which choice is made, the end result is likely to remain flawed in some way, though as with *RENT*, the piece's flaws grant it an attractive emotional quality, reinforcing its valuation of humanity over bland perfection.

Chapter Three

Commissions, Creationists, and Cows Collaborating in the 90s

Take the universe
Spin it all around
Put another generation
on your holy ground

—Sacred Cows

A s LARSON'S ABILITY and will to keep pushing *Superbia* at full power waned, he began drafting material for what would ultimately become *tick, tick... BOOM!* Simultaneously, a series of opportunities to connect with new creative partners in the theatrical community arose, offering new outlets for his work and chances at exposure. While the projects at hand led to mixed results, they gave Larson a sense of participating in the theatre, rather than trying to barge his way in, even if not always in the most successful ways.

Presidential Punch

In 1989, Larson was approached to write material for *National Lampoon's American Tricentennial,* a satirical revue planning to "take a close look at [...] the manners and mores, society and politics, way of life and living, of the 1980's [sic] and 1990's [sic] from the distance of 2076. It's a favorite point of view: hindsight."[1] *Tricentennial* was the brainchild of Michael Simmons, then editor of *National Lampoon* and head writer on the group's popular off-Broadway show, *National Lampoon's Class of '86.* As Simmons recalls: "We'd just done something recent, and so I thought, 'Self, why don't we do a futuristic thing? We can satirise what hasn't happened yet.'" The leading producer was Nelle Nugent, a TV and theatre producer with some hits under her belt.

How Larson became involved with *Tricentennial* is something of a mystery. Simmons lost interest in the project due to conflicts with Nugent, exacerbated by outsiders buying out the National Lampoon company and dismissing him from his editorial position. "To be honest, [*Tricentennial*] wasn't any of our best work, and I can't remember much about it."

Richard Levinson, a satirical songwriter who wrote for *Class of '86* and other Lampoon projects, remembers most of the material being brainstormed at a meeting in Los Angeles in early 1989, but Levinson's and Simmons' timelines conflict, and figuring out the exact sequence of events is difficult. Either way, Nugent had moved past *Lampoon*'s core staff to hiring TV writers and putting out a call for additional submissions.

Larson's own notes about the business side of the arrangement are limited, his production questions going largely unanswered.[2]

---

1. Nelle Nugent. Letter to Contributors. Box 8, Folder 1, Jonathan Larson Papers, Music Division, Library of Congress, Washington, D.C., 1.

2. At least on paper.

According to a paper in the archives, commissions would be due by the end of October 1989, and the show was to have a cast of 10 and orchestra of 12. Larson also had questions about who else would be involved creatively, how contributors would be paid, and even whether his submissions had actually reached Nugent.[3]

According to Simmons, one line of his initial concept (Southern California is destroyed in an earthquake, "Some critics noticed an immediate improvement in the quality of movies.") is in the document Larson received, but Simmons and *Lampoon* colleagues Larry "Ratso" Sloman and Jane Brucker deny writing the document in full.[4] Brucker suggests, "This is something [Nugent] pushed together from things tossed around," and Simmons confirms "There's [sic] too many cute touches that I can't imagine any of […] us coming up with [it]." At the same time, Brucker recalls a set of sketches which *were* included in Larson's papers, from early 1990.

The commissioning brief follows with an outline: In 2076, a historian opens a time capsule from 1989 to find an actor dressed as George Washington inside. Since celebrations for the American Tricentennial are underway, she acts as his guide to get him up to speed on the modern world through the various sketches, spoofing the late 1980s (and early 1990s) throughout. Suggestions are then given for various types of skit, and Larson's copy features an occasional comment, typically to question the logic behind the brief (e.g. why the historian and actor framing the piece needed to fall in love at the end and why there needed to be a plot in the first place).

---

3. Jonathan Larson. 'Production Questions' Handwritten notes. Box 8, Folder 1, Jonathan Larson Papers, Music Division, Library of Congress, Washington, D.C.

Larson would ultimately receive copies of other skits from the piece, which are discussed shortly.

4. Nelle Nugent. Letter to Contributors. Box 8, Folder 1, Jonathan Larson Papers, Music Division, Library of Congress, Washington, D.C., 8.

At the end of the brief, Larson noted three possible subjects to pursue: the making of the next president, televangelism, and the future of Broadway.[5] Another set of notes lays out his creative interests (the show's satirical and futuristic aspects, as well as potential topics) and questions about the piece - how will the future be defined, and by whom? Will there be consistency? Can darker issues be pursued?[6] Ultimately, Larson put these questions aside and pursued his first choice, creating a three-song election spoof and perhaps his best satirical work, *Presidential Politics*.[7]

Politics begins with 'The Vision Thing,' wherein a group of handlers and advertising agents convene to announce and shape Barbara Bosom as the 2076 Republican presidential nominee. Unfortunately for Barbara, being smart as well as sexy is a hindrance. Her handlers constantly cut her off, make uncomfortable changes to her appearance, and ignore her requests in sole favour of approval ratings from the 'experts,' a sloppy group of obese junk food addicts. Incapable of even speaking coherently, the experts answer each request with "La di da," an approval number appearing over their heads, inspiring the team to push Barbara's sex appeal and empty Americana:

> Shake the hand
>
> Smile
>
> And we hear her make the speech
>
> "Hello Albuquerque, Statue of Liberty"[8]

---

5. Ibid., 11.

6. Jonathan Larson. 'Initial Thoughts' Handwritten notes. Box 8, Folder 1, Jonathan Larson Papers, Music Division, Library of Congress, Washington, D.C.

7. Nelle Nugent. Letter to Contributors. Box 8, Folder 1, Jonathan Larson Papers, Music Division, Library of Congress, Washington, D.C., 1-6.

8. Jonathan Larson. 'The Vision Thing.' Box 8, Folder 1, Jonathan Larson Papers, Music Division, Library of Congress, Washington, D.C., 8.

As Larson's workflow increasingly hybridised between print and digital

Still, the experts deem her merely acceptable: Barbara needs to show more patriotism - or rather, to unbutton her blouse to show "how rosy things will be, how strong and firm you are.»[9] As her handlers ultimately reveal, "The message is the messenger" in the year of the centrefold candidate, complete with sponsors including Columbian Worldwide Pharmaceuticals.[10] At the end of the song, Barbara has delivered a series of stump speeches to improved ratings from the experts, and the team break for lunch. Musically, the song shifts between a circus motif full of marching drums and whistles, a factory-inspired buzz of rushing from task to task, and sweeping artificial brass band patriotism:

> Think of America
>
> Land of TV
>
> Think of her shopping malls
>
> Golden arches standing tall[11]

The tone shifts into high gear with the second song, the pulsing 'Do Unto Them,' wherein Barbara is put through her paces and taught how to mud-sling (literally and figuratively) by vicious German aerobics instructor Helga. The handlers continue to apply pressure, presenting Barbara with a bikini to wear at the debate and ignoring her requests for information and intellectual discourse ("Better to be good mud wrestler zan to wrestle wiz za facts").[12]

---

media, he would often work on his computer, print materials, and mark them up, leading to multiple instances of the same page numbers in each folder when he was revising heavily. Unless Library of Congress staff added their own holographic numbering, I use the original page numbers here, though they can be more of a rough guide than exact pointer due to this phenomenon.

9. Jonathan Larson. 'The Vision Thing'. Box 8, Folder 1, Jonathan Larson Papers, Music Division, Library of Congress, Washington, D.C., 10.

10. Ibid., 3, 9.

11. Ibid., 4.

12. Jonathan Larson. 'Do Unto Them' (Draft). Box 8, Folder 2, Jonathan Larson Papers, Music Division, Library of Congress, Washington, D.C., 18.

The tune is relentlessly driving, and shows how in-touch Larson was with the direction of American politics, as political discourse during the 2012 and 2016 elections varied from Larson's lyrics to beyond the most absurd of Helga's insults:

> My opponent hates the American flag
>
> My opponent once was a pinko fag
>
> My opponent polluted your water supply
>
> My opponent's tax return is a lie.[13]

In the final scene, 'Likability,' Barbara and Helga hold a mock debate while mud wrestling as the chief handler sends them through a square dance of maximising appeal while minimising any sort of honour or dignity:

> Wet yer finger, stick it in the air
>
> Which way the wind blows- go there
>
> Campaign America
>
> Like it oughta be—
>
> Likability![14]

Barbara breaks off into a rap on the side, condemning the state of the nation and insinuating that past presidents are weeping in their graves. Ultimately, she rebels, calling for truth and morals in politics, throwing the handlers into the mud and setting off on her own as the public take an interest in her as the candidate who thinks for herself.

Compared to other skits in the abandoned show, *Presidential*

---

13. Ibid., 14, 17.

Larson intended this song to be satire, not a genuine prediction of how far actual discourse would degrade. How could he have known that the last two of the quoted lines would turn out to be actual political issues?

14. Box 8-2 Jonathan Larson. 'Likability/La Di Da' (Draft). Box 8, Folder 2, Jonathan Larson Papers, Music Division, Library of Congress, Washington, D.C., 22.

Politics looks particularly highbrow and professional. Other contributors' works are included amongst Larson's papers, and the quality is sub-par and flat, especially when compared to earlier Lampoon shows like *Lemmings*, wherein an MC instructed the audience in suicidal tactics, or even various skits and songs from the Adelphi cabarets. Samples include a sketch where oral sex is illegal and a man buys giant condoms for the first time in a setup similar to a sequence in the 1987 cult film *Amazon Women on the Moon*. Another is about genetically-engineered custom pets but devolves into baby fur porn, and a series of running gags shows a couple getting lost in the subway system on the way to the Tricentennial parade.[15] Some sketches, such as one about socialising frozen embryos, add a welcome sense of bizarreness, but little about the scripts actually approaches being good.

Gotta Get the Vision Thing

Larson's papers for *Presidential Politics* are historiographically fascinating. As a miniature musical in its own right, the depth of *Politics'* materials allows the reader to see Larson's workflow at the time, both in how he generated and refined ideas. While extrapolating similar information is possible with Larson's larger works, *Politics'* condensed nature makes it an ideal starting point and a simpler journey for understanding his creative process.

As part of his brainstorming, Larson took cues from his usual sources: magazine articles, the *New York Times* (which he read daily, and cover to cover on Sundays), and the world around him. Amongst his papers are photocopies of 'When You Kick a Liberal: A post-election parable' by Garrison Keillor[16] and a modern

---

15. The running gag sequence is the only one remembered by any of the Lampoon staff, and not fondly. I recommend not googling 'baby fur porn'.

16. Garrison Keillor, "When You Kick a Liberal". *Harper's Magazine*, January,

marketing take on the second coming of Jesus.[17] Of greater interest are Larson's copious notes. For something so short (the demo tape runs just short of 20 minutes, including an extended playout) and someone used to working quickly, Larson painstakingly annotated his choices and setups, writing himself questions to try and build an idea for the piece.

A tiny notepad kicks it off: "There's one thing we need - it's a gem or a seed."[18] Notes blossom, starting with a specific point (how would a candidate campaign for green issues and waste disposal in 2076) and growing out to a general view.[19] A newsroom setting, plots, and concepts spill out over the pages before Larson clicks on his first solid ideas: "Write to the pictures [...] The campaign is a movie."[20] Refinement: "Talking heads are boring."[21] Notes cover camera angles, who would be involved in building a campaign, how to mould a candidate for the media, and the state of a nation who would vote for them. Pages of handwritten notes follow, including a list of books to read, such as Ed Diamond's *The Spot: The Rise of Political Advertising on Television*. Creatively, Larson asked himself questions to determine direction:

1989, 72-75. Photocopy in Box 8, Folder 3, Jonathan Larson Papers, Music Division, Library of Congress, Washington, D.C.

For non-Americans, Keillor is best known as the discredited ex-host of the gently satirical radio series *A Prairie Home Companion*.

17. Author unattributed, "Forum: He's Back!!!," *Harper's Magazine*, April 1989, 47-53. Photocopy in Box 8, Folder 3, Jonathan Larson Papers, Music Division, Library of Congress, Washington, D.C.

18. Jonathan Larson. Handwritten notes. Box 8, Folder 1, Jonathan Larson Papers, Music Division, Library of Congress, Washington, D.C.

A reworked version of this line would end up in 'The Vision Thing' - "The one thing we need- to make democrats bleed / is the seed of a notion / to sucker the nation"

19. Ibid.

20. Ibid.

21. Ibid.

- 84 was the year of the 'Handler' - 88 the year of 'Negative campaigning' - What will 1992 be like?

- Assuming we will be around in 2076, what will the issues be? How will the demographics change? The geography?

- What are the unwritten laws in politics? What are the techniques to talking in circles?[22]

Next, who would be his candidate? As Larson sketched out one idea after another, he stumbled into a key aspect: "LIKABILITY - less important to be sound of thought & syntax than to look agreeable on screen."[23] Larson also kept a multi-page list of terms, ideas, and reference reminders as he worked.[24]

In his first draft, simply titled 'Likability: The messenger is the message,' the entire sequence is one elongated skit.[25] The candidate is male and unnamed, and all proceedings occur on a single sound stage. Rather than caged experts, leading handler Big Al supplies footage to newscasters and uses zombified focus groups to get feedback. This draft is satirically sharper, but unfocused in a medium which requires moving quickly. The 'Likability' song refrain ('Wet your finger...') recurs as Big Al brings in an actor to play the opposing candidate in a series of smear videos, creating a scandal which is met with apathy equal to his own candidate's positive images.

Whether this version is complete or not is questionable - the

22. Jonathan Larson. 'Questions' (Typed notes). Box 8, Folder 3, Jonathan Larson Papers, Music Division, Library of Congress, Washington, D.C., 3H

23. Jonathan Larson. Handwritten notes. Box 8, Folder 3, Jonathan Larson Papers, Music Division, Library of Congress, Washington, D.C., 10H

24. Jonathan Larson. 'Likability' (Typewritten notes). Box 8, Folder 3, Jonathan Larson Papers, Music Division, Library of Congress, Washington, D.C., 13H

25. Jonathan Larson. 'Likability' (Draft). Box 8, Folder 2, Jonathan Larson Papers, Music Division, Library of Congress, Washington, D.C.

candidate is not in a secure spot at the end, but Larson ultimately took the idea in another direction. Something was missing in this version, and a sheet of paper contained the single word answer: "Conflict!!"[26] Finally, the idea took shape: "Female candidate. Mud wrestling."[27] Three scenes: "1. Briefing, 2. Training, 3. Practice Debate."[28] The characters became archetypes, the comedy broader. The remainder of the papers for *Presidential Politics* are focused on endless tinkering and refinement. Once Larson got his first draft arranged, he made ever-finer adjustments on lines and finally individual words, especially in the dialogue-heavy 'The Vision Thing.'

Politics still holds up after 25 years, but only in part due to the catchy music. After all, even the best-written novelty songs fade if the jokes stop being topical but, with *Presidential Politics*, the opposite occurred: the piece is funnier now because Larson (unwittingly or not) guessed the decline of civil, intellectual discourse in American political campaigns - and who would be involved.

Case in point: in the song 'Likability,' Barbara calls out

> Pour some ales
>
> For old Roger Ailes
>
> And Danny Quayles [sic], his Protege
>
> Back in '96-

---

26. Jonathan Larson. 'The Vision Thing' (Draft). Box 8, Folder 2, Jonathan Larson Papers, Music Division, Library of Congress, Washington, D.C.

27. Why mud wrestling? Larson wrote out notes on environmental issues and geographical terms, starting with swamp, quicksand, and erosion, moving on to sediment, muck, mudslides, wading, rivers, and branching off to the Tigress, Euphrates, and the Tower of Babel, but ultimately boxed in "wallow" under "mudslide" and fixated on mud for a few more pages, ultimately making the leap from there.

Jonathan Larson. Handwritten notes. Box 8, Folder 3, Jonathan Larson Papers, Music Division, Library of Congress, Washington, D.C., 67-70H, 79-84H.

28. Ibid., 25H.

His looks- his tricks

Make Tricky Dick's crimes

- passé[29]

Larson was focused on two of Ailes' roles: first as a spin doctor and media advisor for Presidents Nixon, Reagan, and the first Bush, and second, as author of the 1988 book *You are the Message: Secrets of the Master Communicators*. *Message* was a guide to public speaking and improved corporate and political communications, using Ailes' access to then-contemporary politicians as his case studies. Larson's lyric "The message is the messenger" hearkens back to the tome's title, a contemporary reference which would be lost to most audiences now, though Ailes' book remains in print.

What Larson could not have predicted back in 1989, however, was that Ailes would almost single-handedly shift American media towards the right throughout the 1990s, first bringing conservative radio host Rush Limbaugh to syndicated television in 1991, then becoming president of CNBC and hosting a nightly talk show in 1993. In 1996, the year Larson predicted as the long-forgotten ex-vice president Dan Quayle's year of scandal, Ailes left CNBC to launch what would become his legacy, Fox News Channel. FNC's openly right-wing agenda and confrontational style towards the American left and critical response would rapidly further the reduction of politics to sound bites and simplified arguments, making Larson's vision of candidates accusing each other of pedophilia and finding safety in parroting feel-good phraseology seem depressingly close to actual 21st-century election coverage.[30]

While *American Tricentennial* would fizzle out before seeing the stage, Larson recorded a fully arranged demo which crackles

29. Jonathan Larson. 'Likability/La Di Da' (Draft). Box 8, Folder 2, Jonathan Larson Papers, Music Division, Library of Congress, Washington, D.C., 25.

30. Most of this book - and all but minor revision work for this section - was written well before Donald Trump's presidential campaign existed, let alone the

with potential. Featuring Scott Burkell as Mo, Valerie Pettiford as Barbara Bosom, Indira Christopherson as Helga, 'Sara' as RJ and other minor female roles, and Larson himself as the other remaining male characters, the tape evokes the hustle and bustle of a political campaign and makes it easy to imagine the stage directions coming to life, despite their absurdities.[31] 'Do Unto Them' also stayed in Larson's mind, appearing on the setlist for his aborted 'Songs 1991' concert.[32]

Getting Naked

In 1986, a group of up-and-coming NYU acting graduates created Naked Angels, a theatre company for showcasing their talents. The group became one of the premiere fixtures on the New York fringe by the end of the 1980s, setting up shop in a disused framing factory and converting it into 'The Space,' their home for seven years.

Founding member and actress Jodie Markell remembers:

> What was interesting about Naked Angels was that it crossed over from the fringe to the mainstream. In the '80s, it really felt like if you were interested in theatre, you'd be going to see something at Naked Angels. It was raw. We never had as specific a style

reality of his winning the election. Final revisions were concluded towards the end of the campaign, and Larson's prescience in this area only became more depressing as the election season went on.

31. Larson's session notes have no last names, and 'Sara' is a generic enough name to be up in the air. The most likely candidate is Sara Weaver, who played Elisabeth in the 1988 and 1989 productions of *Superbia*.

32. Victoria Leacock Hoffman produced Larson's *Superbia* concert in 1989 and *Boho Days* in 1990. The two planned on doing a concert/cabaret night in 1991 and Larson went so far as to put together a setlist and invite participants, but he and Leacock Hoffman ultimately decided to focus on doing *tick, tick... BOOM!* at the Village Gate instead.

as Steppenwolf, but it just felt really fresh, and
we didn't have the organisation and classic leading playwright like the Atlantic had with David
Mamet. It was a company run by like 40 people, so
it was pretty wild. There was a bit of a rock and roll
feeling underneath everything.

Thanks to some personal connections, Larson found work
scoring two shows for the group in 1990: *The Naked Truth*, a collection of one-acts on censorship, and *Tell Them Angel Sent Me*,
a high-end fundraiser. Larson had become friendly with some of
the members at Naked Angels and desperately wanted to join. He
began hanging out at The Space, performing works-in-progress for
the members, and helping out on shows. While the group never
accepted Larson as a proper member, a number of Naked Angels'
actors performed in various productions of *Superbia* between 1988
and 1990, as well as on the demo for *Presidential Politics*.

Larson's first show for the group, *The Naked Truth: Ten Takes
on Censorship (& some music)*, was part of what Naked Angels
called their annual 'issue' shows. For these productions, multiple
playwrights wrote short pieces on a set theme and the company's
members would produce, direct, and perform in them, often with
some outside assistance. The format allowed as many members as
possible to participate and to create something modern and relevant in the process. Writers on *Naked Truth* included Christopher
Durang, Kenneth Lonergan, and Pippin Parker, with Matthew
Broderick and Joe Mantello amongst the directors. Larson composed and played incidental music and, upon the show's extension,
wrote a musical finale, 'The Truth is a Lie'. The song is a forerunner
to 'White Male World,' telling the audience to ignore history and
culture, follow orders from the government, and live in ignorance.

In retrospect, the scripts from *Naked Truth* favoured force-feed-
ing concepts over subtlety. As with the Adelphi cabarets, the 'issue'

plays were written quickly and with topicality in mind, performed for a week, and discarded. As a result, a sense of artificiality pervades the entire collection. The shortest bits discussed corporate influence on TV standards and practices, community standards on libraries, and attacks on the National Endowment for the Arts. Longer plays included a take on violence in the movies (an editor becomes uncomfortable when offered a chance to work on a real snuff film) and another in which a man refuses to undress or talk dirty during sex with a prostitute, as doing either would be inappropriate. Christopher Durang's play showed a family going to extremes of American Nationalism, converting to evangelical Christianity and passing judgement on their coworkers and fellow students, all while minding their language. The highlight, however, is Warren Leight's (*Law & Order: SVU* and *Criminal Intent) Name Those Names,* a game show spoof 'hosted' by arch conservative Pat Buchanan, wherein contestants are held at proverbial gunpoint to out fellow liberals or face ruin.

Tell Them Angel Sent Me was a site-specific work set in a restaurant-turned-1930s speakeasy. Part stage show, part cabaret, and part improv, the cast played a multitude of period characters on the last night of Prohibition.[33] Angel, a bootlegging mobster, is throwing a birthday party for his rival - a toast to forming a new partnership as their bars go legit. Throughout the evening, various scenes took place around the venue, the cast mingled in-character with patrons, and two stages were packed with musical acts - mostly Naked Angels company members and friends - singing songs from the 1930s.

Naked Angels company member Juliane Hofenberg remembers:

33. For non-American readers, the United States outlawed the sale and manufacture of alcohol between 1920 and 1933. This is known as the 'Prohibition Era,' immortalised in fiction for the rise in organised crime around producing and distributing bootleg liquor.

(*Angel*) was our second performance benefit, but it was our first big ticket event, and it was the first time John Kennedy Jr. put his name on something for us. He co-hosted it, and he was on our board, [...] and that was the first really big ask we made of him. That script was written by 10 writers. We had 60 people in the cast and 400 people in the audience paying an absurdly high ticket price for us, like $150 per ticket. Nobody in New York was doing that kind of thing back then. We got a lot of complaints from people, like "How dare you ask $100 for people to go to dinner and see a show?"

The audience had to come dressed for a speakeasy in 1933, and we made that very clear. We were in character from the moment the doors opened. The guys outside, the staff, the waiters, everybody was doing improv. The show itself was only an hour, but the evening was six hours and everybody was in that space and time for the duration.

Larson, appearing as pianist Johnny Fingers, played piano in the restaurant's upstairs bar where early arrivals mingled before dinner was served in the main space below, as well as for late arrivals unable to get seating after tickets were ultimately oversold. In addition to backing the Naked Angles crew for six hours, he also performed an original composition, 'Break out the Booze.' 'Booze,' another rarity released from Larson's archives, is sung by a down-on-his-luck fellow jazzily lamenting the state of the world and suggesting everybody do as the title says and drink their troubles away.[34]

Larson made his final contributions to Naked Angels in 1991

---

34. 'Break out the Booze' was sung at the 2006 Library of Congress concert

for the play *A Darker Purpose*. A noir-inspired gambler's tale, the piece was cursed with a rocky production. Not only was it playwright Wendy Riss's first show with Naked Angels, but it was also the company's first work neither written nor directed by a member of the company.[35] According to Naked Angels member and *Darker Purpose* producer Beth Emelson, a company member had promised to act in the show and brought the rest of the group on board. Emelson asked Larson to contribute, as the scene changes were punctuated with singing showgirls and required a music director. Riss also wanted an original song to open the show, which Larson composed in addition to incidental music.

As much as the script for *A Darker Purpose* aimed for edge, the show ultimately tried too hard. Philip is a lucky guy winning nightly on the roulette table, but has an unlucky past and even unluckier acquaintances: everybody wants a piece of his winnings, either through befriending him with fraudulent intent, sleeping with him to clear out his bank account, or ultimately rigging games to drive him off. Philip's distant brother, Wolf, appears with news of their father's mysterious death before learning the truth behind his brother's circumstances. Complicating matters is Wolf's ex, Louise, who initially seduces Philip for his money, but ultimately falls in love with him.

Based on listening to Larson's MIDI files, *Purpose*'s music was far from his best work. Riss wrote the lyrics for *A Darker Purpose*'s opening number, a jazzy tribute to Las Vegas, though the music is closer to the score from a *Peanuts* special than anything tonally appropriate for the script's gritty noir atmosphere.[36] All other songs

---

celebrating the induction of Larson's papers to the Music Division and Larson's demo was included on the 2007 CD *Jonathan Sings Larson*.

35. Riss would go on to find success in television, working as a writer and story editor on shows including *Hung* and *The Killing*.

36. Jonathan Larson. Music for 'Naked Vegas,' stored as multiple files

used in *A Darker Purpose* were catalogue tracks, such as Johnny Cash's 'Ring of Fire'.

Adame & Yves[37]

Larson's final collaboration in the early 1990s was also his most ambitious, but also not his own. In 1992, an alumnus of the prestigious BMI Lehman Engel Musical Theatre Workshop named Paul Scott Goodman began an offshoot project to create new works with support from BMI's infrastructure.[38] Calling the group Multi Media Musicals, Goodman sought collaborators to bring new developments in musical theatre past the stage and to find a new niche for the genre in film and television. Assembling an up-and-coming 'dream team,' he first turned to his fellow composer and neighbour, Jonathan Larson.

"I always had this thing with him," reminisced Goodman at a memorial evening in 1996:

> [We were] rivals - there was no other way to say it. When I met him, and he met me, it was like "Oh fuck - here's this guy, and he's got as much ego as I've got, as much passion and talent, and he wants to change things." I thought I was the only one in New York doing this, and I found somebody else doing it. That's what it is in New York. Ambition

---

(Microsoft Word and Digital Performer Files). Contained within disk40.img. Jonathan Larson Papers, Music Division, Library of Congress, Washington, D.C.

37. A previous edition of this section was originally published on Playbill. com as 'How the Feverish Imaginations of Jonathan Larson, Rusty Magee and Friends Birthed the Musical *Sacred Cows*'. An earlier draft was also included with the liner notes for the *Sacred Cows* digital audio release. I have since rewritten the piece for tonal needs, as well as to include new material from additional research.

38. Goodman is best known as the composer of *Bright Lights, Big City* and *ROOMS: A Rock Romance*.

equals competition. In reality, you should be close
and go to each other's shows and be friendly, but it
wasn't like that. We had this grudging respect. We
wanted the same thing.[39]

At the time, Larson was reaching the end of his work on *tick,
tick...BOOM!* and recently finished his first full draft of *RENT*.
Hoping to get further work in TV after providing incidental music
years earlier for *Sesame Street*, Larson jumped at the chance.

BMI Workshop director Maury Yeston suggested his own candidates, leading Goodman to invite Jeremy Roberts - then working in-studio with *Jekyll & Hyde* composer Frank Wildhorn and
as Linda Eder's musical director - to come on board.[40] Goodman
also knew Rusty Magee, a composer working the commercial and
comedy scenes.[41] At the time, Magee was serving an extended run
as musical director at the West Bank Cafe Downstairs Theatre
Bar, which he ran in partnership with comedian Lewis Black and
actor Rand Foerster, and where he first met Goodman.[42] While
production of Magee's new Off-Broadway musicalisation of
Moliere's *Scapin* would take him away from the project at times,
he served as Goodman's unofficial second-in-command at Multi
Media Musicals.

Also participating was Bob Golden, who had made a name
for himself in television and played in a band alongside theatrical

---

39. Vicky's Larson Evening, Tape #1. Video. February 1996. Privately held by
Victoria Leacock Hoffman, Washington, D.C.

40. Yeston's key works include the scores to *Nine, Titanic,* and *Phantom,* an
alternative take on *The Phantom of the Opera*. Linda Eder is a theatrical singer and
actress, and was married to Wildhorn at the time.

41. Magee's best known works include *The Green Heart* and *Ubu Rock*. He
died of cancer in 2003.

42. The West Bank Cafe Downstairs Theatre Bar is now known as the Laurie
Beechman Theatre.

composers David Yazbek and Adam Guettel.[43] A mutual friend at BMI introduced Golden to Goodman and the workshop. Golden decided to take a chance on the project, seeing it as a learning experience to work with stage composers - an area largely outside his professional interest.

The five collaborators - along with early departure Larry Kirwan - first asked themselves what they were even looking to create.[44] Goodman's outline from August 1992 on the group's goals suggests three options: short works for targeted broadcast demographics, a musical soap opera for MTV, and an annual revue featuring rock and theatre stars from the New York area. The document concludes: "It will be the express purpose of MULTI MEDIA MUSICALS to return The Musical to the forefront of the entertainment world."[45] An uncredited document in Larson's papers suggested three items for both TV and video, almost entirely for children. One, *A Day In the Life*, would follow children around town for a day, featuring a

---

43. Golden's career has largely been in film and television composition, his work being heard in *Sesame Street, Insomniac with Dave Attell*, and *Fahrenheit 9/11*.

David Yazbek wrote the stage adaptation scores (music and lyrics) for *The Full Monty* and *Dirty Rotten Scoundrels* and the theme song for the children's game show *Where in the World is Carmen Sandiego?*

Adam Guettel is the grandson of Richard Rodgers and son of Mary Rodgers. Richard Rodgers, along with Oscar Hammerstein II, kicked off what is considered to be the golden age of musical theatre with their show *Oklahoma!*. The show was the first musical to fully integrate the script, lyrics, music, and choreography in service of the story. Rodgers & Hammerstein went on to write a series of massive hits, now considered standards in the musical theatre canon. Guettel's mother, Mary Rodgers, was a composer and children's novelist, most famous for writing the score for *Once Upon a Mattress* and the novel *Freaky Friday*.

44. By 1992, Kirwan had been fronting his Irish punk rock band 'Black 47' for three years. In addition to his music career, he has also written numerous plays and musicals dealing with Irish history and issues from an Irish-Republican perspective.

45. Paul Scott Goodman. 'Multi Media Musicals..A New BMI Workshop'. Box 21a, Folder 1, Jonathan Larson Papers, Music Division, Library of Congress, Washington, D.C., 74H.

song about all the places where kids spend their time.[46] Other early ideas included musicalising fairy tales and an album of songs about daily routines, such as brushing one's teeth.

From November 1992 through March 1993, the group met weekly at Roberts' studio to discuss ideas, bring in songs, revise the script, and record the demo. "Everyone contributed," recalls Roberts. "We all wrote on it, we all performed on it." Tempers flared, but in expected ways, as everybody had strong ideas about the project, especially Larson. "Part of the challenge [...] was to see if everyone could collaborate," remembers Goodman, "[but] when we fought, they were always healthy fights."

Despite the drama, outlooks grew enthusiastic as the show came together, though Golden also remembers ideas taking precedence over order: "Everybody would go home and write, then bring something in. It was totally the opposite of what I was used to in TV." A week after the first meeting, the five collaborators began bringing in material, and within three weeks, the first recordings were laid to tape, with Roberts producing and engineering the sessions in addition to his writing duties. For the next five months, songs were written solo in every collaborative arrangement imaginable, then reworked and performed by all five members of the team.

While the show's exact format never solidified (would it be live with an audience or strictly studio-bound?), the first Multi Media Musicals project, now titled *Sacred Cows*, was devised and pitched as a weekly anthology with each episode taking a different Biblical or mythological story and giving it a '90s celebrity twist (for example, casting Prince as Icarus) using contemporary music and visuals. "We decided on Bible stories," explains Goodman, "because they were in the public domain and we wouldn't have

46. 'VIDEO/T.V. IDEAS'. Box 21a, Folder 1, Jonathan Larson Papers, Music Division, Library of Congress, Washington, D.C., 76H.

to pay royalties on them." For the pilot, the team reworked the Garden of Eden story. Other ideas tossed about for the *Sacred Cows* header included a 1950s take on Siddhartha and Tina Turner telling the story of Sodom and Gomorrah.[47]

A New Beginning

As the music rises, a lone Angel (Goodman) documents the apocalypse: one morning, and without warning, God (Larson) has destroyed the world and, as grunged-out heroin-chic Angels gather, they ask for a cosmic redo. God, an outburst-prone rock diva a la Axl Rose, is *so* over the old world, but now he's bored and agrees to the Angels' request — but this time, it's going to be different. Creating paradise from a bombed-out parking lot, God creates Adame (Magee/Golden), a modern, urban alpha-female with a taste for pop iconography.[48]

Unfortunately for God and the Angels, Adame is a little too modern. Despite living in paradise, she frets in rap about how she can't talk to her girlfriends without a phone, let alone find a decent curry. Bored from the start, she wants to leave and find something to do - even bowling - rather than simply hang around and taking it easy. To complicate things further, her sex drive is unstoppable: "I want some action and I DEMAND satisfaction."[49]

Finally, Adame's complaints are too much, and amidst a tantrum, God takes one of her ribs and creates Yves (Goodman), a

47. 'SACRED COWS'. Box 21a, Folder 1, Jonathan Larson Papers, Music Division, Library of Congress, Washington, D.C., 75H.

48. Magee was no longer involved by the time the 'Tree Montage' was recorded, and a recording script assigns the Adame lines to 'BG', aka Bob Golden.

49. Bob Golden, Paul Scott Goodman, Jonathan Larson, Rusty Magee, & Jeremy Roberts. *Sacred Cows: Episode #1 "A New Beginning" (The Story of Adame and Yves)*. Cover Dated 29 April 1993, Pages dated 5 May 1993. Box 21a, Folder 2, Jonathan Larson Papers, Music Division, Library of Congress, Washington, D.C., 5.

naked hippie with a guitar affixed to his crotch. Unlike his counterpart, Yves is perfectly happy enjoying the quiet, strumming out folk melodies and rhyming variations of "Yippie aye oh" into drippy love poem:

Yippee Aye-Oh Yippie Aye-Ay

Give me an order and I'll obey[50]

Adame is not amused and resorts to increasingly drastic measures to woo her asexual mate and strip him of his instrument.

The story isn't complete without a snake, and in *Sacred Cows*, the Serpent manifests as a stogie-chomping, three-headed advertising agent who looks to draw the hapless humans to the Tree of Knowledge with a series of catchy jingles. In another modern twist, the tree is a tower of televisions with CDs, VHS tapes, and game cartridges hanging off wire branches and boasting a bright red remote. As the serpent lures them in, the Angels fret: the same mistakes are happening all over again. Adame is down with the idea of the tree, but Yves hesitates. As the Serpent woos them ("Move a little faster. Let it be your master"), a four-way counterpoint of fear and desire builds.[51] When Adame and Yves succumb, God appears on the screens and condemns them not to banishment, but to house arrest: the pair are doomed to live with the Serpent in the garden, bored for all eternity. As the parking lot is replaced with an idealised set, Adame grows bitterly depressed from the lack of stimulation, Yves celebrates, and the Angels torture the Serpent, asking, "What would you do, stuck in paradise forever?" before departing, content that it will remain "morning forever, in paradise."[52]

---

50. Ibid., 9.

51. Ibid., 11.

52. Ibid., 15.

God Gave You a Temper, So Use It!

Sacred Cows could have been indulgent, crude, or an incoherent mishmash of individual styles. It wound up being none of the three. The music builds on early-'90s trends, invoking early alternative-rock bands like Live and Nirvana, plus key female rappers such as Queen Latifah and Salt-N-Pepa. While the lyrics were tongue-in-cheek, such as the Serpent arguing with itself about corruption tactics, we can still feel the Angels' tenuous position as they're forced to watch humanity repeating its doomed history and Yves' fear of corruption.[53]

Musically, the score ran on character motifs: ethereal pop for the Angels, early-'90s pop-rap for Adame, country-western for Yves, hard rock for God, and jazz for the Serpent, supplemented by big 1950s-esque advertising jingles. Running in and out of the individual tunes is the Angels' apocalyptic piano motif, a reminder that, despite the jokes, disaster is just around the corner. Production-wise, all five collaborators played instruments and sang on the recording, and Roberts handled arrangements and mixing, deftly pulling individual styles together and incorporating both levity and an unearthly air into the recording.

Introducing God was the team's greatest challenge. According to Larson's notes, they needed to discover the creator's motives in creating a new world, find an appropriate tone for Generation X's supreme being, and ultimately break down why it was all doomed to fail again. Goodman drafted the first God song, 'Get it Right This Time,' which would be replaced by the bouncy, power-pop Larson/Goodman collaboration 'Another Go' (using the motif from finale

---

53. Ibid., 7.

There are two unique editions of *Sacred Cows* in Larson's audio archive. One is a copy of the final version, as subsequently released commercially. The other is an earlier edition, which alters the order of some Yves/Serpent bits in 'The Tree Montage' and a few alternative line readings.

'Eden'), and ultimately, the crunchy, shouty 'I'm God'.[54] According to Goodman, he and Larson co-wrote the song at Larson's apartment, but the session deteriorated as the two began arguing over who would play God in the show, shouting "I'm God!" "No, I'm God!" At a memorial in 1996, Golden explained that, "Jonathan wanted to do this hardcore one-chord thing [...] and the brilliance of the song was that you needed to explain how the new beginning was going to come about. Jonathan finds the path of least resistance and writes 'I'm God and I just blew up the goddamn world!'"[55]

Larson's contributions also included lyrics for the Snake's 'Gotta Get a Jingle' (music by Rusty Magee), lyrics for 'No More Mister Nice Guy,' (music uncredited), and music and lyrics for 'Eden,' minus Bob Golden's 'Apocalypse' motif at the end. Another collaborator wrote an alternative, early lyric for 'Eden,' but the handwritten lyric lacks a credit.

Unfortunately, the satire-happy networks weren't ready for a work so casually undermined a core myth behind American religion. Golden remembers "going with [Goodman] to a meeting with MTV, but nobody knew what to do with it." Despite liking the songs and the ideas, the producers had no idea how to bring the show to life, and passed. The theatrical world responded much the same way: "We did a presentation of the demo for like 30 people at the BMI Workshop, and afterwards, they were silent. I've never been that uncomfortable in my life." At the same memorial service where Golden shared his stories, Goodman admitted "it wasn't ready."[56]

---

54. A recording of 'Another Go' exists in Larson's audio archives, attached to the end of his 1993 interview with journalist Barry Singer. Larson's MIDI files for 'Another Go' and 'Eden' are also present in his digital files.

55. Vicky's Larson Evening, Tape #1. Video. February 1996. Privately held by Victoria Leacock Hoffman, Washington, D.C.

56. Vicky's Larson Evening, Tape #1. Video. February 1996. Privately held by Victoria Leacock Hoffman, Washington, D.C.

Even so, the project might have fit in well as a bound-ary-pusher on cable TV. In the early 1990s, MTV was a haven of quirky and offbeat programming, providing an outlet for outsider animation in *Liquid Television*, plus rising alternative comedians such as Denis Leary and Colin Quinn, and would soon be home to cult sketch comedy heroes *The State*. Comedy Central, meanwhile, carried Canadian surrealists *Kids in the Hall* and the derisive, smart-alecky *Mystery Science Theater 3000*. Even network comedy was slowly getting its edge back as old stalwart *Saturday Night Live* was entering a renaissance with Phil Hartman, Dana Carvey, Mike Myers, Adam Sandler, and Chris Farley leading the bill, while *The Simpsons* topped primetime ratings. "We were years ahead of the game," recalls Roberts.

Come Spring 1993, Magee was becoming increasingly involved with *Scapin*, which took him away from the final recording ses-sions. That summer, *RENT* entered development at the New York Theatre Workshop, drawing Larson away from the project as well. With two of its core creatives unable to commit the extra time required to refine the show, *Sacred Cows* was left to fade into the background. The premature deaths of Larson (1996) and Magee (2003) would subsequently keep the material confined to archive: "After Jonathan and Rusty died, we didn't want to feel like we were exploiting their memory," explains Goodman.

Out of *Sacred Cows*, however, came close working relationships between its creators, especially for Golden, who worked frequently with Magee until the latter's untimely passing. The pair performed in early readings for *RENT* at New York Theatre Workshop, and much of *RENT's* final creative team would subsequently go on to produce Goodman's *Bright Lights, Big City* at NYTW in 1998. In the meantime, the collaborators would all remain close and keep in touch personally and professionally.

Looking Back

How do the creators feel about their project 20 years on?

"I'm amazed by how many ideas we all had — there's so much going on. You hear the personalities of the entire team, [everyone's voice] really comes through," says Roberts. "Some of the creative choices we made back in Spring of '93, before the whole animated thing, before irreverence, including a rap...»

"It's weird to hear Jonathan Larson singing "I'm God" and talking about heaven," mentions Goodman. 'We were all so hungry back then...»

"It was a chance for five creators to get together and create," says Roberts. "With most projects, you have a master — such as a producer — but here, we didn't have one. We just got together and did it. It was a true collaboration."

As for Multi Media Musicals, Goodman reminisces: "*Sacred Cows* was meant to be the first project. We started on a few more things, but after *Bright Lights, Big City* went to workshop, [MMM] fizzled out. Jonathan's death also took away a lot of the appeal."

While *Sacred Cows* remained consigned to archive for two decades, the recording and ideas are still fresh today, despite the early '90s aesthetic. While perhaps not as scathing as the *South Park* creators' treatment of religion in that series or Broadway's *The Book of Mormon*, *Sacred Cows* flashed a rebellious spark from creative people given the freedom to make something for themselves on their own terms, and now grants us a musical snapshot of five talented young artists on the edge of ascension.

Chapter Four

Fear and Self-Loathing at Popular Prices
tick, tick... BOOM!

Cages or Wings
Which do you prefer?
Ask the birds
Fear or love baby, don't say the answer
Action speaks louder than words

—tick, tick... BOOM!

I F *SUPERBIA* WAS Larson's theatre of ideas, a grand sprawling world built around fears of yuppie excess, *tick, tick... BOOM!* was Larson dipping his toes into theatre of the self, of theatre as therapy and raw emotion. A reaction to the chief complaints about *Superbia* - too big, too out there, too much focus on concept over character - *tick* was all about character, with Larson looking at himself and wondering where he'd gone wrong. A fan of the 1980s boom in performance art practitioners like Laurie Anderson and Eric Bogosian, Larson set out to write an intimate, personal work which could connect with the hip crowds at PS122 and the Franklin Furnace: just him, a piano, and, if funds allowed, a couple guys in a band. "He was inspired by Denis Leary," says friend and producer Victoria Leacock Hoffman. "He didn't think he was better than Spalding Gray or Bogosian, but he knew he could write something better than Denis Leary, and he wanted to be able to keep performing and carrying on."

According to Larson's sister, Julie Larson McCollum, *tick, tick… BOOM!* was written "out of frustration." *Superbia* had failed to catch on, and early work on *RENT* with Billy Aronson had fizzled out, leaving Larson without an ongoing project. By comparison, big sister Julie had established herself in Los Angeles working on television commercials. After spending the remaining money from his *Superbia* grant on a shoestring-budget trip to Europe, Larson returned to New York to face his 30th birthday: one where he continued waiting tables, wearing crumbling shoes, and watching his closest friends advance while he felt he was staying put. His response, first called *30/90* (Larson, born in 1960 would turn 30 in January 1990), shows a confused, frustrated creator faced with the romantic question artists constantly face: stay true to your work and likely live forever in poverty, or get a day job and reduce creative work to a hobby? Larson's friend and creative sounding board, Eddie Rosenstein, remembers those days well:

> I was paying my bills off [by] working as a free-lancer, and I'd take anything that came up to pay those bills, and I would squeeze my work in between that - which meant I often had projects that would fizzle out because I couldn't see them through. Jonathan was my role model, and somebody who had the courage to work in a restaurant and pick up just a few little bits here and there, but to use his most productive hours on his most productive days focused on his goal, even though it seemed as far away and absurd as all of our goals at that time.

A Rock Monologue

Unlike *Superbia* or *RENT*, which saw heavy revision to their core storylines, *tick* stayed fairly consistent throughout its four years of development. From its initial incarnation as *30/90* through *Boho Days* and, finally, *tick, tick... BOOM!*, the structure remained constant: Larson spends the weekend leading up to his 30th birthday confronted by his waning career prospects and disintegrating romance. He gives up on the theatre to take a market research job on the big day itself, only to find he's unsuited to working in advertising, and ultimately returning to his true calling.

Two large monologues from *30/90* were cut early on. The opener, about Larson selling tickets for his ex's dance show, would be replaced with his own surprise birthday party when *30/90* became *Boho Days*, though the following scene would be repurposed: instead of Larson interacting with Susan after the post-show party as a lead-in to 'Green Green Dress,' the action would shift to the aforementioned birthday party.[57] A second, extensive monologue about working at the diner - capped off with a nightmarish family ordering breakfast, only for their daughter to vomit all over their food - would be cut entirely.

Musically, the first casualty was 'London Faces,' wherein Larson expressed his disappointment about visiting the UK.[58] 'Swimming,' a song about Larson's workout habits being interrupted by nagging concerns, and 'Debtor Club,' a Tears-for-Fears-esque track about credit cards and keeping up appearances, made it into *Boho Days* for its September 1990 run, but were cut when the show became

---

57. The ex in question, named Marta in the script, was Brenda Daniels, a Merce-Cunningham-trained dancer. Larson would also base aspects of Maureen in *RENT* on Daniels, and their collaborations are discussed in Appendix A.

58. 'London Faces' is on the 2007 *Jonathan Sings Larson* CD, and Larson wrote an extensive journal entry on his computer about his trip to London and Paris, perhaps in anticipation of turning it into a monologue for *30/90*, but no scripted edition ever materialised.

tick, tick... BOOM! in 1991. The song 'Boho Days', envisioned as an encore, would be tried as an alternative opening in the eponymous edition of the show and again discarded, as was wistful love song 'See Her Smile,' replaced with the darker, more contemplative 'Find the Key'.[59] New songs would also be added: 'Johnny Can't Decide,' a late-night contemplative ballad added for *Boho Days*, 'Real Life,' contrasting the differences between Larson's bohemian existence with his upbringing and the expectations of someone his age, and 'No More,' a rocking tune about the joys of moving from a hellhole apartment to a luxury flat, all premiered during 1991's run of the ultimately named *tick, tick... BOOM!* The remaining songs: '30/90,' 'Green Green Dress,' 'Sugar,' 'Sunday,' 'Play Game,' 'Why,' 'Therapy,' and 'Louder Than Words' remained in the show from start to finish.

Real Life

Larson's solo version of *tick* gives off a more complicated aura compared to the reworked 2001 edition most readers will know. On the one hand, Larson's performance is raw, inherently personal, and emotional - perhaps too much so in the *Boho Days* iteration, as he wailed during the show's final monologue. While director Pippin Parker reined in Larson's character-actor eccentricities for the 1991-1993 productions of *tick*, Larson's authenticity as a shabbily-dressed composer remained apparent. As in real life, this was Larson not just afraid of waiting tables and losing his girlfriend, but fearing where America, the theatre, and his generation as a whole were heading. Unlike *RENT*'s bohemians or *Superbia*'s

---

59. Larson's demo of 'Boho Days' can be found on the 2001 *tick, tick... BOOM!* Off-Broadway cast recording. A version performed by Anthony Rapp, Michael McElroy, and Jeremy Kushnier is on the *Jonathan Sings Larson* CD. 'See Her Smile' was reintroduced to the show in 2001.

rebellious youths, though, Larson could only answer for himself. Says Rosenstein:

[T]he entire artistic dialectic [was] do you choose to be true to your soul to the very end, at whatever cost that is, or do you sell out? And is that okay, too? It's not a choice between the nice apartment and the much nicer apartment. It's not about how much you sell out; it's whether or not you sell out. It's a black-or-white. It's love versus fear, and what world do you want to live in? It's cages or wings. That was anthematic and it was important. Because he was willing to live that life, he accumulated wisdom, and that's what resonates.

Despite Larson's convictions, the scripts for all three editions of *tick* are full of references to his failures to make good on his potential and goals: "I don't blame Rosa Stevens for avoiding my calls. No one invests in new ideas. They invest in Market Research."[60]

Guilt over not having financial stability: "Before [Dad and I] both wonder about why I couldn't have been content, taking over his business [...]"[61]

Over failing himself and his lovers: "I've let fear control me, and instead of facing it, I've spent my life worrying about my career, or trying like some dumb Catcher in the Rye to teach women what love was about, but I haven't been there for them [...]"[62]

Over never having contributing to a world changing event: "The biggest decision we've ever faced is what jeans to buy or if we want fries with our Big Mac."[63]

---

60. Jonathan Larson. *Boho Days*. Box 34, Folder 1, Jonathan Larson Papers, Music Division, Library of Congress, Washington, D.C. 8.

61. Jonathan Larson. *Boho Days*. Box 34, Folder 1, Jonathan Larson Papers, Music Division, Library of Congress, Washington, D.C. 17.

62. *tick, tick... BOOM!* 19 Apr 1993. MAVIS 187232-3-1. Jonathan Larson Recordings, Recorded Sound Division, Library of Congress, Washington, D.C.

63. Ibid.

And, in one of the best lines cut from the show in its published edition, of failing his parents by being a product of his generation:

My heritage is television. My religion is shopping,

My parents are ageing, yet I haven't paid them back for anything they've lent me over the years.

And I feel guilty because my sister and I had shag carpeting installed in our bedroom[s] and my parents never even changed the wallpaper in theirs.[64]

Larson's notes and concept sketches reveal the genuine nature of his introspection. While certain of his talents, Larson was equally aware of his flaws, as demonstrated by his notes: "My griefs are minor compared to ghetto kids."[65]

Poor Poor Cynical Me

Who am I?

A spoiled, impatient to sell out, but petrified if I do, sugar addicted, fame obsessed, compassionate, bright, self-conscious, opinion-seeking composer - afraid if I'll be exposed as talentless or derivative."[66]

"I fee [sic] GUILTY.[67]

Despite the angst in Larson's notes, scrawled out in rough pencil and worked into varying monologues, he kept his deepest concerns largely to himself: "It's not that I don't share my feelings", he said in the 1991 version of *tick*, "I just convert them into songs

64. Ibid.

65. Jonathan Larson. Handwritten Notes. Box 32, Folder 8, Jonathan Larson Papers, Music Division, Library of Congress, Washington, D.C. 12H.

66. Ibid., 13H.

67. Ibid., 19H. Caps and underline in original

and perform them for complete strangers at popular prices."[68] Julie Larson McCollum confirms:

> I know there were moments when he was struggling, and working and working and still working at the diner, and he would hear things like "Oh, I got a promotion," or "I'm working with this great, well-known director," and unbeknownst to me at the time, sometimes it made him feel like he hadn't been a success yet, whereas, of course, we were looking at it completely the opposite way, and I was in awe of everything he was doing.

> If he felt [like he was letting us down], he didn't generally express it, at least to me or my parents. We never felt he was letting us down, and if he felt that way, that wasn't generally expressed. You write something and it's how you're feeling in the moment.

Rosenstein sympathised with Larson's frustrations, but is fully aware of *tick*'s dramatic license: "He was living a full life in the way he lived it. We were in the epicentre of where we thought we were. He was really very close to the middle of what he was involved in, just on the periphery a little more than he'd like."

Michael's Gonna Have It All

At *tick*'s core is Larson's relationship with Michael, a semi-fictionalised version of real best friend Matt O'Grady. O'Grady remembers:

---

68. *tick, tick... BOOM!* November 1991. MAVIS 186798-1-5/186798-3-4. Jonathan Larson Recordings, Recorded Sound Division, Library of Congress, Washington, D.C.

He dedicated it to me, which was kind and sweet - and any production they've had, I've made sure they do that - 'cause it was my 30th birthday present. We were both turning 30. It's a very emotional and moving piece for me, and perfect that it's one act because I have a short attention span. I feel incredibly lucky and honoured, but the whole thing is bittersweet and painfully ironic. He's sitting there writing about me and other people and our friends who have died, and here it is 20 years later and I'm still around and he's not. That's not how anybody thought the story was gonna go.

Larson and O'Grady had been close for their entire lives, starting as children in White Plains, NY:

Jon was always in my life. Somebody asked me when I met [him], and I don't know. I just know he was always there. He was a kid in the neighbourhood, but then, when I was in 7th or 8th grade, we just became inseparable. Jon was so above the fray. He never really gossiped about anybody. He just didn't have time for that.[69]

The two remained close, and when it came time to start dating, O'Grady confided in Larson that he was gay. His best friend accepted him fully, as did the entire Larson family, a true blessing in the late 1970s. The pair were like friends in a teen movie, visiting New York together throughout high school and university and getting into suburban teenage mischief.

While *tick, tick, BOOM!* was built upon Larson and O'Grady's friendship, Larson took plenty of dramatic license in constructing

---

69. Vicky's Larson Evening, Tape #1. Video. February 1996. Privately held by Victoria Leacock Hoffman, Washington, D.C.

their relationship in the piece. For example, 'Michael' in *tick* was Larson's roommate and an actor before pursuing market research - two things O'Grady never did:

> I was not an actor in high school. We did a lot of things together. We were at the Y together as kids, and he was my best friend through high school and college, but I was never in the performing arts. However, when we were getting out of school, I went into market research and did try to get him jobs in market research or to write jingles at agencies. I wanted him to have work and didn't know if anyone would listen to his music or if he'd be successful, so I was very concerned about his well-being as a person, and he was incredibly committed to it, which is obviously honourable and it was his passion, but did I start making money? I didn't have a BMW, but I did have a car that I owned. I didn't get to live in a high-rise tower, but I had a lease in my own name and my own apartment. Back then, everybody was just living with whoever had an open room. I don't think anybody had the lease.

> I wouldn't live with him - I found some old notes, but I found what I said when the [RENT] movie was being made. Everyone thought I was his roommate. I never lived with him. He set it up like there was an Odd Couple scenario, and that's what it would've been, but I'm much cleaner than he ever was. He was like 100% straight bachelor guy.

I *was* giving him clothes, but they were shirts, not three Gucci belts, they were three really nice Perry Ellis shirts, or I'd find clothes for him or give him clothes I never wore. I wanted him to look good. He just wanted a t-shirt and jeans, probably, but he was like a brother. I took great pride in him and what I could convey and bring to him.

As far as how Larson handled his best friend working in a field he regarded as evil, O'Grady recalls:

He didn't feel like I was a sellout. He acknowledged what I was doing and probably saw a lot of other people in his own trade that sold out, and he worked with people. There was an exploding burst of talent colliding with frustration. Of course you're gonna point the finger at somebody. If it was at me, it was just for artistic purposes. He knew I needed health insurance to stay alive.

While Larson embellished aspects of his life (and his friends' lives) for dramatic purpose, his sweet tooth was, if anything, underplayed. According to O'Grady,

He liked sugar. We both liked sugar. When you grow up in the suburbs, Hostess products are on your table all the time, not just when growing up. We'd go for a late-night ice cream. He made a great milkshake. Every important discussion I had with him was at the diner, because then I had his undivided attention.

O'Grady was not the one responsible for introducing Larson to market research brainstorming, though - that honour belongs to friend Lynn Blumenfeld, who also suggested Larson collect attendee surveys after a performance of the show. However, subsequent editions of *tick* have no significant changes to reflect any input from the surveys, implying Larson used them either as a way to extend engagement with his audience or as a form of time capsule, whereupon he could look back at that point in his life, even filling one out himself.

HIV - already present in Larson's world - complicated his own life during his work on *tick*. The first time was at the 1990 production of *Boho Days*. Matt O'Grady, having only been informed that the show was a birthday present about his friendship with Larson, brought his sister to a performance. While Larson knew his best friend was HIV+, O'Grady had kept the news from his family, only for the news to hit from the stage. Amazingly, their friendship survived: "I was blown away," remembers O'Grady. "It was so beautifully done, and such a testament, and I was the guy with the bicentennial eyes. He just got it all, but it was obviously so painful and personal as well."

Susan and Karessa

Larson faced his greatest creative struggle on *tick* with writing female characters. Following *30/90*, a set of notes in a feminine hand commented "[women] look witchy, dumb or obnoxious (or lesbian)" and later "voice of [women] is one dimensional."[70] In *30/90*, Larson's ex, Marta, is a jealous, easily angered shrew, and in all editions, Susan is a naive, new-wave practitioner frequenting a questionable ashram, while Karessa Johnson is a vain bimbo hanging onto wealthy high-society boys.[71]

---

70. Unknown Author. Handwritten Notes. Box 33, Folder 2, Jonathan Larson Papers, Music Division, Library of Congress, Washington, D.C., 94-95H. The female symbol is used for 'woman/women' in these notes.

71. According to Victoria Leacock Hoffman, nobody caught the sexual pun in the name Karessa Johnson during the 1990s, and it was only when an investor on *tick, tick... BOOM!* pointed it out to her in 2001 that she noticed it herself.

Pippin Parker, who directed *tick* from 1991-1993 agrees with the criticism:

> I remember [addressing Karessa] very specifically. Those characters weren't his strengths going into it, but not outside what you'd expect in that kind of process. We always looked at the female characters with more scrutiny, to make sure they had a life which not only existed as a part of the protagonist, but as a sense of something more.

For Marisa Miller - a fellow performer hanging out at Naked Angels and regular to Larson's shifts at the Moondance Diner - Larson's reimagining of an awkward late-night encounter is a riotous tribute to their friendship:

> I had run into him maybe a couple months before [the *Boho Days* performance in 1990] in the middle of the night with my new boyfriend. It was so mortifying for him, being on that Twinkie run, and little did I know about it.
>
> [It was in] Sheridan Square in the West Village, and I always called it the 'Nasty Corner'. There's a place there called Village Cigars with a mini-mart that was just disgusting. [My boyfriend and I] were probably going to pick up condoms or clove cigarettes or something, and there I ran into Jonathan. Funnily enough, my boyfriend at the time was by no means a hunk or a stud. He was a wiry New York downtown theatre type of guy, but [Larson] saw me as a single girl having fun at these parties and chatting with him and stuff like that. I liked him so much, and we were sympatico, so running into him, I was just excited, but he was mortified. I

was exactly like he portrayed. I was just like, "OH MY GOD! JONATHAN! I'M SO EXCITED TO SEE YOU!" and he just wanted to slink away.[72] Of course, I introduced him to my boyfriend and told him what Jonathan did, and kept engaging him when he just wanted to get the hell away. That's what was so cute about it. I knew that the spirit of [the gag] was that he wanted to get away, and I just kept wanting to talk to him.

It's funny, because I'm not a fan of later Andrew Lloyd Webber, but I have a feeling I must have said - because I did like *Jesus Christ Superstar* and I did think it was superior to like *Cats* and other things - so I might have said without even realising it, "He writes rock musicals, like *Jesus Christ Superstar*" or something like that.[73]

I love ['Sugar']. I think it's great. You use things from everyday life [as a writer] and hopefully people are good sports, and a lot of times they're not, and so writers have to deal with that. It's great when people know it's just in good fun. We really had a laugh about [his performance] - like "Thanks! That's such a lovely portrayal." But I knew life's like that, and it was good fun. I knew he didn't think of [me that way] - that's why I laughed - and why it was such a warm thing when I realised it was me.

---

72. When performing 'Karessa,' Larson punctuated his bubbly ditz voice with exaggerated arm waving and bouncing on his piano bench.

73. When Larson performed in *tick*, Karessa's introduction of "What do you do? Oh, he writes musicals - like Andrew Lloyd Webber" is punctuated by the guitarist playing the chorus from *Cats*' 'Memories' and Larson audibly cringing in disgust.

Susan, however, was a much more complicated character based on Janet Charleston - Larson's long-term girlfriend who he'd been with for a year when *30/90* debuted. A Cunningham dancer alongside Brenda Daniels, Charleston began dating Larson in March 1989, and much of Larson's commentary about Susan came from his own observations and concerns about the relationship. For example, both Larson and Charleston worked jobs outside their fields to pay the bills while pursuing their artistic endeavours, and Charleston, like Susan, did seek solace at an ashram. She remembers:

> I often went to a yoga ashram called Kripalu. The residents there were not paid; they maintained the ashram and programs through selfless service, called *seva*. There were disciples of Kripalu's guru and people who weren't disciples, like me. Kripalu was a haven of healing and learning for me. One time, I remember, I was going to go to the ashram for a week and Jonathan spontaneously drove me there. Usually I would take the bus. So he drove me up there in Rusty [his car], and he stayed and had lunch there and we went swimming in the lake. I remember listening to Suzanne Vega or Ricky Lee Jones during the drive and some song hit him, and he told me he was afraid I wouldn't come back. There was never a job I was applying for there, as he mentioned in [*tick*], but I did think of staying there for a longer period of months at a time. I also didn't want to give up my dancing, and I didn't want to be away from Jonathan, so I never did go there for that long.

Likewise, Larson commissioned one of his fellow wait-staff at the Moondance Diner to make Charleston a real 'green, green dress:'

> This was the tightest, shortest, sexiest dress I've
> ever had. It's beautiful. And it is made of dark
> green wool. When he gave me that - he was such
> a poet and so romantic - he gave me a printout of
> the Legend of Tam Lin. It's a Scottish legend about
> a strong young woman named Janet and her fairy
> knight lover. This particular version begins 'Janet
> put on her green green dress,' and goes on.

Even as *30/90* became *Boho Days* and finally *tick, tick...
BOOM!*, Larson continued to draw upon what was happening
in his life. For example, as his relationship with Charleston hit a
rough patch in 1991 and the two decided to put things on hold, he
changed Susan's perspective on the ashram from a place of healing
to one of escape, adding the risk of her leaving and his anxiety over
losing the love of his life. 'See Her Smile,' with its warm, gentle
desire for Susan's happiness, was replaced with harsher self-eval-
uation in 'Find the Key' as Larson tried to musically convey his
emotions in the wake of her departure. As Charleston recalls:

> ['Find the Key'] is revealing. We did talk about
> his difficulties in knowing how he felt and being
> able to express it. He often felt more comfort-
> able expressing his feelings in writing, both in his
> work and personally. In 'Find the Key' he asked
> himself, "How do I feel?" He was always very
> romantic throughout our relationship. He was
> expressive, but sometimes it was hard to sit down
> and talk about things. It came out so much in his
> work. Sometimes he would write things to me,

rather than say them, and he wrote songs for me. I remember once when Jonathan needed to tell me something very important and emotionally intense, he wrote it in a letter because he felt more able to say it that way. He sat with me while I read the letter.

Waiting

The first production of *tick, tick... BOOM!* (then *30/90)* occurred on 25 March 1990 - two months after Larson's 30th birthday - at the office of his agent, Flora Roberts.[74] A small audience was in attendance, and one can only guess how some reacted. While some of the parties in Larson's life - Charleston, O'Grady, and ex-lover Brenda Daniels - had their names changed, Roberts, Stephen Sondheim, and others in the theatrical industry were directly referenced. One of Larson's first tasks after the reading: create a list of aliases to protect the innocent (and guilty).

From there, Larson teamed up with Victoria Leacock to produce the show - now in its *Boho Days* iteration - for a handful of nights in September 1990 at Second Stage, off-Broadway. To raise the $10,000 necessary to rent the theatre, Larson and Leacock appealed to family members to invest in $1000 shares. David Saint, an up-and-coming director, helmed the staging.

Robyn Goodman, one of Second Stage's top artistic staff, helped Larson and Leacock produce:

> I can't remember who brought Jon to me, but I remember listening to the tape [of *tick*] that my dramaturge gave me, and I thought, "Where is this guy from? He's so talented!" I just remember

---

74. Roberts also represented Stephen Sondheim.

his integrity and his exuberance. His arrogance, his naiveté, everything all together, and that show which meant so much to him. He was onto something, and I knew it. I told him I wanted to produce the *Hair* of the '90s, and he said, "I want to WRITE the *Hair* of the '90s!" And he did and, schmuck that I am, I didn't get to produce it.[75]

One night, Beth Emelson from Naked Angels brought a young producer named Jeffrey Seller to see the show. Seller, then working for Broadway producers Barry and Fran Weissler, wrote Larson to say he was "bowled over. Your work — music, lyrics and spoken words — has an emotional power and resonance that I rarely experience in the theatre."[76] Seller asked to meet with Larson to discuss ideas, and the composer quickly accepted.

Leacock Hoffman remembers the Second Stage production of *Boho Days* being well-attended and received.[77] Critics were invited, and Goodman managed to get a second-stringer in from the *New York Times*. While he said privately that he loved the show, he would not be able to get the column inches to cover it. The lack of publicity meant Second Stage were unable to commit to the risks involved with an extended production, and Larson and Leacock were back at square one.

Work on *Boho Days* continued while Larson concurrently

75. Goodman would team up with Victoria Leacock Hoffman in 2001 to produce *tick, tick... BOOM!* off-Broadway.

76. Jeffrey Seller. Letter to Jonathan Larson. Box 34, Folder 9, Jonathan Larson Papers, Music Division, Library of Congress, Washington, D.C.

Barry and Fran Weissler are top-tier Broadway producers who are known for putting on large-scale musicals, mostly revivals, with star casting. The 1998 revival of *Chicago*, still running around the world in various forms, including on Broadway at the time of this writing in 2015, is their biggest hit.

77. Recordings from this production and the subsequent 1991 run of *tick, tick... BOOM!* support her memories.

began pursuing *RENT* as a solo project. In November 1991, Leacock produced two performances of *tick, tick… BOOM!* at the Village Gate nightclub (where she had produced Larson's *Superbia* concert two years before), advertising the show in the Village Voice and classified ads across New York. The ads, headlined "sex, drugs, rock & roll and twinkles" were stark, and tickets cost a whole $10. Pippin Parker of Naked Angels directed, Roger Bart sang backup, and Flora Roberts still failed to return Larson's calls.

Parker's input proved vital in shaping *tick* as Larson performed it: initially working as a dramaturgical assistant, Parker went over the script with Larson in detail, refining the outline and then going into the details, trying to bring depth to the characters flittering in and out of view. As director, Parker scaled back the over-the-top nature of Larson's performance in *Boho Days* and fixed some of the tonal inconsistencies, such as the actions causing the audience to laugh during the final, emotional breakdown of a monologue:

> We worked on the characterisation. It was very personal, so the cast of characters was close to him. We talked a lot about [Michael] and what that meant, how to have the best impact on the audience. In some ways, it's the emotional anchor of the script, which we spent extra time on. In some of the characterisations, it was attempting to give them as much colour and shape as possible, which is difficult because they're popping in quickly and have a very small amount of time to present themselves.

For Parker and Leacock Hoffman, the 1991 edition is definitive, predating Larson's most cynical adjustments and performing at his peak, crammed onto a tiny stage with the band and playing off Bart's vocals and presence in an intimate high-energy space.

By the end of 1992, Larson was dedicating himself creatively to *RENT*, starting work on *Sacred Cows* and *Blocks*, and revisiting *tick, tick... BOOM!* for its final iteration at New York Theater Workshop's 'O Solo Mio' Festival of one-person shows. Following two performances on 4 December 1992, interactions reached their nadir between Larson and Roberts, culminating with the young composer firing his million-dollar agent that January.[78] *tick* would be performed two final times at an 'O Solo Mio' mini-festival of encores in April 1993 before ultimately being shelved.

Parker, who also directed both 'O Solo Mio' runs, remembers the '92 and '93 editions with regret:

> All the material is basically the same, but they were very different experiences. Obviously, Jonathan was comfortable performing, but less comfortable performing as himself alone on stage [...] It was under-directed. It was really Jonathan at the piano and a little working at the mic, but it was not as engaging or energetic. The actual physical setting at the Gate was a better situation for it than sitting in a [proper] theatre, and I think audiences were more receptive. We were able to give the right context for the experience at the Gate [versus] the Workshop. It was also under-rehearsed [at NYTW,] and we didn't crack that nut as a one-person show.
>
> Jonathan was really learning as he was going along through the first [run]. He was from a really traditional musical theatre world, and [at] 'O Solo Mio,' things were coming from a lot of different

---

78. In practice, Roberts' agency had all-but-formally dropped him the month before. Unlike with Larson's first agent, Wiley Hausam, this parting was far from amicable.

directions. He was in touch with the East Village and Soho, [but] his background was more standard musical theatre than other stuff, and expectations were possibly not right for that.

Play the Play Game

For three years, Larson pushed his monologue, producing his standard run of demo tapes along the way and trying to sell the piece as a concept album to record companies. He also discussed his options with Jeffrey Seller, who liked the material, but was wary of Larson as a performer. According to Emelson, Seller expressed concern over Larson's ability to command the stage when tied to the piano during all the musical numbers. On paper - and even on audio recordings - the show works fine with a single person filling so many roles, but videos reveal Larson's limitations in effectively staging himself: he never wanders far from the piano bench, preferring to stay seated and cutting off his body language, as though remaining semi-foetal at the instrument. By working at a full piano versus a more concert-friendly keyboard on most songs, Larson also made ineffective use of the stage, distancing himself from the show's band.[79]

Victoria Leacock Hoffman recalls the breaking point being when Seller asked Larson who was going to play him in the actual production. The idea of anybody else performing the show never occurred to the composer, and he recoiled at the thought, unwilling to hand over what was, at heart, an autobiographical work. According to Emelson, who routinely visited Larson at

---

79. 'Swimming,' 'Debtor Club,' 'No More,' and 'Real Life' used a small synthesiser positioned by the band, along with 'Pioneers of the Extreme,' a scene wherein Larson describes a potential idea for a Western-themed show about Generation X slackers. 'Play Game' was the only song wherein Larson was freed from keyboard duties and moved extensively around the stage.

the Moondance Diner during the negotiations, there were "a lot of painful conversations - playwrights can be possessive, nobody understands it as well as you do." However, Emelson felt the work contained a universality which would benefit from other voices - something Larson did not want to hear.

As Larson went from freshly turning 30 before the first reading to a more disillusioned 33-year-old, the tone changed from *30/90*'s naivete and *Boho Days*' sass to *tick, tick... BOOM*'s embracing of his acknowledged frustrations:

> And Rosa Stevens? Fuck Rosa Stevens! My friends are coughing and screaming from viruses that rage like runaway wildfires, yet the men in power send them nothing but autographed copies of their 8x10's. And I want to help, but I don't know what to do. I'm afraid to die young, and afraid to grow old in a country being ruined by greed, and hate, and ignorance, and I need to laugh but I'm forgetting how.[80]

Victoria Leacock Hoffman feels the show got increasingly sour, wallowing in self-pity and becoming too whiny and bitter: "Jonathan was struggling and wanted to follow his dreams."

Likewise, Emelson recalls problems with connecting to the audience by the time the show reached New York Theatre Workshop: "Most of the people [attending] were around 24 years old, and 30 was far away. They thought it was interesting, but couldn't hang their hats on it, and the audiences felt distanced - some of it was too far from their daily understanding."

It looked like one of Larson's notes may be coming true: "Stay

---

80. Jonathan Larson. *tick, tick... BOOM!*, stored as "!93 TIXK TEXT" (Microsoft Word File). Contained within disk8.img. Jonathan Larson Papers, Music Division, Library of Congress, Washington, D.C.

up & coming - you'll never be a has-been."[81] Unable to secure interest in the theatre for *tick* and turned down by record companies when he pitched the piece as a concept album, Larson put the show to bed in order to more productively focus his energy. As invitations for new collaborations came in and his friends began falling ill to the plague ravaging the arts, he decided to revive a previously abandoned collaboration - one he could make entirely his own.

41/01

In 1999, Victoria Leacock Hoffman and Robyn Goodman teamed up to bring *tick, tick... BOOM!* back to life. Leacock Hoffman intimately knew the work, and Goodman filled in a gap in production experience which Leacock Hoffman lacked. Two backers' readings were held and enough investments were secured to proceed.

The pair initially approached Diane Paulus (*Finding Neverland, The Capeman*) to direct, but ultimately hired Scott Schwartz, son of Broadway composer Stephen Schwartz.[82] Goodman and Leacock Hoffman agreed that the script required additional work to make it a full-on piece of theatre, and sought out a playwright to handle adaptation duties. Goodman had recently worked with soon-to-be-Pulitzer-winning playwright David Auburn on his Manhattan Theatre Club debut, *Proof,* and reached out with an offer.

From the start, it was clear to the team that *tick* needed to be expanded beyond a single actor. As Auburn explains, "He was taking on an impossible task: he had to perform these very complicated, Bogosian-style monologues and sing the songs as all of

---

81. Jonathan Larson. Handwritten Notes. Box 32, Folder 8, Jonathan Larson Papers, Music Division, Library of Congress, Washington, D.C., 31H.

82. The elder Schwartz's work includes *Godspell* (which Larson starred in at Adelphi), *Pippin*, and *Wicked*.

the characters, and accompany himself on the piano, and conduct the band that was accompanying him. You watched it and you felt like, 'This is just too much for anyone to do as a performance,' and you could feel the strain of that." The first reading of the revision expanded the show to two performers - Jonathan and Susan, played by Anthony Rapp and Amy Spanger - before Michael and other incidental characters were split off for a third actor. This dynamic allowed for more natural interchanges between the characters (versus Larson talking to himself via two or three exaggerated voices), as well as reducing the load on a single actor.

Building the new *tick*, however, required as much forensic work as dramaturgy: "What I recall," says Auburn, "is having several versions of the script that he used and his performances, and then I had a videotape of him doing [it], and several cassettes of songs - I remember a lot of songs, everything that was in the final show except "Come To Your Senses." I was [told], 'See what you can do with this, what are your ideas of how this can be reshaped?'"

Auburn also set about rewriting Larson's dialogue and structure. Whereas Larson started *tick* with his birthday party and went through a weekend of hell, ending with a rain-soaked moment of clarity, Auburn restructured the story to end with Jonathan's birthday party as a high note and allowing Larson's angst to fizzle, rather than explode and burn at the end:

> [Among] the ideas that I contributed was that it should really end with his birthday, and that the show should be restructured so that it built up to that birthday party, and we should build in the experience of the workshop of *Superbia* so that was something you could experience and have the disappointment of along with the Jonathan character. [...] I [also] remember thinking immediately, there was a song called 'Why,' [which was halfway

through the show,] but I thought, "That's the 11 o'clock number," and it screamed out to be the second-to-last song in the show. A lot of what I did initially was just say, "All right, if you put that next to last so it's the emotional climax of the piece, what happens to the rest of it," and that clarified a lot of things for me.

Auburn and Schwartz also made the decision to cut references to Larson's chest feeling tight and thinking he would explode: "They were there," remembers Leacock Hoffman, "but the argument was that nobody would believe us. They'd think we were being overdramatic and making it up, so [the lines] went." Says Auburn:

> It wasn't so much removed as de-emphasised. You didn't really want to feel like you were going for cheap sentiment or pathos by preserving a lot of that original language that would have such a dark undertone with our retrospective knowledge of what happened to him. [Larson] was a very ambitious guy who was very frustrated, and that kind of language is typical of what artists use when they're pissed off that their work isn't getting the recognition it deserves and they're feeling that they're not young anymore. In a way, it's more innocent than that, and I didn't want the show to be about this doomed artist. I wanted the show to be about this very ambitious and driven artist.

The *Superbia* workshop, which Larson monologued about with increasing bitterness, became a more important aspect of the story, with Jonathan pinning his hopes on that one night. By staging the workshop, the team were also able to add 'Come to Your Senses,' a cut song from *Superbia,* to *tick,* giving the actress playing Susan a big number in a show dominated by the male performers. Leacock Hoffman recalls going through her tapes of *Superbia*, looking for a song, when a cassette of 'Senses' fell off the shelf and grabbed her attention. The team chose 'Senses' over top alternative, 'I Won't Close My Eyes,' as the latter was likely to be used in any future editions of *Superbia* and was more downbeat in tone.

Schwartz and Auburn also questioned how much to deal with the actual people behind the source material versus staying true to Larson's semi-fictionalisations. O'Grady recalls:

> I took a lot more interest [for the 2001 version] and kept an eye on it, because I knew the press was going to come out. I didn't ask them to change anything. When Scott Schwartz was working on it, he was like, "Y'know, I'm sort of mixed about talking to you, the real one, because I need to create something," so we actually talked very briefly, and I got that and respected it. "It's artistic license, you guys need to do what you do." I was really pleased with how it all came out. I just wanted to make sure that tribute to the guy with the bicentennial eyes is still there. That's the only thing I asked for. I think they did a very good job of it, and I knew they were going to deal with my HIV status - that's such a pivotal point in it, and I was already outed [during *RENT*'s publicity] - so once it's in the *New York Times*, there's really no turning back.

Expanding *tick* also required new material to hold the expanded structure together. Auburn remembers,

> I knew from the beginning that it would be an editorial job, and there would have to be some additions made on my part, but I tried to stick to

Jonathan's language as much as I could. I remember worrying about being maudlin - that was the thing that really concerned me. I really didn't want the show to be feeding off of our sadness or regret about what happened to this man. I wanted the show to be - if it was going to work or be moving or exciting or whatever - I wanted it to be that on its own terms and not rely on whatever other knowledge we were bringing to it.

I wrote an argument to set up ['Therapy']. As I recall, Susan and the relationship with Susan was [what] changed the most over the various drafts, and the starkest of choices to be made editorially were about what kind of character Susan was, and what she wanted, and what she was doing, and what the problem with the relationship was. In some drafts, the crisis in the relationship didn't climax in the same way and wasn't as severe, and she was a less serious person, a bit sillier. Her character varied a lot. [It] was a running gag [in Larson's versions] that she was a slightly spacey character. I thought that the point shouldn't be that the relationship wasn't falling apart because she was spacey, but that they wanted different things, and Jonathan's problems were making it difficult for the relationship to thrive. As I recall, some of the sillier stuff with Susan ended up being given to [Karessa]."

Auburn ultimately re-wrote many sections of *tick*'s book.[83] The

83. When I interviewed Auburn, he said the published script for *tick, tick... BOOM!* was "about 80% Larson." A more accurate description would be 80% Larson's story, but, at most, a third of the dialogue (excluding the songs, which had

introduction, all of the scenes relating to *Superbia*, Rosa's calls, and Jonathan's back-and-forths with Susan are new to the 2001 edition. Jonathan's conversations with Michael are used to recontextualise the song 'Real Life,' shifting the action from a creative struggle to showing adult choices and their consequences. As a result, Auburn's script is dramaturgically better than what Larson originally wrote, utilising the original events as a framework to create a new piece which highlights Larson's themes, but also paints a softer image of pastel naiveté versus the original's bold, brash, and more emotionally charged collage.

Being a musical, the new *tick* needed someone to bond the new text to Larson's compositional soul and intentions. Goodman brought on a young musical director named Stephen Oremus, who had recently worked on Andrew Lippa's *The Wild Party*. Prior to that, Oremus spent a year on the road conducting and music-directing the second (aka Benny) U.S. national tour of *RENT*, and was already in touch with Stephen Schwartz - then beginning work on *Wicked* - and by extension, director Scott Schwartz. Serendipity struck.

If going through piles of paper drafts was difficult for bringing a script together, the musical materials were even rougher. As Oremus recounts:

> [Larson] had a couple very basic lead sheets. Victoria gave me pretty much every audio and video recording of [him] performing the show that existed, so I basically pored through them to see how the songs were being used and got together with Scott and David Auburn, and we all sat down and went through these different versions of the

three or four lines changed and one extensive rearrangement by Stephen Oremus) is Larson's. To determine this number, I took Larson's scripts and recordings and highlighted every line in the published script which appeared verbatim in both editions.

show. David and Scott took a pass, and then I sat
down with them and then talked about the different musical moments and how we were going to
use them and what the songs needed, and we continued to build the show from there.

Larson had begun composing digitally by the time he started
working on *tick*, but even that was of little help to Oremus: "It
was very rudimentary, very early days for [digital composing,] as
well. We were all working in *Finale* at that point, but it was not the
easiest thing in the world." Ultimately, *tick*'s score would become a
labour of transcribing, reworking, and fiddling.

Moving to three characters also freed Oremus to expand
the vocal arrangements and engage in Larson's beloved uses of
counterpoint:

I wanted to make sure that I could build on what
[he] had originally done, so there were a lot of
very challenging moments where I had to sit there
and go, "What would Jonathan have done with
this?" when we were putting together the opening number [or] 'Johnny Can't Decide'. What I've
always said is that it's a great testament to the universality of Jonathan's writing that I was able to
take his lyrics about all these situations and put
them in the mouths of different characters, and it
worked for those characters when it wasn't meant
to be. He wasn't becoming those characters in the
songs, but he was describing the experiences, and
it was beautiful and amazing to do that.

Auburn and Oremus also sought to free the show from its early
'90s confines. "What he was writing about," says Auburn, "which
is ambition and frustration and self-flagellation and self-belief, all

those things are very salient. It's raw. And you get the feeling that that's what it took to get to *RENT* in a way - he had to purge this, and then he could go on to do *RENT* once he'd gotten all this shit out." Oremus agrees: "I wanted it to be universal in encapsulating Jonathan's creative time during a period without saying, 'It was this period.' The show does - he talks about it, he goes to a pay phone, the show kinda does that for you, but it was about trying to stay true to Jonathan's original vision and building on it."

Part of freeing the score from its original era was changing the sound. While Larson had no issue using trendy MIDI arrangements and an electronic score, Oremus aimed for a more timeless and unified palette:

> There are very subtle differences in almost every single song in the piano patches - I used very different patches for several of the songs, so for example, 'Green Green Dress' has that honky-tonk piano, but we also wanted to make it sound like a Cramps song, and I wanted to stay true to different kinds of music Jonathan evoked. The important thing is that the piano was his voice, which is why it's featured so prominently in [the] orchestration - it was all about him at the piano presenting this, and this is how we got to know him.

As *tick* prepared to open in April 2001, buzz began building in New York City for the first Jonathan Larson work to open since *RENT* - and production mistakes began being made. The producers - assuming they had a hit - refused to discount the show during previews, a common practice of offsetting audience risk while final changes are implemented. Leacock and Goodman also wished to hold top producer billing and sought smaller investor-producers versus a strong general manager. The 2001 show opened with solid - but not rave - reviews from the *New York Post* and *Times*, and the show struggled financially through the summer, a time when most shows see peak ticket sales from heavy tourist traffic. Despite the show only breaking even, at best, some weeks, the decision was made to record a cast album, and Leacock Hoffman's long-time friend Paul Shaffer (band leader on *Late Night with David Letterman*) recorded a series of radio commercials.

Then, disaster struck: On 11 September 2001, the day *tick, tick... BOOM!*'s cast album was set to reach stores, two airplanes crashed into New York City's iconic Twin Towers. The city ground to a halt, shows were cancelled, and the United States entered a state of shock and mourning. While *tick* did not suffer financially, thanks to insurance payouts, it would prove difficult in the following weeks to lure audiences back to a piece about fear and whose advertising campaign relied on the phrase 'an explosive new musical'. Sales would recover slightly as teen icon Molly Ringwald (who had been rehearsing for the show when 9/11 hit) made her stage debut as Susan. Ex-New-Kid-on-the-Block Joey McIntyre took over a week later from Raul Esparza, but sales dropped off when Ringwald left. The investors Leacock Hoffman and Goodman brought on wanted to cut their losses and close the show immediately, but the lead duo - along with Larson's father - made the case for advertising the closing as a last-ditch publicity attempt. The scheme worked, and the final weeks sold out.

BOOM BOOM BOOM

While important to Larson on a personal level, it is worth re-examining *tick, tick... BOOM!* within the wider breadth of his catalogue: *30/90* and *Boho Days* may have been the focus of Larson's 1990 (culminating in the Second Stage production), but he never gave the show the time he devoted to *Superbia* or *RENT,* which both overlapped *tick*'s earliest writing. 1991 saw work for Naked

Angels, conceptual work on at least one abandoned show, co-performing *Billy Bishop Goes to War* with Roger Bart, composing an incidental commission, and work on the first solo-penned draft of *RENT,* plus the evolutionary reworking from *Boho Days* to *tick, tick... BOOM!* Larson subsequently made only minor revisions for *tick's* 1992 and 1993 productions as *RENT* became his focus and he aged out of being able to play himself.

In other words, Larson meant for *tick* to be a personal showcase to highlight his skills and spend some time performing, rather than an enduring piece of theatre, and it likely would have been fondly - but fleetingly - remembered, were it not for the show's autobiographical reflection providing insight after Larson's death. Writing to David Maness – a close family friend whom he reverentially referred to as 'Uncle Dave' - Larson unpacked the events of a meeting whereby his mentor, Stephen Sondheim, had reservations about the piece:[1]

> On Boho Days- His main objection was that he's seen this type of show (highly personal bloodletter) from many young writers- He felt that compared to SUPERBIA, which was "so highly original, etc." it was a step backward. [...] I asked how I could improve it for him and he said- Don't change it on MY account.. [sic] If your audience is relating to it- that's what counts.. [sic] Also- he felt there was nothing quirky about it. But I replied that to my younger audience- being an aspiring writer of musicals IS quirky. He couldn't disagree.. [sic] When I told him that young producers are serious, asking if I was slitting my wrists by going on, he said- "Not at all- it'll be a good experience- Just

1. More specifically, Maness was a close friend of Larson's father, Al Larson, and the families were neighbours. A former editor at *Life* Magazine, Maness was one of the younger Larson's go-to confidantes in his early career.

promise me your next piece won't be about this experience!!"[2]

And *tick* does provide insight: across Larson's three solo-penned musicals, *tick* is the one wherein Larson establishes his future on a metatextual level. In *Superbia*, the composer asks how his hero can cope with creativity and emotion in a bland, corporatised world and if he is capable of forging a path. In *tick*, he makes his decision: art is his life and livelihood, regardless of the financial or social consequences. The result of this choice subsequently manifests across the characters and issues in *RENT*.

Despite its musical proficiency and raw heart, *tick, tick... BOOM!* is a departure from *Superbia* and *RENT*'s early in-your-face political writing and shows Larson developing a more character-driven style. Other composers – such as fellow Sacred Cow, Paul Scott Goodman – were working on similar pieces, but it took until1998 when John Cameron Mitchell and Stephen Trask unleashed *Hedwig and the Angry Inch* off-Broadway that a rock monologue captured the attention of downtown audiences. *Hedwig*, with its gender-bending punk sensibility, also featured an actor performing almost solo with a backing band, and attacked similar themes as *tick*, such as fear of being left behind in a changing world and seeking emotional completion. However, whereas Larson focused on the emotion and immediacy of a single moment, Mitchell & Trask aimed for a greater sense of universality by tapping influences ranging from ancient Greek philosophy to David Bowie. The mix of Larson-esque rock aesthetic, unforgettable central character, and emotional depth quickly rocketed *Hedwig* to cult status, and the show ran over two years at the Jane Street Theatre (where it would be followed by the reworked *tick, tick... BOOM!*) before being adapted into a film in 2001.

---

2. Jonathan Larson. Letter to David Maness, stored as 'uncl D 3/15/91' (Microsoft Word File). Contained within disk78.img. Jonathan Larson Papers, Music Division, Library of Congress, Washington, D.C.

Chapter Five

The Harshest Critics
Mowgli, Away We Go!, & Blocks

Who am I?
As you can see
I'm no one anyone'd want to be
Up to and including me
Especially me

—*Blocks*

W HILE LARSON WROTE shows about mudslinging
politicians, biblical heresy, and dancing dollars, he
also had a flair for writing material worthy of the
world's toughest critics: children. Larson's sister Julie remembers his
relationship with his nephews well: "He was truly a Pied Piper. Kids
gravitated to him, and he was the one who'd play with the kids and
roll around on the floor with them and pay attention. He adored my
two sons, he was intensely close to them, and it was magic."

In 1984, Larson began collaborating with life-long New
Yorker Seth Goldman on a stage adaptation of Kipling's *The Jungle
Book*. Goldman wanted to create a musical unlike Disney's car-
toon adaptation, one tonally aligned with the source. Keeping the

original's dark, often violent moralism, *Mowgli* presents the ruthless nature of wild living, balanced with the emotion of musical expression. Goldman intended for *Mowgli* to be a large Broadway show, with elaborate sets and costumes plus a sizeable cast playing both Mowgli's wolf pack and human villagers, but such ambition turned out to be both the show's selling point in the age of the mega-musical and its downfall, as the scale came across as daunting rather than inviting to producers.

Looking for a non-traditional composer to set his script and lyrics to music, Goldman discussed the project with high school friend and tap dancing classmate, Victoria Leacock, who suggested Larson. Goldman saw one of the composer's J. Glitz club performances, introduced himself, and the two met to discuss their options.[3]

For the next few months, Goldman and Larson got down to business. Larson would suggest lyric changes, and Goldman extensively revised the script over the course of their collaboration. The two worked to bring the show together across different lifestyles and works schedules, meeting during lunch breaks, after late nights at the theatre, and on weekends. Larson would receive updates at these meetings, score what he could, and call Goldman with the results.

Hoping to attach some big names to the project, Goldman reached out to children's author Maurice Sendak to create conceptual set designs, but was declined. Despite working in the industry (Goldman was then employed at Circle in the Square theatre in Manhattan) and extensively shopping the show around, the pair failed to find interest from producers, even for development work. Larson became increasingly focused on *1984* and its transition to *Superbia*, leaving Goldman to continue working solo before he ultimately abandoned the project. The two remained on good terms, and Larson would run early drafts of *Superbia* past Goldman

---

3. See the appendix for more on J. Glitz.

for feedback, but their collaborations ended with *Mowgli*. Despite drifting apart, Larson and Goldman remained acquaintances and kept in touch through Leacock until Larson's death.

Two sets of *Mowgli's* songs were recorded: a rough recording of six tracks with Larson at his keyboard, and a fully produced demo of four songs with arrangements by Steve Skinner and featuring vocal performances by Larson, Scott Burkell, and Marin Mazzie. The opening, 'Call of the New Day,' combines a keyboard line similar to Elton John's later theatrical work with an animalistic barking chorus and African percussion. The sound is unique, and while the elements sound disparate on paper, the actual recording is pleasant and sets the location. 'Ruler of the Jungle' is the young Mowgli's 'I Want' song, a synth-driven pop solo. Another ensemble song, 'The Birth of Fear,' uses a similar syncopation (and identical synth patch) as 'Introduction to Superbia,' with a different vocal melody. The song is intimidating and drives home a sense of dread and anticipation. The final song, 'We Be of One Blood,' is a soft-pop buddy song between Mowgli, Baloo, and Bagheera.

Goldman still looks fondly on the material and the times:

> You certainly can't knock the talent on [the tapes]. I've always been a musical theatre fan, but at age 14, I had fake IDs to get into CBGB's. I always liked what Jonathan was doing, and I liked that this had a sense of something other than 'traditional Broadway musical' in the synths and the sound of it."

Meanwhile, utilising his alumni network, Adelphi instructor Nicholas Petron found Larson his first paid work as a composer, connecting him with producers at Children's Television Workshop to underscore three stop-motion films for use on *Sesame Street*, a job which would net him small but much-needed royalties for over a decade. Petron also found Larson work writing music for a series of licensed children's books on tape. These cassettes, for franchises including *An American Tail, The Land Before Time,* and *Sweet Valley Twins,* would be packaged with a picture book, allowing children to read along with the recording. Larson also wrote 'Close Harmony,' a pop song promoting the *Electric High* series and 'Don't Look at Me,' a pop-rap song for Theatreworks USA's *Ethics Revue,* about a boy who feels guilty for not intervening after watching as a cool kid frames the class outcast for shoplifting. In 1992, Larson would be commissioned to write a new song for *Sesame Street* and handle arrangements for another, but neither piece would ever see transmission.

Destination Sky

One day during development on *Sacred Cows,* Larson vented to fellow *Cows* collaborator Bob Golden about his difficulties in breaking back into *Sesame Street* and television work. Golden registered his surprise, feeling Larson was his equal - if not superior - as a composer.

In late 1993, fortune struck. Michael Rosen, an area real-estate mogul and one of Larson's regular customers at the Moondance Diner, had seen an advertisement in the *New York Times* Sunday magazine for a children's video about construction vehicles. Upon completing some basic research, Rosen found the video had quite a backstory: a laid-off father of two noticed his children were transfixed by a construction crew building a highway across the street from his house - the sight of bulldozers and such in action keeping their attention rapt. The man shot some footage on his camcorder, hired an editor to cut the footage into a 20-minute tape, and set it against royalty-free music. The tape first surfaced in local shops and subsequently took off via mail-order, making its creator rich.

Rosen thought he was onto an idea: could his favourite waiter (whom he knew was also a composer) make a kid-friendly tape on a reasonable budget? Larson was sure he could, and Rosen agreed to finance the production in exchange for the distribution rights. By this time, Golden was not only writing for *Sesame Street*, but also one of PBS's new children's show darlings, *Lamb Chop's Play-Along*.[4] Larson and Golden knew they could come up with the songs, but the question was what to make them about - and how to do it within Rosen's budget.

Golden remembered the project at a memorial evening in 1996:

> There was a real sense of playfulness [to it]. [The video] was not an easy collaboration - ever - but looking back on it, it was a really fun experience. Anything Jonathan wanted to do, he would do, and it was with the simplicity of childlike wonder. He came to me saying, "It doesn't need to be developed, let's outline this thing." And I said, "If we're gonna meet with the backers and try to raise $25-30,000, we should have a plan here," and he said, "No, no, I've got all we need. It'll have a sock puppet and a video camera." Within about two hours, the idea was sewn up, and we were ready to go to the backers' meeting. Jonathan put everything we talked about in this magnificent proposal, and we go to the meeting, and Jonathan reigned. He did so well in meetings. And he was just himself and so confident and really eager, and the backers said,

---

4. The show starred ventriloquist Shari Lewis and the eponymous puppet. It ran for five years on PBS and contained a mixture of skits, songs, and storytelling.

"Look, we don't want to hear your credits. We're money people, you just go and do your thing."[5]

Together, Larson and Golden wrote *Away We Go!*, the story of two siblings (played by real-life brother and sister Sal and Mary Cunningham) seeing the sights of New York City through different modes of transport, from a high-rise hotel lift to the Staten Island Ferry and an airplane. Led by happy puppet Newt the Newt (voiced by Tony Hoylen, who played Roger in various *RENT* readings, and puppeteered by Doug Skinner), each segment would begin with a factoid and introduction before going into a song about a different type of transportation. Larson and Golden shared songwriting duties, with each contributing four songs to the project and tweaking the other's work.

At the same memorial, Golden also recalled:

> [W]e started having the typical disagreements on how to proceed. I wanted to shoot on beta[cam, a professional format], [he] was convinced it should be low-end video. I thought we needed something like a Muppet, and he was convinced you don't even need a Muppet, you just need the sock.[6]

As arranging contracts and legalities stretched through the winter and spring of 1994, time began getting tight: Larson was mired in rewrites for a workshop of *RENT* that October, and permits were required for filming around the city. The pair were also trying to perfect the design for Newt the Newt: early drawings looked more frightening than cuddly. Larson turned to his artist friend and ex-roommate, Anne Egan, to build Newt, always

---

5. Vicky's Larson Evening, Tape #1. Video. February 1996. Privately held by Victoria Leacock Hoffman, Washington, D.C.

6. Ibid.

winning her over despite an aggravating back-and-forth on the final prop. Egan described the experience as such:[7]

> He idealised his friends. He could be this publi-
> cist about himself because he believed that about
> you as well. He never badmouthed people. Even
> when we were doing [*Away We Go!*] and he had
> the problem that the puppet looked too much
> like a Muppet. He called me up, and the project
> was dragging on, and we didn't want to see Newt.
> Newt was finished, and he was mailed, and I did
> NOT want to hear Newt was coming back to me
> one more time. And all of a sudden, Jon's on the
> phone like, "I've got a problem with Newt. Newt's
> eyes just aren't gonna work, he looks too much like
> a Muppet." And I'm just like, "I don't want to deal
> with this…" And my husband's in the background
> with two green tennis balls like [does a dance for
> the group with her hands in front of her eyes] and
> I'm like, "Jon? Okay, send Newt over," and sewed
> on the tennis balls. "Jon, I've got this really crazy
> idea. How about like two tennis balls?" "GREAT!
> GREAT! THAT'S GREAT! Anne, it looks great!"
> Even my five-year old was like, "Mommy, those are
> two tennis balls." It was that energy [of his] that
> pushed it through.[8]

Filming for *Away We Go!* took place on 28-30 August 1994, with Larson directing. "Some of it was pure luck," remembers Director of Photography Jonathan Burkhart. "We found a bus, asked the driver if we could film, had the kids sing along as we

---

7. More on Anne Egan and sharing Larson's apartment in Appendix B.

8. Vicky's Larson Evening, Tape #3. Video. February 1996. Privately held by Victoria Leacock Hoffman, Washington, D.C.

played the song, and ran with it." Larson and Burkhart completed the majority of work on the 28th and 29th. Golden missed the end of pre-production and first day of shooting due to a trip to Europe, and returned to a surprise:

> "I come back and on my doorstep is a 100 page binder that says, 'When Bob Comes Back,' and it was this incredibly detailed, organised listing. He had organised a crew, everything. There was a camera crew, these two kids, and their mother that he got for $100 each. I couldn't believe it. He had this giant crew. In addition, we had a Checker Cab lined up. We had a bus with a driver. We had clearance at an airport without insurance, and it was all attributed to Jonathan's wide-eyed sense that you can do anything."[9]

Golden shot pickup footage on the 29th and joined the rest of the production on the 30th, making a cameo with Larson in the lift song, 'Down.' Filming was assisted by working entirely to prerecorded sound, thus eliminating a potential time and cost sink, and every favour possible was called in, including to Larson's ex-roommate Todd Robinson, who flew the team in his own airplane to get skyline footage. Postproduction continued through 1994, with editing done by Jon Vesey at Broadway Video, and design on the box art and release planning carried over into the spring of 1995.

For anybody used to working in film and video, projects moving at a snail's pace is routine as approvals and contracts are passed from hand to hand, signatures are sought, and deals are arranged. As *Away We Go!* slowly made its way to duplication, Golden and Larson knew they had a quirky gem of a project behind them. Golden recalled:

---

9. Vicky's Larson Evening, Tape #1. Video. February 1996. Privately held by Victoria Leacock Hoffman, Washington, D.C.

It was this beautiful project, but we had no idea how we were gonna sell it, and the backers called us and said they wanted to do a second one. It was at that point that we started discussing the second video, and we were thrilled about it.[10]

Unfortunately, the timing on *Away We Go!* proved tragic: On 26 January 1996, the day after Jonathan Larson's untimely passing, a parcel containing the finished box art and a handful of screener tapes arrived at his flat. The video would see commercial release in late 1996, with Larson's family subsequently acquiring the rights from Michael Rosen and keeping it in print on DVD ever since.

Musically, *Away We Go!* holds up well, as befits a film created by musicians. The songs are simple, catchy, and ideal for repeat viewings. Larson and Golden's styles meshed well, with Golden's songs ('Get Ready,' 'Driving in a Taxi,' 'Bus Ride,' and 'Here and There') leaning towards the upbeat and bouncy, and Larson's ('Down,' 'On the Water,' 'Destination Sky,' and 'Away We Go!') slower and more melodic, excluding the title song, which mirrors 'Get Ready' in tempo. Hoylen sang lead on most of the songs, with the children's roles sung not by the screen actors but studio performers.

However, *Away We Go!* will always be best remembered for is its climactic number, 'Destination Sky.' Penned by Larson, the song is nostalgic, bittersweet, and magical, as the children bid farewell to New York and return home:

> So Auf Wiedersehen
> Gotta catch the plane
> But don't be sad or cry
> 'cuz we'll met again
> But my friend, 'til then

---

10. Ibid.

Destination: Sky.[11]

The lyrics would take on an additional meaning in 1996, when the song was played at Larson's memorial service and performed in February 1997 at a concert in his honour.

Visually, *Away We Go!* betrays its budget and rushed shooting schedule. Shots occasionally flash out of focus or get reused within the same song, and sharp-eyed viewers can distinguish between footage filmed on the principle camera and pickup shots from consumer grade Hi-8. For the target audience, these flaws are irrelevant when there's a colourful puppet and adventures to be had. For grownups, the flaws are charming and reflect the project's handmade, independent nature.

Blocks That Keep Us Blocked Up

While working on *Away We Go!*, Larson also scored a commission for Broadway Arts Theatre for Young People. The brainchild of founder Karen Butler, Broadway Arts had three goals: first, to move beyond fairy tales and traditional 'children's' theatre and produce shows relevant to the issues facing young, inner-city students. Second, to make them quality productions with professional, union actors. Third, to pair established and up-and-coming talent behind the scenes.

"Karen wanted to make a difference, unlike what she'd been seeing," says ex-production manager Michael Murnin. From the start, the company had three projects in mind: a show for elementary schoolers, using songs licensed from the Joe Raposo (*Sesame Street*) catalogue, a piece about racism for high schoolers, using the stories of Harlem jazz legends by André De Shields, and a third

11. Bob Golden & Jonathan Larson. *Away We Go!* Directed by Jonathan Larson. New York: Unky's Music LLC, 2004.

work for middle schoolers about issues faced directly by the students in their everyday lives.[12]

This third show, ultimately titled *Blocks*, would bring Larson and the Broadway Arts team together with veteran Broadway lyricist Hal Hackady in a cross-generational collaboration:[13] Karen Butler, Michael Murnin, and director Karen Azenberg were in their late 20s, Larson was 32, and Hackady, 70.

Input for *Blocks'* content came directly from students and potential audiences: a series of questionnaires was sent out to schools, and students were asked to list issues which they felt were important in their lives and also to write a bit about themselves. The responses were mature, with the children listing AIDS, alcohol/drug abuse, and single parents as the most pressing issues in their communities. The accompanying essays were eye-openingly positive - the pupils knowing and openly mentioning their flaws, but balancing them with an optimistic outlook, secure in the idea that they aren't *bad*, but imperfect.

From here came the commission: a 40-minute musical for a cast of 2-6 (*Blocks* would have five), and a minimal technical crew. The students needed to be entertained, pulled into the material, and spoken to as equals with clarity and directness, not lectured to. For *Blocks*, the focus would be on self-esteem and self-worth, encouraging students to pursue their own paths and make smart choices for themselves: "We must focus on the everyday choices our young people make. By acknowledging the difficulty of these 'simple' choices, we make the first step toward showing

---

12. For non-Americans, the rough age breakdown is 5-11 for elementary school, 12-14 for middle school, and 15-18 for high school.

13. Hackady's work includes the musicals *Minnie's Boys*, about the Marx Brothers, and *Snoopy!*, based on the *Peanuts* cartoons and regarded as an unofficial sequel to *You're a Good Man, Charlie Brown*.

our audiences respect, and in turn help develop a sense of self-esteem."[14] Says Butler: "We wanted to devise something that was pulled from the whole genre that MTV had pushed forward: a short musical, short music pieces, each staged separately."

Larson's involvement began with Butler's colleague Richard Berg, another of the composer's regular customers at the Moondance Diner. According to Butler, Larson saw Berg reading over some scripts and struck up a conversation. The two hit it off, with Berg attending early *RENT* readings and befriending Larson. When the choice was made to go with a youth-accessible sound for Broadway Arts' new show, Berg asked Larson to partake. Similarly, Hal Hackady, then working on a new adaptation of *The Hunchback of Notre Dame*, came on board via Arnold Engelman at Westbeth Theatre Center as lyricist and book writer alongside director Karen Azenberg, who also directed *Somebody Come and Play*, the Raposo show.

By all accounts, Larson and Hackady were successful collaborators: the former provided the necessary sound and learned from the latter's expertise. While disagreements would arise over language and authenticity - Butler and Larson often suggested changes to make the wording more contemporary - Butler feels "it was a learning experience for all of us, and I think they got along really well, creatively. Each knew what his domain was."

"They were a fascinating duo," says Azenberg. "It was a very haphazard, odd pairing of people - but successful. Jonathan was clearly brilliant without a doubt, but he was also a really great collaborator." Hackady also was able to tap into his established theatre network, spreading word of Broadway Arts and bringing not just attention, but much needed donations.

---

14. The Broadway Arts Theatre for Young Audiences. 'Authors' Information Sheet'. Box 3, Folder 6, Jonathan Larson Papers, Music Division, Library of Congress, Washington, D.C., 2.

During the writing process, the full team met once every two weeks to go over new material, ensure the educational goals were being filled, and decide upon revisions. According to Butler, "Jonathan would call and say 'Okay, this song is done, I wanna play it for you,' and we'd go to his place, or he'd record it and bring it in and play it for us. Because it was episodic, it was easier to do that."

"In some ways, it was a challenge," reminisces Azenberg. "Hal was trying to write in the language of 14-15-year-olds and, at the time, he must have been 70. [He] had the right intentions and ideas, but the language was from a different era. Jonathan worked really hard to find a middle ground so that we were gonna be speaking to the audience we were playing to, and they were wonderful about listening to feedback." Larson's papers supports Azenberg's memories, with faxes coming in from Hackady, followed by notes and revisions in Larson's hand, particularly on the songs 'Blue' and 'Identity Crisis (Madonna)'.

Blocks would run for one week of two-performance days per semester (spring and fall) at Westbeth Theatre Center, followed by a one-week two-performance day tour of schools in New York and New Jersey in 1993 and 1995. Due to potential work conflicts and stylistic needs - especially on *Blocks* - casts would stick to a single show versus performing for Broadway Arts in repertory. As Azenberg remembers, "It wasn't quite as prevalent that you had somebody working in musical theatre who could sing like a rock/pop/rap singer, so finding people who could actually *do* the material was trickier." The audience was definitely pre-Giuliani New York: "At the time," says Butler, "it was almost exclusively - I hate terms they use - it was underserved schools, at-risk children. We were going to some pretty rough neighbourhoods. The kids were rarely shocked by it."

The hardest thing about finding schools willing to take the

show, according to Butler, was keeping Larson from cranking the volume too loud during pitch presentations and scaring off the older administrators who controlled the bookings. At one conference, Azenberg kept sneaking in to adjust the soundboard pre-show to the point where Larson would smack her hand away from the controls. Plans had been made to take the show up to New England during 1996, but were ultimately cancelled due to Larson's death and funding cuts at Broadway Arts.

In each production, the actors called each other by their real names, and the script assigned lines to "#1," "#2," and so on. Each 'character' had a description on the script's first page, suggesting Larson and Hackady aimed for as much audience self-insertion as necessary, adding to the show's impact. Each cast would be rehearsed from the ground up, the music being adjusted to fit their needs. For *RENT* fans, *Blocks'* 1995 productions featured some soon-familiar names: Rodney Hicks, Anthony Rapp, and Yassmin Alers. Murnin recalls that girls in the audience would often rec-ognise Anthony Rapp from his films (*Dazed & Confused* being a recent hit), and the attention was well-appreciated.

Despite originally aiming the show at urban middle school-ers, the show would ultimately play to audiences as young as 10, despite containing some strong language ("Blue ain't for faggots / or for niggers or hymies or spics / or the rest of them maggots") and intense themes.[15] Murnin defends the decision: "We were always upfront with educators about what they'd see, so that we wouldn't have any problems or objections." While changes would be made due to feedback - particularly from students during early post-show talks - *Blocks* was generally well received. According to Azenberg:

---

15. Hal Hackady (Lyrics) & Jonathan Larson (Music). *Blocks*. Box 3, Folder 5, Jonathan Larson Papers, Music Division, Library of Congress, Washington, D.C., 11.

[The reception] was the genius of the songs and the material they created. It was a musical style that [the kids] had never heard when they went to see 'theatre,' so it sounded more like the music they listened to than any kind of show they had seen. Immediately, they listened, and it was fascinating to see the change in the audience as they realised they could relate to the sound of it, and it allowed them to listen to the message.

It was equally important that "[the cast] be very comfortable portraying what they were portraying, so it could come across honestly to the kids. If you were 'acting,' they would read it in a minute," highlights Azenberg. Honesty and approachability were important and, in keeping with Larson's cabaret background, delivering the message took priority.

For Rodney Hicks, new in New York and still uncomfortable with his own sexual identity, the show was a confusing experience:

I didn't realize that the character I was playing was so NOT me at the time. My character was this gay teen who was all about loving and being young and his song was a rap about just that. A lyric was, 'I wanna be Madonna' and another character retorted 'You're never gonna be Madonna so get real.' What I identified with at that time was the need to want to be anything other than who I was, a gay young man who hadn't yet come to terms with his sexuality.

Jon wrote deep not just lyrically, but melodically. Even though his melodies seemed very simple on the surface, there was an aching quality to them. [He] was one of the first people to believe in me, WAY before I believed in myself. He was both music director, composer, and truth seeker. He was writing for you and your truth. What you brought to the table. Although I was still in the stage of my life where I wanted to be anything but gay, I remember Anthony being the first bisexual identified person I had ever met, and I found him so fascinating. That he could be so comfortable in his own skin and simply be. I so wanted to obtain that quality and longed for it to be a driving force in my life. It took many years for that to happen.

Similar to *J.P. Morgan Saves the Nation* and *RENT*, *Blocks* shows Larson's mastery of genre-crossing composition, jumping from MC Hammer-esque rap ('Reasons to Fail') to vaudeville ('Parents for Sale') to grunge and pop in a mere 35 minutes. Highlights include 'Blue,' an introspective folk song on working-class close-mindedness and masculinity, 'Identity Crisis (Madonna),' a poppy party song on finding self-worth versus attempting to imitate a celebrity, 'I'd Forgotten Sky,' a ballad sung by an older girl (Yassmin Alers in the 1995 cast) about rediscovering life and kicking a drug habit, and 'Bruise,' a haunting, vicious grunge number similar in style to Nirvana's 'Heart Shaped Box,' about covering up abuse:

> This scratch right here
> My dog did that
> I got no dog
> I mean my cat
> Slipped on a rug
> Make that wet grass
> No, make that ice
> Try broken glass[16]

---

16. Hal Hackady (Lyrics) & Jonathan Larson (Music). *Blocks*. Box 3, Folder

Staging on *Blocks* was largely minimal: the cast were tied to standing microphones, and according to Azenberg, "It wasn't dancey, but movement connected with the style. It was more traffic patterns. [The cast] were hired more for their singing style, so we tried to capitalise on that." Each cast member had different block props with issues written on the side, first used to build a wall - knocked down at the end of the show - before a hidden side was revealed and the blocks were rearranged to build a rainbow.

After each performance, members of the audience would be invited to interact with the cast and production team. Larson would attend when possible, though Azenberg and Butler typically led the discussions. "The most moving of all was when a high school kid came out at an after-performance discussion. Every other kid in the audience was so wonderful with him, so supportive. It was one of the highlights of the post-shows," remembers Butler. Says Azenberg: "I remember several experiences during the talkback when, after the kids had left, the teacher would hang back and say, 'That kid that asked that question or said this comment never speaks, so clearly you touched him, connected with him/her in some way.'"

While Larson's death brought *Blocks* to an end at Broadway Arts despite solid buzz among educators and increasing demand from school districts, the show found a second life in 1997, when Housing Works, a New York organisation offering housing, counselling, and classes to homeless AIDS patients, spun off a children's theatre company for patients' families. The organisation's artistic director, Victoria McElwaine, knew Larson and reached out to the team at Broadway Arts after his passing.

Building a new show upon most (but not all) of the songs from *Blocks*, the children at Housing Works told their own stories amidst

---

5, Jonathan Larson Papers, Music Division, Library of Congress, Washington, D.C., 17.

a high-fantasy concept, adding a framework to the loosely structured original and performing their own creation, *I Make Me A Promise*. Michael Murnin oversaw the adaptation, and additional songs were written by Christine Talbott. Murnin remembers, "It was exciting for the kids. A lot of them were inner-city, but they'd had a wide variety of lives and backgrounds." *Promise* was performed off-Broadway at the McGinn/Cazale Theatre, then home to Second Stage.

Amongst the enthusiastic audiences were representatives from the U.S. Department of Housing and Urban Development (HUD) - Housing Works' chief sponsor. According to Murnin, the representatives were blown away by the show and insisted it be performed for HUD staff in Washington, D.C., promising the young performers a presidential visit from Bill Clinton. The federal agency paid for the cast and staff to be flown to Washington and put up in a hotel, and the performance went off with just one small hitch: it took place on January 17, 1998 - the day the Monica Lewinsky scandal broke. While the kids still got a tour of the White House, the presidential meeting was cancelled.

Unfortunately, Broadway Arts proved financially unsustainable. Despite ever-increasing demand for their work, funding cuts from organisations including the NEA trickled down, and the company never reached self-sufficiency. Azenberg ultimately moved to Salt Lake City, where she now runs a regional theatre company. Michael Murnin directs community theatre in Delaware, and Karen Butler teaches through applied drama at a private school in New York City.

Chapter Six

A Gentleman's Agreement
J.P. Morgan Saves the Nation

For I regard this contest
As one to determine who shall rule this country-
The government of the people
or a few domineering and ruthless men?

—J.P. Morgan Saves the Nation

I N MARCH 1995, producer Anne Hamburger commissioned
Larson to score a musical for En Garde Arts, her non-profit
company dedicated to site-specific productions.[1] En Garde
had a show opening that summer, and the original composer had
dropped out. For Larson - buried amidst *RENT* revisions - the
request provided a chance to take a much-needed break from his
epic, provide distance from the material, and recharge his creative
batteries while engaging in a new project - one guaranteed to be
staged. The show might not have been 100% his own, but it was
still close to his politically charged roots: *J.P. Morgan Saves the*

---

1. The e in 'Anne' is pronounced.

Nation, a satirical pageant about American economic history via a larger-than-life financier's biography,.[2]

Hamburger created En Garde Arts in 1985 and dedicated the company to engaging with New York City's public spaces (especially those in a disused or dilapidated state), colliding the city's past and present through text and staging. "I come from a visual arts background," recalls Hamburger:

> When I was an undergrad, I did performance art and earthworks, and when I came to the city, I started working with Anne Bogart, and she had something called the Emissions Project, where she was doing environmental theatre with a collective of actors. I just became very inspired by the whole notion of theatre in relation to its environment, to reaching out to new audiences, of the serendipity of people and things running into a piece of work. I love the idea of theatre really being able to embrace spectacle at the same time it embraced story, so I started doing these shows. My way of working as a producer, as a creative producer - and I think there are very few of me around - is I love putting people, projects, and ideas together. I love talking to artists.[3]

En Garde policy was to choose the sites first, then commission or select plays to fit their needs once permits and funding were

---

2. Whenever possible, quotes are taken from the published version of *J.P. Morgan Saves the Nation*, available from Sun & Moon Press. Quotes from early drafts and last-minute revisions will be cited accordingly.

3. James F. Schlatter covers the company's goals and methods in detail in his article 'En Garde Arts: New York's New Public Theatre' in *PAJ* Vol. 21 No. 2, and this author shall refrain from rehashing it in depth.

secured. No cool location, no need for a project. "I was very moved and driven by working with the community," says Hamburger.

"Anne had a wonderful visual eye," remembers Carol Bixler, En Garde's assistant producer from 1995-1998. "She was intrigued by space and theatre coming together, and laid the groundwork for a lot of relationships between artists and the city. She was also a master of PR, doing work in the summer and getting coverage when little else was going on. It got us huge amounts of PR and built the company's reputation."

Anne Hamburger first encountered *J.P. Morgan's* book writer and lyricist, Jeffrey M. Jones, during En Garde's infancy:

> I got to know Jeff through Mac Wellman. Mac wrote two pieces for me - *Bad Penny*, which we did by the Beau Bridge in Central Park, [and] *Crowbar* at the Victory Theatre, [which] was the first live theatre piece [there] in over 60 years.[4] Mac wrote a piece about the [Victory's] history, and the audience sat on the stage and the action took place in the house.

Hamburger and Jones had discussed working together early on, though other commitments kept Jones from participating in the company's first decade of operations. However, as time passed and the financial district provided a series of day jobs, Jones had a revelation: "It occurred to me that [En Garde Arts] might just as well site a piece that represented what Manhattan is really known for: money and power."[5]

Mac Wellman was also responsible for inspiring Jones to look at J.P. Morgan. Like many readers with an interest in history,

---

4. The Victory had been converted to a cinema.

5. As of this writing, Jones is currently working at investment bank Goldman Sachs in addition to writing.

Wellman had read Ron Chernow's then-recently published *The House of Morgan: An American Banking Dynasty and the Rise of Modern Finance.*[6] As Wellman and Jones talked, the former asked if Jones knew of how Morgan once bailed out the New York Stock Exchange by personally walking down Broad Street with a cheque for US $25 million to cover the day's trading. Jones had not - but was fascinated, picking up his own copy of the book and devouring it.[7] The Morgan story, as told in *The House of Morgan*, would form the backbone of Jones's parable, and Chernow's book became the creative team's go-to source.[8]

Jones and Hamburger subsequently chose the site: Federal Hall, at the intersection of Wall, Nassau, and Broad streets – the heart of New York's financial district. Says Jones:

> The details of the site turned out to be too good to be true: Stock Exchange; Morgan Bank; Former Treasury w/ George Washington in front; Statue of Liberty behind the Exchange but known to everyone. The [Bankers' Trust] was founded by Morgan partners who earned their spurs in 1907, but it wasn't until I saw it from a distance and realized there was a step pyramid on top that I understood how it completed the square.

Jones began to write his show, initially turning to friend and long-time collaborator Dan Moses Schreier for music. Schreier had composed incidental music for some of Jones' plays, and initial compositions were scored to Jones' stand-in lyrics, including a take

---

6. Chernow's later biography of American founding father Alexander Hamilton would be musicalised to far greater commercial success.

7. Jones ultimately employed Wellman as *J.P. Morgan*'s dramaturge.

8. Director Jean Randich compiled a chapter-by-chapter summary of Chernow's book with key quotes and excerpts, including it along with a rough chronology of events in Morgan's life and surrounding economic history for members of the creative team.

on the finale which Jones describes as "ravishing and complex." However, Schreier ultimately decided against seeing the project through to fruition, leaving Hamburger and Jones in search of a new composer. Meanwhile, Jones had chosen a director: Jean Randich, who had directed some of Jones' *Crazy Plays* in New York's Tweed Festival.

Conveniently, a hip, young composer lived across the street from En Garde's office: Jonathan Larson. While Hamburger has since forgotten how the two first met, his work instantly made an impact: "He was a real menschy guy, a real doll. He was very stressed out about everything with *RENT*, not sure if it was very good, but I loved it, and that's why I wanted to hire him to do *J.P. Morgan*." Hoping to get Jones on board with her choice of replacement, Hamburger sent him a tape of Larson's late 1994 demo from *RENT*. Jones was impressed and agreed to engage Larson on the project.

Larson, however, was initially hesitant: "He was so involved in *RENT* at the time," recalls Victoria Leacock Hoffman. "He wasn't sure if he wanted to do it, and it would be a big rush, but I told him he should do it. The *Times* always covered [En Garde]'s stuff, and I said he should let them review this before seeing *RENT*. I remember saying, "Do you want to introduce them to your work with your big show?" - I think that stuck with him."

According to Jonathan Burkhart, Larson "in no uncertain terms [...] loved the *J.P. Morgan* experience." Working quickly on a show about the American condition, combined with a budget, a hot company known for operating on the edge, and a real production in New York, made for an excited composer. Buried under seemingly endless delays surrounding *RENT*, *Morgan* was a fast-tracked project from heaven - the sort every composer dreams of: no producers making endless demands for rewrites, no artistic director refusing to set production dates, just writing music and putting up a show. Despite the disappointment of having limited input on the story, Larson unleashed his artistic wild child, engaging in Jones' anarchic script on an equally chaotic level.

Getting Paid to Sing You This Song

Larson's musical proposal, to "encompass a variety of turn of the century styles as well as modern popular music - everything from J. P. Sousa & Scott Joplin to Madonna & Pearl Jam," clicked with Jones, who says:

> There was never any thought of doing 'period' music. What would be the point? Jonathan early on had the idea of sampling as broad a range of American musical styles as possible. Since that was his field of expertise, it never occurred to me to question him, but the idea also made a lot of sense.

Director Jean Randich explains that she found the music ideal for the production:

> I think it's pretty astonishing how much [Jones and Larson] gave each other - if you think of how unusual the book and the lyrics for *J.P. Morgan Saves the Nation* are, it's almost like an Andy Warhol idea, and yet I think Jonathan found musical language for all those different characters and songs, and he found a wonderful choral feel. Whenever the chorus was going on, it was just like PARTY! Jonathan's music had a physicality - these people physically changed the world, they were running up and down the stairs, there was a physical energy going on and they were singing this music which was propulsive, and I think he captured that thing

Jeff obsessed about, and even the fact that Jeff could visualise the currency moving - it exists on a lot of levels.

The decision to span eras and styles also corresponded with Jones' belief in the material's contemporary relevance. At a fund-raising presentation, Jones introduced the song 'Greenback Dollars' thusly: "For reasons that may not seem mysterious to any of you, the Civil War was not financed principally by bonds or by taxes. It was funded by bad money. Greenback Dollars - that is to say, dollar bills unbacked by specie, were pumped into the economy at an enormous rate [...] Our metaphor is Madonna."[9] In 1995, the stock market was rising on the verge of the dot-com explosion, and monetarist policy had seen wide deregulation of international banking and trading. Following a brief recession in the early 1990s, the economy had recovered and was growing faster than ever, and the glam and throb of '80s dance pop lent itself to the financial party that was the late 20th Century - ironically or not.

One problem, however, faced all involved: time. The first script from *J.P. Morgan* present in Larson's archives is dated 3 February 1995, and rehearsals were to begin on 2 May of that year, leaving him under three months to compose a planned 17 songs. Worse, songs in the first drafts were often tagged as placeholders or were written to fit Scheier's now-discarded compositions. If writing 10 songs for an Adelphi cabaret was a trial by fire, composing *J.P. Morgan Saves the Nation* would reveal a composer adept at bat-tling the flames, honed by an additional decade's experience and confidence in his ability to work at speed. *RENT* may have been plaguing his mind, but for Jonathan Larson, overt, satirical polit-ical theatre must have felt like returning to a comfortable home.

---

9. *J.P. Morgan Saves the Nation* (Producer Backing Performance). Spring 1995. MAVIS 187206-3-3. Jonathan Larson Recordings, Recorded Sound Division, Library of Congress, Washington, D.C.

Jones, who in a 1995 interview admitted he "[didn't] know anything about musical theatre," was at least on the right track.[10] Certain scenes and songs, such as a sea shanty-cum-lullaby for Lady Liberty to sing to young J.P., a lyric about financially mismanaging railroads were in place from the earliest drafts, along with the aforementioned 'Greenback Dollars,' though often with temporary lyrics or significantly more verses. For Larson, the challenge was to figure out what worked, what needed to go, and more importantly, what remained to be musicalised. For Jones, clarifying the narrative and characters came at the same time.

While the writers worked on their end, Hamburger and Bixler set to work handling the logistical arrangements. Bringing *J.P. Morgan* to life required six permits from agencies including the National Parks Service (to use Federal Hall), four different city organisations, and a sound permit from the police department ("They threw a shit fit about that one," recalls Bixler.) Rudy Giuliani was in his first term as mayor, and his new policies to clean up the city and change procedure, complicated affairs, as did the costs for permits. Bixler and Hamburger sent every application with letters begging the city to waive various costs: "The $35 per day [for a street permit] is, of course, quite modest for a one-day event, such as a street festival. However, when applied to a production running for six weeks, the total charge is considerable."[11] Hamburger tended to play up the company's consistently perilous financial state in her letters: "We are facing a potential 50% cut of our Department of Cultural Affairs money and hope that we can

10. John Istel, 'Rescuing the Musical'. *Village Voice*, 4 July 1995. 74. Clipping held in Box 6, Folder 4, Jonathan Larson Papers, Music Division, Library of Congress, Washington, D.C.

11. Carol Bixler. Letter to Ron Maiorana. Box 5, Folder 13, En Garde Arts Records, Billy Rose Theatre Division, New York Public Library, New York, NY.

receive government support by fee waivers to help offset the difficulties we are experiencing."[12]

Getting Morganised

As Jones and Larson worked through March and April 1995, *J.P. Morgan's* book underwent dramatic revisions. By March 1995, Jones' discarded many of his original lyrics, and Larson had pushed to musicalise three additional scenes. As rehearsal began, Larson and Jones would go back and forth, Larson often pushing for lyrical revisions (or writing them himself) until Jones demanded a halt: the script's publication deadline was approaching, and the show needed to conform as closely to what Jones submitted as possible.

True to form, Larson recorded a full demo of the show, arranging the music with Steve Skinner and singing all the parts.[13] These recordings, created as Larson moved from song to song, primarily featured lyrics from the drafts dated March and May 1995.[14] "He really cranked it out," remembers Bixler. "The first time we listened to his work, he'd already done six songs. He was lovely, and never a problem."

"At one of the first meetings, Jonathan himself laid out the work and the time - 'I need to get X songs to you in Y weeks' - and executed," says Jones. "I'm telling you--consummate professional! There was never any question that he would deliver anything less than a first class score."

---

12. Anne Hamburger. Letter to Fran Reiter. Box 5, Folder 13, En Garde Arts Records, Billy Rose Theatre Division, New York Public Library, New York, NY.

13. This recording also contains 'Let Go The Line,' a song Larson wrote for the film *White Squall*. The song is discussed in detail in Appendix A.

14. Jeffrey M. Jones (Lyrics) & Jonathan Larson (Music). J.P. Morgan Saves the Nation (Rehearsal Draft). Box 5, Folder 10, Jonathan Larson Papers, Music Division, Library of Congress, Washington, D.C.

Something, however, was missing. As Jones tells it:

> My favorite memory — not just of this production
> but of my whole career — was Jonathan's decla-
> ration that we needed a new song early in Act I
> to introduce Morgan sympathetically, as a young
> man. I believe we may have been 3-4 days from the
> first preview. I wrote a bunch of lyrics overnight
> and sent them to him, but they were incomplete;
> he came back with music and a finished song,
> which we tweaked before the runthru, [sic] sitting
> in a stairwell in front of the Stock Exchange to get
> a little shelter from the wind.

Prior to this last-minute insertion, Morgan's first song came
almost half an hour into the show, when he mourned the death of
his first wife. In adding this song, 'The Office Down There,' Jones
and Larson show a wide-eyed Morgan hoping to do good and rise
to greatness, providing pathos to his subsequent journey as he loses
his emotional and ideological cores. Randich remembers Larson
demanding the number as well:

> [Jonathan kept saying] "J.P. Morgan needs an
> 'I Want' song!' He played it [when] we were at
> Federal Hall. He had it on a tape on a boombox,
> and we were looking for a place to plug it in so we
> could play it. I remember sitting on the sidewalk
> by the steps of Federal Hall, and he pushed play,
> and there was this song. It really was at the last
> possible moment, and he was going 'I NEEEED
> THIS' and it comes from basic musical theatre and
> 'What does your main character want?'

In addition to speed, Larson also had an extra bonus to offer:
an archive. Three songs in particular - 'Greenback Dollars,' 'Jack

'o' Diamonds,' and 'Run That Railroad' - feature new vocal lines over existing music. While 'Jack' slightly reworked the tempo and overall arrangements to 1990's 'Break out the Booze,' 'Greenback Dollars' reused the complete scoring for 1993's 'Identity Crisis (Madonna)' in an altered key with minimal refinements to the synths in order to fit the new structure and take advantage of revised synthesiser patches. Meanwhile, 'Run That Railroad' uses the guitar hook from 'Cool/Fool,' a discarded number from early editions of *RENT*.

As performed, *J.P. Morgan Saves the Nation* follows the titular character from birth to death. He is surrounded by his hawk-like father, duty, and conscience - represented by George Washington on the one hand - and the distant women in his life as portrayed by Lady Liberty, on the other. In his rise to glory as the most powerful banker in America, Morgan locks horns with the country's not-so-consistently moral needs in the form of a smooth-talking, snake-oil-selling Uncle Sam, and flirts with the temptations of greed and unchecked capitalism personified as a sultry female Devil. Surrounding him are period businessmen and a chorus of money girls, clad in skin-tight dollar-bill-print spandex.

If Larson's puckish inner Brechtian was running amok with audial imagery and intensity, he was doing so through an increasingly confident grasp of motif. Liberty's theme, 'I Loved a Sailor,' is *Morgan*'s key musical theme, recurring in most (if not all of) the character's songs and, with minimal rearrangement, varies from gentle and mournful, as in its original incarnation as a shanty, to powerful and imposing as an underscore whenever Morgan is summoned by George Washington or Uncle Sam. A second motif, this time for death, comes through in 'The Woman Died' and 'The Telegram,' and is reprised again at the start of the 'Railroad Wars' scene, albeit with different lyrics. Jones contributes equally, with lyrical themes set up for reprise in 'Proceedings,' the rap number surrounding Morgan's downfall.

Getting On Board

For its cast, *J.P. Morgan Saves the Nation* was something of a reunion: director Jean Randich and actors Buzz Bovshow, Stephen DeRosa, Julie Fain Lawrence, and Robin Miles all pursued MFAs at Yale Drama School during overlapping years.[15] The group stayed in contact after graduating, and calls were made. Larson's training at Adelphi - inspired by Burdick's time at Yale - quickly got him on the same page. Rounding out the principal cast was James Judy, who, along with Bovshow, lent experience to the production as the title character and George Washington, respectively.

Randich knew she was in for a challenge from the start:

> I was pretty naive - I had no idea how complex [the staging] would be, and now I think it would be impossible. After 9/11, you can't even get near [the Stock Exchange], but I didn't realise [it then]. I just thought, "This'll be fun! Let's put on a show!" I finished Yale in '94, and then I got a Fox Foundation grant to go to Norway, as I'd done *Peer Gynt* as my thesis, and I was fascinated with everything Norwegian at that point. I went over, I was working as an assistant director at the Nationaltheatret, and I think we started talking about it when I was over there.[16]

"I remember, in trying to cast it, thinking 'I have to have

---

15. En Garde Arts founder Anne Hamburger also received her MFA in Theatre from Yale Drama School, though years before Randich and the *Morgan* cast.

16. The Nationaltheatret is the National Theatre of Norway in Oslo.

people who are smart, they have to understand this,'" continues Randich:

> Sometimes a director will try to explain it or find a parallel, and I thought "Ooh, this is really hard. I barely understand this. I need to have people who can." Stephen DeRosa walked in, and he understood what Jeff was doing with Uncle Sam, and he has that generosity and openness and "We're all gonna have a good time here!" which dovetailed with what Jeff was saying about how we like government that always seems non-hands on and that kind of thing."

"It was unlike anything I'd ever done before, and I'd venture to say [for] the whole cast, unlike anything anyone had ever done before. It was really exciting," recalls Robin Miles, who played 19th Century Market Capitalism (aka the Devil).

Dance Captain Neil D. Seibel auditioned,

> [...] for anything I could audition for. Everybody on production, we were all kids for the most part. Everybody in the ensemble, we were young, in our early 20s, trying to break into the city. At that time, En Garde Arts was a hot-ticket item. They had the buzz 'cause they were doing all this really cool work. It was like a gig that everybody wanted to be in because they'd just started winning Obies, so it was a legit credit and they used big casts.[17]

To En Garde Arts, *J.P. Morgan* was a financial and

---

17. A dance captain is a performer charged with maintaining choreography standards in a production and calling additional dance rehearsals as needed. The captain typically holds an otherwise minor ensemble role in the show or serves as an understudy.

logistical challenge, as well as a creative one. The budget clocked in at over $300,000, and the company's future depended on the show making money. "That was business as usual, really," remembers Hamburger. "We were always trying to figure out where we could get our money from. We did have pretty good foundation support in those days, but it was insane to do these shows." Even after favours had been called in and such necessities as rehearsal space were secured through donations, the budget remained high and continued growing as additional stagehands and run crew were brought on board, exploding from 8 people on crew to 18. "You don't know what you don't know, and we didn't know how many people we were going to need for turnovers," recalls Bixler. "It was my first site-specific show, and the budget had already been sorted as well. Fortunately, Anne was good at making friends and calling in last-minute favours." Presentations were arranged for donors, and the money came in to get the show off the ground.

As Seibel mentions, *Morgan*'s cast was particularly large. DeRosa remembers, "It definitely felt like the cast was outnumbering the audience." Boasting a cast of 34 (five principals and 29 dancers/singers), the show filled the steps and archways of Federal Hall, and work began on the show's additional set pieces, such as a platform to line up with the building's statue of George Washington and two giant lighting towers, both sturdy enough to support cast members climbing them during the show. Powering the electrics would be its own challenge as En Garde staff scrambled to find neighbouring buildings willing to let the company run lines after hours.

Despite its unusual location and quirky script, *J.P. Morgan*'s casting was structured in the same vein as an opera or an old-fashioned musical, with the cast neatly divided into principals, a small singing choir, and two choruses of dancers. The groups were often kept separate in rehearsals, coming together only during tech or as absolutely needed. Dance Captain Seibel recalls: "A friend of mine was a singer, and we thought 'Great! We'll see each other all the time!' - and then barely got to talk to each other during the entire run." Given the short rehearsal time and limited facilities, such a setup minimised full-cast rehearsals and allowed the team to focus on necessities, especially with the dancers often off-stage.

Security proved to be another nightmare. Because the show was being performed on the steps of a working government building with close access to the New York Stock Exchange, the company needed to strike the entire production after each performance, rebuilding it the next evening as soon as office hours ended on Wall Street. Actors had to submit to background checks, and guards were posted at all dressing rooms to ensure no suspicious items were brought in or left behind.

Even going to rehearsal required security access, as the cast were rehearsing on the 51st floor of the nearby Bear Sterns office on Water Street - a floor which had been gutted for renovations but not yet converted back to a functional business space. Besides its view of the performance site, the ongoing renovations made it easier to rehearse without noise concerns - plus it was easy to secure as a donation from the owners, as its unfinished state temporarily took the space off the rental market. The space was divided into multiple areas, allowing the actors and dancers to work simultaneously as needed, as well as to provide a small library with research materials on Morgan and his era for the cast and crew. Miles remembers the location's physicality: "We had natural light coming in and lots of windows. There was a strange kind of beauty to it. It was down and dirty to a certain degree - you'd come home and just be so dirty with this concrete dust."

"Being in that space," says Julie Fain Lawrence, "it felt really guerrilla-theatre-like, which En Garde Arts was about anyway."

Seibel remembers:

> When you got off the elevator and went to the left,
> that was set up as the dance studio where all the
> dancers were, and at the other end, that's where the
> singers were all set up, and they were working with
> Jonathan, and at the other end was the actors, and
> they were all working with Jean. The cool thing
> was that we used the windows as mirrors, as it was
> almost floor-to-ceiling windows, and because we
> were rehearsing in the evenings, we used those as
> our mirrors in the studio.

The speed of production affected the entire cast and crew: "We were all really thrown into it," remembers Stephen DeRosa. "Or at least I was. I was still at school when I auditioned. You're on the steps of Federal Hall. You're rehearsing this thing without mics, just to get the blocking, and you look like a group of homeless people running around, and Jean's trying to block something with minimal lights." Says Seibel: "We were only allowed to rehearse at certain times of day and on specific days, because it was a crazy schedule. It didn't bother me, because I was so used to doing downtown theatre, I was used to a nutty schedule."

Rehearsals proceeded at a clip at 55 Water Street, and the creative team quickly gelled. As Seibel observed:

> Jeff was there doing the rewrites, and Jean was
> working with the actors and getting to talk to her as
> the director, and Doug as the choreographer, and
> Annie as the overall producer - she was really con-
> sistently there as well. Everybody was, really - for a
> show that big and that was that disconnected - I do
> remember all of those personalities very well and
> working with them very closely for a show of that
> size and being as young as I was at the time. I have
> since realised that not all units are that cohesive.

While Jules Cohen is credited as music director, Larson worked extensively with the actors during rehearsal, teaching songs and making revisions as necessary. Because the outdoor location required all its space to be used for acting and seating, a live band was out of the question. As such, once Larson finished teaching songs to the cast, rehearsals would be conducted to backing tapes - restricting for improvisational acting, but excellent at keeping the large cast and its varying components in line: unlike standard cassettes or a band, DAT tapes always stayed on tempo, thanks to operating on a fixed timecode.

While *RENT* was never far from Larson's mind, his overall passion for the project grew during rehearsal, for better and for worse. As Seibel describes:

> Sometimes choreographers and composers feel this need to tear people down. [Larson] was never like that. When he was passionate and feisty, it was always about the work, trying to make it the best it could be. It was never about cutting someone down, which I appreciated, and he could be so generous with compliments at times. At certain times, it was beautiful to watch. People would miss something and miss something and miss something, and he would say, "You have such a great voice. You'll get this, you just gotta get out of your way," and then he'll say, "Dammit, you missed your entrance five frickin' times, how frickin' hard is it?" He was really funny out of rehearsal. In rehearsal, he was one way, and out of rehearsal, it was fun to just watch him kick back and get flirty and giggly. I never saw him giggle in rehearsal, but out of rehearsal, he could be this funny, silly, giggly, laughy guy, which was really cool.

Randich found Larson's passion infectious:

> [Larson] was really gung-ho. He was extremely
> energetic, always positive - never negative. I always
> felt he was very encouraging. He had that pluck.
> Drive, comedy - he was very funny. He was brave.
> I think the music was brave. Fun - and maybe
> almost homespun. It didn't try to be edgy in that
> way. I think he picked up on the 19th-Century
> feeling, because it was happening at the end of
> one time and beginning of another, and he really
> pulled from that. It's very similar, the way Kurt
> Weil's music is so listenable and so seductive, and
> there's something bouncing and upbeat.

The cast retain fond memories of working with Larson: "I had a lot of one-on-one time with [him]," says Lawrence. "I hadn't pursued musical theatre much since high school and hadn't had the best experiences [...,] so working with him individually gave me tons of confidence. He was a great support. He was very generous."

"We all got to know Jonathan well, and some of us got to know him better than others. He was an interesting guy, but he was a young, struggling artist, as well," says Seibel, who Larson encouraged to audition for *RENT*.

> He was like, "Yeah, yeah, you should come, you
> should audition. You're fun and we've just had
> a great time." I was moving to Paris. I was like,
> "Jonathan, I'm not auditioning for anything, I'm
> gonna work and make some money and then be
> over there for nine months or a year at least," and
> [we were all] like, "No, we can't do it."

Larson also asked Robin Miles to audition for the role of Joanne in *RENT*,

but I had no money - I had just done *Morgan*
for like $250 a week, and the coffers were empty.
I agreed to do a Shakespeare somewhere and
couldn't do *RENT*, because I had to pay my rent.
[But with *Morgan*], I remember standing at the
piano and trying to find the right keys and worrying that I wasn't going to hit some of the notes,
because the range was pretty wide, and [Larson]
had total confidence and relaxation. He knew I was
gonna be able to do it. That completely set me at
ease. Given the other elements I was trying to integrate, I really thought, "My gosh, this is too much
to handle," but he didn't bat an eyelash. That kind
of support, that kind of confidence, when it comes
at you, it bleeds onto you, and I went, "Oh, okay, I
can do this." And I did. But I really was grateful for
all that work at the piano. He was always willing to
go over something one more time - always. Real
generosity of spirit. All that support was really,
really generous.

As with Larson's music, *J.P. Morgan*'s choreography paid
homage to American dance, with a firm grounding in the modern.
Choreographer Doug Elkins kept his units separate, giving the
male and female ensembles different styles, with the leads and
singing ensemble taking on their own directions, as well. Seibel
describes the overall style as:

The first show I did which had a street edge to it.
It's funny now, but there was a lot of 'Vogue'-esque,
a lot of fun and edgy, ambisexual [stuff]. The guys,
we'd do a lot of stuff which was really thuggish and
edgy, and really grounded and heavy 'cause we were
all in these black suits with bowler hats, and we

were wide-stanced and really gruff and very ath-
letic choreography, and then we'd turn around and
do a straight-up drag queen sachet. The women
were in skin-tight unitards painted like dollars,
and some of them had little tails or would steal our
bowler hats. They would have really Afro-centric
choreography at times, and then very old-school
jazz, classic jazz choreography, and also turn
around and do really fun, sexy, at the time MTV/
street choreography. That was the early '90s, so you
were starting to see a lot more contemporary choreography going into musical theatre. Now, it's so
much the norm.

Elkins also integrated background interactions and non-
dance elements into his choreography, creating a visual language
backing up the script. Individual performance skills were empha-
sised in places, such as a dancer with bullwhip experience beating the Businessmen characters into shape, maintaining a carni-
val-like atmosphere in line with Uncle Sam's huckster persona.
Businessmen dancers would also work with specific dollar girls
throughout the show, with Elkins building a visual relationship
between financiers and easy money, before ultimately taking the
money away in 'The Bailout,' a topsy-turvy number on the 1907
stock market crash: "One of the coolest visuals," remembers Seibel,
"was the section where we jumped out the windows onto the steps
and you'd [lift] your jacket up. The combination of that and the
lights, [how] the breeze [caught] your jacket, I felt like it was a
really cool image. The visuals were so important, because the space
were so huge - you were so small as a single person that it was easy
to get lost, and there wasn't this real sense of personal ego - you
were more of a visual."

Lawrence remembers moving out of Water Street and onto the

steps as a cause for excitement: "It wasn't that crazy difficult. I love performing outside, and site-specific performance just gives you so much more of an environment to work with. We were excited that we actually had the steps and space to travel. It was such an experience, such an adventure."

"I was afraid I was going to break my neck half the time," recalls Miles. "People [were] walking by, and [we were] performing, and I loved that."

The dancers, however, needed extra rehearsals to adjust to the location's physical limitations: "Visually, we were on the steps, and levels, levels, levels, and if you were on the steps and trying to do any acro[batics] or combat on the steps vs. on the flat in front, or if you were up above in the alcoves or pedestal areas, those [would be] saved for a lot of the acting work," remembers Seibel. "So many people that I knew, they wanted to know 'what are the rehearsals like, what are you guys doing down there, what's it like?'"

Randich remembers the location from a more pragmatic approach:

> You're trying to find an entertaining way to tell this
> story that we're all still pawns in, and at the same
> time, the fact that it was done outside, and we had
> to move everything in and out, and the streets are
> narrow, and Jonathan would be pushing the seat-
> ing risers. It was kind of epic and heroic and excit-
> ing, and also terrifying. It was very frightening.

The cast also looked forward to interacting with the audience, separated by little more than the sidewalk in front of Federal Hall: "I remember the fact that we had this large ensemble sometimes coming at you or being in the aisles. That was both exciting as a performer and seemed to be fun for the audience," says Stephen DeRosa, who was struck by the surreality of the whole affair:

I was literally fresh out of school and in a state of shock on some level. It didn't really feel like my first real show in New York. It felt like this strange, experimental theatre thing we were doing and throwing together so quickly. It felt like we'd barely been in the room a couple weeks before we were on site. To do a full-length musical outside with three days of tech, and I was commuting back and forth from Yale after classes and don't know how I was doing it… It was just insanity, but when you're in your 20s, everything seems fun and adventurous.

Seibel also remembers excitement in the air:

You were in your 20s and in this cast with all these young, beautiful people, and everybody in New York wanted to know what the hell was going on, because En Garde was just known for doing this interesting work that was really visual, and people wanted to see it, so we had that buzz going for us, and we fed into it. It was such a high [to be on the steps]. It was so cool to just go and be in such a big show and with all those people and the vitality and fun. And everybody was pretty. I know it sounds shallow, but everybody wants to be one of the pretty kids.

During performances, Federal Hall and the New York Stock Exchange closed at 6 PM. The streets would be blocked off at 6:30, with the lighting towers and seating risers trucked in or pushed down the streets from storage. Power would be hooked up to outlets at Federal Hall and 30 Wall Street, with Larson and anybody else available from the En Garde office helping out to ensure things

were ready by the 8 PM start.[18] Due to the show's open performance, tourists and passers-by crossing through the district would
stand around and watch part (if not all) of the show for free from
behind the bleachers. "It's hard to believe the whole thing came
together," says Bixler, "but we had a lot of determination, and Anne
was good at inventing systems and ways to make things happen."

Fielding the Critics

While the participants enjoyed the *J.P. Morgan* experience, the
same cannot be said for New York's theatre critics. In the *New York
Post*, critic Clive Barnes damned the show as 'horrendous,' saying
of the score:

> Equally, a musical needs music, and Larson - here
> with a score that sounded so vaguely second-hand
> that had it been either memorable or hummable,
> you might have hummed it on your way to the site -
> seemed capable of only very marginal assistance.[19]

Reflecting upon Larson's work in 2001 when he reviewed *tick,
tick... BOOM!* off-Broadway, Barnes described *Morgan* as "inde-
scribably awful" (though recanted on Larson's overall talent).[20] In
the *New York Daily News*, critic and science fiction author Thomas

---

18. Larson attended every performance of the show, often standing at the
back, sitting on the roof of a newsstand, or curled up in the J.P. Morgan building's
windows.

19. Clive Barnes. 'Nothing Saves "J.P."' *New York Post*, 16 June 1995. 44.
Clipping held in Box 6, Folder 4, Jonathan Larson Papers, Music Division, Library
of Congress, Washington, D.C.

20. Clive Barnes. 'Larson Tops at Tuning Into Musicals.' *New York Post*,
22 July 2001, accessed 25 January 2016, http://nypost.com/2001/07/22/
larson-tops-at-tuning-in-to-musicals/.

M. Disch headlined his review, "Save the Nation from 'J.P.'!" and focused on the script and cast, ignoring the music entirely.[21]

Mixed reviews came in from Jan Stuart at *New York Newsday*, who felt the show was interesting but also outstayed its welcome, despite praising Larson's music as "eclectic and often catchy [...]" and enjoying the choreography despite wishing they would "let any single song expand and thrill in good old Broadway tradition."[22] Michael Feingold in the *Village Voice* appreciated the imagery and found it "extremely diverting, on a pleasant summer night, but is also a handy way of not coming to grips with any meaning that Morgan's career and its consequences might hold for a contemporary audience."[23] Feingold also praised Larson's score, calling it "a cheery survey of folk-pop modes from honky-tonk to post-Motown, [which] keeps them bouncing along appealingly."[24]

The key review, which was reservedly positive, came from Ben Brantley at the *New York Times*. Brantley opened: "But has [Wall Street] ever had the chance to witness a chorus line of paper dollars pulsing carnally to a disco beat? The seductive powers of filthy lucre have been given very literal-minded life in an anti-materialist musical spectacle [...]"[25] While Brantley praised the choice of location and enjoyed the evening, he wished the show carried more bite and

21. Thomas M. Disch. 'Save the Nation from "J.P."!'" *NY Daily News*, 16 June 1995. Clipping held in Box 6, Folder 4, Jonathan Larson Papers, Music Division, Library of Congress, Washington, D.C.

22. Jan Stewart. '"J. P. Morgan": Trading on Wall Street's Power.' *New York Newsday*, 16 June 1995. B19. Clipping held in Box 6, Folder 4, Jonathan Larson Papers, Music Division, Library of Congress, Washington, D.C.

23. Michael Feingold. 'Uncertain Tones.' *Village Voice*, 27 June 1995, 90. Clipping held in Box 6, Folder 4, Jonathan Larson Papers, Music Division, Library of Congress, Washington, D.C.

24. Ibid.

25. Ben Brantley. '"J.P. Morgan" and Some Heavy Site-Specificity.' *New York Times*, 16 June 1996. C2. Clipping held in Box 6, Folder 4, Jonathan Larson Papers, Music Division, Library of Congress, Washington, D.C.

relied less on historical obscurities. For Larson, however, there was nothing but praise, with Brantley calling the score "peppy [...] in a post-modernist medley of musical voices" and stating "Mr. Larson works adroitly in an assortment of musical pastiches, from ragtime to rap: his music hall hymn to capitalist hunger, 'Appetite Annie,' winningly performed by Mr. Judy and the chorus, is charming."[26] DeRosa agrees with Brantley's opinion: "The big takeaway for me, and probably for the audience as well, was how wide-ranging the music was, and how fun it was."

Unfortunately, neither any of the reviews nor a profile piece on Larson's quest to reinvent musical theatre running in the 4th of July edition of the *Village Voice* provided a much-needed money quote and low ticket sales forced *Morgan* to close a week early, on 9 July 1995 instead of 16 July. "I didn't read the reviews until after the show had closed," says Seibel:

> I remember when they said that we were closing early, and that surprised us. We were all kinda like, "Well that sucks," because we thought we'd be able to finish out that run. There were a lot of times when we were choreographed to look out at the audience, and [they looked] thin. I didn't think it was that drastic, but I had no concept of what it was costing to put that show on. I remember in rehearsal, talking about, "Well these are challenges, and these are things," and also laughing because "This is so off the wall, this is so different" from anything that was really going on, on the Broadway scene, because at the time, the Broadway scene was so traditional, and even the Off-Broadway scene... When they're talking about how *Sylvia* is really

---

26. Ibid.

edgy? Really? We were laughing because we were thinking, "This is really different."

"There's *nothing* commercial about this show," says DeRosa:

Off-Off Broadway had a kind of cachet and respect at that point, which is virtually non-existent now. Even Off-Broadway now is non-existent, because it can't sustain itself financially. En Garde Arts had an artistic excitement to it. [Brooklyn Academy of Music] was coming up at the time, and it had that kind of audience and enthusiasm, and that's useful. It's a necessity in New York and for a budding young artist, which most of us were.

Bixler was unsurprised: she and other members of En Garde Staff had questioned Hamburger's desire to run the show for six weeks instead of the initially-planned four. For one thing, the bleachers held 400 seats - massive for an En Garde show - and in Bixler's opinion, "so much of what En Garde did, worked by being limited." Combined with the high costs and lukewarm reviews, it made sense to bring the show down when they did.

Unfortunately, Wall Street agreed with the press, and Jones' fellow finance workers stayed away - except to occasionally express their hostility towards the company. Randich remembers, "Trying to do a show like that between the Morgan Bank, Federal Hall, and the Stock Exchange, it felt like [they thought], 'Who are these people to come in here and make fun [of us]?'" Bixler recalls: "Fridays on Wall Street were grim. The traders would leave work early to go and drink. One week, a guy was weaving drunkenly down Wall Street, yelling [at] us that this was his world, and we had no right to enter [the traders'] world."

Brecht, Brecht, Brecht

Brantley's concern - that *J.P. Morgan* "[uses names] in the way a comedian would refer to Lorena Bobbitt or Dan Quayle" - reflects the academic nature of the material, but also misses Jones' point:[27] "Morgan's life is the frame, but the economic history of the United States is arguably the real story." Jones' goal in writing *Morgan* was to passionately explain American economic development, a subject bypassed in history classes for the gloss of battlefields, demonstrations, and high idealism. *J.P. Morgan Saves the Nation* subverts all of these concepts: battles are waged in board rooms and the trading floor, reference is made to the New York Civil War draft riots, and the man's ideals - a firm hand and a consolidation of wealth for the greater good - are everywhere.

Every reference to a historical figure has relevance, even if the audience is unaware of the immediate implications in Morgan's life or the wider state of American economic forces. For example, Uncle Sam's discussion of the economy - it should always go up, and deflated currency can be wiped away by pumping it into abstracts on the stock market - is mirrored later in the show when Morgan competes with Edward Henry Harriman and John D. Rockefeller for control of the Northern Pacific Railroad - leaving behind a wake of economic carnage as the men rush to gather shares. The stock market crashes as outside shareholders began shorting against inflation caused by the competition. The dramatic representation, staged as a boxing match-cum-street fight, results in what Uncle Sam tells the audience to avoid: the economy went down and the dollar tanked, leading to 'The Panic' and the industrialists' subsequent pledge to shore up the stock market out of pocket as trusts and banks fell, is capped off with the central incident of Morgan walking down Nassau Street, cheque in hand, to keep the New

---

27. Ibid.

York Stock Exchange afloat. The scene would play out again in 2008, but this time, the banks were bailed out by taxpayers, not a wealthy industrialist.

Brantley, however, wasn't the only one to focus on the historical particulars - Randich herself got caught in the same trap:

> At the time, what I think I thought was, "This is a historical piece," and I wasn't aware of how timely it was. That idea about, "If what makes this country run is making money, and the best way to make money is to sometimes be a little unscrupulous about it, and that the people who do that - whoever can understand that and get more of it can help other people out by giving them money, but also make them beholden and inspire their hatred, and it spirals around like that," then we're always going to be subjected to a force that's larger than any human being. There were a lot of subtleties in it. Whether or not people saw all that, I don't know. It's a giant picture.

Morgan's sense of charity is also called into question. In the play, Morgan dismisses a homeless Liberty while making a speech at the opening of the Morgan Library, giving with one hand while refusing to help the impoverished in front of him with the other, and building on a trend that those who do not understand money should be allowed (if not encouraged) to fail at it without assistance. Morgan's sense of guilt ultimately sends him in pursuit of Liberty, following her mournful analysis, 'I See a Man,' but it is too late. His image as the greedy egoist is locked in place: that of a cold figure concerned with preserving his legacy despite his desire to conquer and belittle his fellow man.

Structurally, *J.P. Morgan Saves the Nation* is equal parts pageant, mystery play, and Brecht.[28] The steps of Federal Hall may have provided direct relevance to the plot's events, but also functioned the same way as a town square would during a Passion: an outdoor gathering spot where the community comes together and joins the ritual - except that *Morgan*, the religious foundation is capitalism. Both, however, end with a crucifixion, even if J.P. Morgan's was only proverbial. The characters are part of a religious iconography - in this case American patriotism and capitalism - telling a morality tale. The stations of the cross are even mirrored in the surrounding landmarks: the New York Stock Exchange, the Drexel-Morgan building, the Banker's Trust, and the Statue of Liberty in the background. As Randich remembers:

> When I read it, I realised that it's a piece about ideas, so it falls into the theatre of ideas and not necessarily the theatre of argument. It's not "J.P. Morgan was wrong and you shouldn't think like this," but I think Jeff and Jonathan were interested in the carnival canvas of capitalism and the driving force of money that can lead you - and leads all of us [astray]. What he describes is heightened now when you read it 20 years later and go, "Ooh boy, that actually happened even worse." When you watch, you don't think, "Money is mammon, it's the Devil, bad bad bad." The piece is more complex than that. [The show's] religion is more the Protestant Work Ethic - that somehow, if you do good work, it is its own reward, and there's a part

---

28. Mystery Plays were performed in medieval times by amateur actors from town guilds. The performances took place in multiple public locations, often took several days to finish, and told various biblical and religious stories. The form mixed the sacred and profane, and shifted towards the latter during the 16th Century. (Pavis, 227) In America, one can easily argue there is no greater god than the U.S. Dollar, making Morgan a canonised saint in the religion of capitalism.

of Morgan who wants to believe that, and that's reinforced by the George Washington character. I think maybe [Jones] was getting at the point that the Founding Fathers didn't realise what capitalism was going to become, and average people making stupid choices, and what makes our country what it is. Democracy is as strong as its weakest link. It's really about a problem we all live [with]: "How can we be humane and do good work that is well done?" and that means it helps other people. How can we do that if what we define as successful is your personal success and who cares what happens to anybody else? That's still a problem.

At his core, J.P. Morgan is motivated by simple, good-natured desires: to be successful and to do good deeds well. His adherence to law and order, however, distanced both the real Morgan and the character from the public, creating an image of one looking down at the people rather than engaging with them. George Washington instils this belief in Morgan at the start of his career: "You see they hate us, fear us, call us moneylenders - usurers - behind our backs. You just remember who we are."[29] Morgan's faith in money leads to his doomed first marriage, great success, and blindness to society when lording his ability. After saving the Susequehanna Railroad, Morgan speaks:

> Still, if you believe what I did was right,
>
> Let me sit on your board...
>
> Just let me be there in the background
>
> Fighting for the little guy,

---

29. Jeffrey M. Jones & Jonathan Larson. *J.P. Morgan Saves the Nation.* (Los Angeles: Sun & Moon Press, 1995), 29.

The ordinary everyday fool who understands nothing at all about financial matters,

Yet puts his savings into the hands of American business only to see them wiped out in an instant.

If it were only up to me, there'd be no hope for them, yet it can't be so.

I alone must reorder the entire economy of the United States in the 19th Century...[30]

Morgan's desire to raise society to his level culminates in the song 'Gentlemen's Agreement,' wherein he gathers a group of businessmen and sets a code of conduct: no lawsuits, no dirty deals, and no arguments without Morgan moderating. Musically, the song begins with a harpsichord minuet duetted between Morgan and George Washington before shifting to crunchy rock guitar and the remaining businessmen joining in, starting fights, and ending with Washington's death on the line:

And so dear gentlemen, farewell;

If I don't see you all in hell

I'm sure I'll see you all someday again

In court...[31]

Jones and Larson also invoked Brecht's core beliefs in theatricality. There is never a doubt that the audience is watching a fiction, with set pieces marked up with safety tape and the dollar bill girls taking the symbols of American independence for a waltz. The pair also made extensive use of the alienation effect: Uncle Sam breaks character to deliver a lecture on the economy, and Jones recalls Larson had a "recurring desire to irritate the audience," fighting to bring the coda on 'Gentleman's Agreement' to "earsplitting" levels.

---

30. Ibid., 52.

31. Ibid., 62.

Randich brought her own Brechtian sensibilities, backed by European training in Germany and Norway, to the show and her direction. Despite her struggles to keep up with the material, she knew a naturalistic staging or performance style would fail the text, and encouraged all to look past the surface:

> A lot of people are used to doing naturalistic performance, and because this is also theatre of ideas, it's important that you're putting forth this idea or referencing something from the Bible - excavating what myth is being dealt with here, talking about that, but wanting it to feel very immediate. Trying to honour the material and make it live. [T]hen there was the balance between the principals and the businessmen and the dollar girls. I think that felt really good. There are intricate parts of the story which you lace together. The costuming for the chorus was fantastic, the dollar girls felt great in those costumes, they looked like moving, sensuous, sinuous dollars, and that gave them a lot of freedom. It helped with the Brechtian thing.

Music and volume also contributed to *J.P. Morgan*'s Brechtian nature at its climax, when Morgan is put on trial in front of the US Senate and forced to testify about his level of control in American finance. Morgan, who twice bailed out the nation's economy, is indignant and confused: he's a hero looking out for the state of corporate affairs and wondering why a simple deal is incapable of fixing any problems as a result. Politics, however, are fickle, and Uncle Sam and George Washington pepper the financier with questions, the latter's ringing with disappointment. Initially, Larson wished to stage this scene as a circus, but Jones and Hamburger resisted: it was a valid metaphor, but tonally and thematically out of touch with the rest of the piece. Despite pushing for his choice, Larson ultimately conceded. He subsequently returned with a better idea: using the Devil as a rapping commentator, like Judas in the title song from *Jesus Christ Superstar,* mocking the hero on his fall. As the Devil sings the chorus, "Look at what you've done," Uncle Sam, Liberty, and Washington join in with their disappointments and wishes. Larson hoped the aggressive style would make rich patrons in the audience uncomfortable. Jones was thrilled with the imposing drums and arrangements, which both highlighted how the government imposed its will on business and cast Morgan as a gilded age scapegoat.

Finding the Devil's inner menace, however, would be a challenge. For most of the show, the Devil is sultry and seductive - not inherently evil, but chaotic and corrupting. The change, from playfully sexy rival and mistress to the American public to industry turning against its hero, hits hard from the first note of the song. For Miles, getting the tone right proved difficult:

> [I have] a jazz background, very mellow stuff. My first thought was, "Me? Rap? How can I do that? I'm from the Jersey Shore!" I'm the epitome of not cool, so a lot of it was trying to masculinise my performance and almost neuter myself. I wanted to embody more of the male rapper energy, because that's how I was going to be able to access it. [It] was tremendously empowering. I remember intentionally wanting to be up in peoples' faces, cause them to get uncomfortable, because it's so not how I am normally. By playing that role, I was able to let go of myself completely and go for the other thing.

Did Larson succeed at unnerving the audience? Miles believes so:

> It's a funny thing. Because I was playing the
> Devil at that moment, I didn't care what anybody
> thought. I did scare a few people. My now husband
> - then boyfriend - he looked at me afterwards and
> had flowers in his hands and was like, "Should I
> get any closer to that? I don't know." He looked a
> little uneasy. I'm going to go from his reaction and
> say that it worked.

The principal actors - aside from James Judy as Morgan - were also tasked with finding their characters in ideological archetypes over actual historical figures or contemporary people. For DeRosa, Uncle Sam was thrilling, but complicated - much like the show:

> It was an exciting idea, figuring out this man who
> bailed out the government. There was this one
> capitalist who was richer than everyone else, and
> it was fascinating - allegories and this Brechtian
> idea of the government being Uncle Sam and
> essentially a huckster, trying to sell the public one
> thing when in reality he was poor and freaked out
> and insecure and was coming off with all this bra-
> vado and bravura. The character itself was a lot of
> fun. Both Robin [Miles] and I had roles like the
> Emcee in Cabaret, where we were playful with the
> crowd. It wasn't a hostile confrontation or a punk
> rock relationship. It was a charming narrator-
> takes-you-on-a-journey experience. You had these
> tempting forces who, to be honest, were kind of
> vague, influencing this man's life and seeing what
> his choices were.

George Washington and Uncle Sam foreshadow Morgan's rise and ultimate decline: Washington pays $300 to exempt Morgan from the draft, and proceeds to lecture Sam: "He has a different purpose, now you cannot see it, but someday you will. And you'll be glad you spared him then," to which Sam replies: "Don't matter to me, it's just the law. And nobody's better'n the law, sir."[32]

Given the era of J.P. Morgan's life and how it dovetails the late Industrial Revolution with Southern Reconstruction, *J.P. Morgan Saves the Nation*'s focus on economics makes the Devil, in many ways, the main character: the Devil shifts Morgan's focus from solely doing good to doing *well*. She inflates and crashes the national economy through battling Morgan, and has both Morgan and Uncle Sam playing by her rules, such as when she rips off Uncle Sam's arms and arranges a loan through Morgan for Sam to buy them back. Even if not directly responsible for Morgan or his activities, the Devil provides a catalyst for events in every scene of Morgan's adult life. Miles found the intricacies exhilarating:

> I played a lot of supernatural beings in the early parts of my career. What sets the Devil apart is that the Devil does things and never even considers apologising or explaining a damn bit of it. Not a motivation, not an explanation. The Devil just does whatever the Devil wants, and there's a certain freedom that comes with that. There's complete and total freedom from guilt. What does a person do when they don't have societal guilt? As an actor playing the Devil, you have to remove your conscience, and I found it really difficult to do, but at the same time, part of it was very empowering. [As] a woman, playing that kind of role is empowering, because, as a gender, we are constantly explaining ourselves.[33]

---

32. Ibid., 28-29.

33. The Devil's costume consisted of a top hat, large red fright wig, a tight bodice, fishnet stockings, and tall, high-heeled boots. As Seibel puts it, "Robin

As Morgan's adversaries, Uncle Sam and the Devil provide both the comic relief to Morgan's ea rnest work ethic as well as the temptations to pull him away from the path of righteousness. The two also make for uneasy allies on stage, with the Devil frequently duping Uncle Sam into a substandard deal. However, the inverse is true in presentation: DeRosa played Uncle Sam with a menace, sneering at events and relishing his image of power and strength, while Miles played the Devil as a purely chaotic force:

> It's an archetype, not a stereotype. The Devil, as an archetype, morphs into what he or she needs to be to cause the victim to come towards them or to fall into their clutches. It could be frightening them into it, seducing them into it, or making yourself so alluring that the other is so curious about what the Devil has going on that it lures them in. I feel like I played the latter two, and then the rap piece, and in a way, that was when the scarier part of that archetypal energy comes out. I love archetypes and hate stereotypes, but I think we Americans don't get archetypes as well as Europeans do in terms of their theatre.

Randich feels the Devil's chaos amped up the character's appeal to Morgan, the character, preying upon his lawful nature and the spirit of Kipling:

> [The Devil] is chaos, 19th Century Market Capitalism. [The Devil] tempted the way the market tempts, because if you can manipulate the chaos better than other people and make a killing, there's certainly gratification, and there's lots of jokes about

---

was very visual, she had all these big, red feathers, and it was almost like a *Moulin Rouge* aspect before *Moulin Rouge* was there."

that. I don't think Morgan is portrayed as a predator,
but she tempts him to show his prowess, and they
show that with the dollar girls and the businessmen,
and it evokes those archetypes of business as a hunt
and the man as the Great White Hunter.

As Morgan fights with the Devil (or, more accurately, thinks
he is fighting while falling prey to her), his pursuit of money and
power comes at the cost of all around him, such as discarding and
ignoring his second wife, played by Liberty. As Liberty and the
Devil duet on 'Your Loving Wife/Jack O' Diamonds,' Liberty sings
her love of the man, and the Devil responds in counterpoint with
a jazzy siren's call to wealth. The song provides an inverse of 'The
Office Down There,' seeing Morgan consumed by his mission,
no longer driven by Liberty's motif (present in 'The Office Down
There'). Says Randich:

> I think Jeff saw J.P. Morgan as a tragic figure, and
> in order to be a tragic figure, you have good qual-
> ities which also contribute to your fall. That kind
> of laser focus, aggressive entrepreneurial spirit, or
> "There's no gold, I've got to help the government
> out" - that relationship was intriguing to him. It's
> tapping into *Citizen Kane*, that eternal loneliness.
> The audience knows something about this man
> that he doesn't know himself. I don't think Jeff is
> interested in any kind of psychoanalysis, but it's
> not a biopic.

While Uncle Sam, the Devil, and even George Washington fell
into line, Jones admits he found the Liberty character a struggle
and "never felt I achieved what I wanted. I wish I could have done
her justice but of all the characters, she didn't fit the irony tem-
plate." Randich agrees:

There were a number of things going on with
Liberty. There was a conflation of the Statute of
Liberty, of our country as a place where there's
kindness and refuge, and his first wife, Amelia
Sturges, who died of tuberculosis, and I think Jeff
was using that as a pivotal moment for Morgan,
where he realises he can't control everything, [like
in the story of] Nebuchadnezzar: 'You can be a
king, but if that's because of your power, you've got
another thing coming to you.'[34]

Liberty also represented Morgan's conscience after the American
Civil War. A piece of said conscience dies with Morgan's first wife,
and as Liberty passes from role to role - from the Susquehanna
Railroad to Morgan's second wife and ultimately a homeless
woman - Morgan's ability to do good beyond the financial sphere
and his willingness to listen to his inner doubts diminishes. Liberty
represents the appeal of goodwill and humanitarianism, a desired
superego over the Devil's id. As Randich describes her:

Liberty is a force for good, but if you don't listen
or you ignore her, there's some kind of choice with
it, whereas with the Devil there's temptation, and
if you play her game, you may think you're beating her, but can you win? What does Liberty represent? There's some kind of freedom, and it's a lot
different from the compulsion and the id, and the
pure sexual nature of the drive to make money.

34. The Nebuchadnezzar myth, as presented in the biblical *Book of Daniel*,
is a story about pride and power. God can bestow power and status upon a king,
but an arrogant man will fall either by incurring God's wrath or through his own
devices. In the mythology, God curses Nebuchadnezzar to seven years' insanity as
punishment for lacking humility - the king loses everything because he claimed it
was created through his own power and ability. At the end, the king praises God
and is restored to rank and wealth. The myth is directly referenced in the *Morgan*
song 'Proceedings'.

What Jones ultimately presents is a portrait in silhouette of a complicated figure, leaving the audience to draw their own conclusions about J.P. Morgan the person. For every sympathetic portrayal of Morgan's motivations in his pursuit of wealth and control - that bringing the railroads into line under combined management and controlling the price of gold to keep the US Treasury in the black is a good thing - Jones counters with an alienating incident, such as Morgan all-but-forcing his first wife into marriage, screaming at his second wife for considering him ugly, or messily stuffing his face at a banquet. Brechtian influences abound, with Jones demanding the audience not give in to the personified forces manipulating Morgan, but rather to engage them intellectually and see them in our contemporary existence, both in the economic glory days of 1995 and now: "The play has been and will continue to be incredibly relevant every 10 years." Robin Miles was already aware of the show's contemporary parallels:

> I used to be a paralegal at [a large New York law firm], who handled a large number of mergers and acquisitions [in the 1980s]. I was there for the craze and stayed through until the mid-'90s. After the mergers and acquisitions had been accomplished, all these companies who merged began to fail, so the law firm began to go more and more into bankruptcies. Being in the thick of that, seeing that excess up close, learning more about J.P. Morgan and that era and even the Coolidge era - learning about the robber barons and all that, it felt like, "This could happen again. What's the relationship to now?" You can't help but feel like, "Is this gonna repeat?" but I can't say I dwelled on it too much, because my financial situation wasn't as stable as it could've been - and isn't that what

we need? We need the luxury to be able to actually think about that stuff, and if we're running around playing catch-up, we don't have time to apply ourselves to political stuff. When you're talking about something like *J.P. Morgan* being prescient looking forward, [while] trying to make my ends meet at the time, I didn't have a lot of time to look at it too closely, but I knew enough about it to know it was not a happy time.

Jones' heavy Brechtian influence both made *J.P. Morgan* fascinating to play and an intellectual playground for engaged attendees, but also ran the risk of turning off general audiences. Looking back on the show, Stephen DeRosa reflects:

[The] American tradition is to enter through the heart, and Brecht didn't do that. He wanted you to enter with your brain, and you had to be thinking while you were watching this. You couldn't simply get lost in the emotional life of the characters or you wouldn't be getting the point. Brecht constantly tried to do things in his plays to remind you not to simply get emotionally involved in the characters, but to remember that we're telling this story to make a point. We don't do that. It's like *The Sopranos* or *Breaking Bad*. They're bad people who do bad, bad, bad things, but American audiences love to fall in love with the people they're watching and to culturally identify with them and then ultimately make them redemptive, and that sometimes can be a flaw - especially in political theatre, where the goal of a political piece of theatre is not for you to care about the people, but for you to be, on some level at the end of the day, angry at

the people. You're not supposed to feel sorry for
[them].

As mentioned above, Jones wants the audience to like J.P.
Morgan enough to follow his story, to see his motivations, and even
approach one of the greatest and most ruthless business tycoons
in history with sympathy as his motivations lead - as in all true
tragedies - to his downfall: Jones "love[s] so much how Jonathan
captured the rage and the righteousness and the certainty of the
congressional crowd that they were going to take the Monopoly
Man down." The emotional draw runs counter to Brecht's desire
for alienation: rather than focus on why the government takes aim
at Morgan (financial power surpassing state power for a start), the
show switches back and forth between theatre of ideas and biography when it needs to win over the audience.

The Spirit Lives On

The nearest thing *J.P. Morgan Saves the Nation* has to a spiritual
successor is Lucy Prebble's 2009 play *Enron*. The latter presents
corporate larceny on a grand scale through the structure of Greek
tragedy, while also tackling questions of economic activity and
business culture. Both shows utilise music and physical production
to interpret events and regularly break the fourth wall to explain
more complicated aspects of economic theory in simple ways for
the audience (*Enron* does it far more frequently, using the economics lessons to establish scenes).

Morgan and *Enron* also require audiences to look at complicated, often villainous historical figures through a sympathetic -
if not compassionate - perspective. The great industrialists of the
Gilded Age, such as Morgan, Rockefeller, and Carnegie, may have
been philanthropists, but also concentrated wealth on a level previously unheard of - even preceding the abolition of serfdom - and

were ruthless to the workers actually building their empires of railroads, steel, and trade. Likewise, audiences at *Enron* are shown the Gilded legacy through Jeffrey Skilling, Andy Fastow, and Ken Lay: men for whom greed has been taken to extremes past the point where their fate escapes control, and audiences want their schemes to succeed, not to cheer for their undoing.

Both plays were also savaged by the New York critics, though *Enron* had a happier ending than *Morgan*: the Broadway production may have flopped, but the show was a critical and commercial success in London, with a continuing life in European and American regional companies. How much of the reaction to either show comes from cutting too close to the bone is hard to judge: neither show lets the audience off the hook, appealing to the inner capitalist to support the core figures while simultaneously confronting them head-on with the consequences of following such a path. Randich nails the issue on the head: "In our country, we don't want to talk about what [Morgan] talks about. Look at all the government decisions - the scene with Uncle Sam getting his arms ripped off, and I'll buy this and that."

Whether *J.P. Morgan* could find a new future is questionable, but highly likely. Jones has expressed an interest in revisiting the script, but the question is how to make it work outside of its original space. Likewise, too much tinkering could ruin the magic. As Stephen DeRosa says after revisiting the script nearly 20 years later: "Part of what made the show work was how experimental it was. The experience for the audience was site-specific. The fact that you were in the presence of these buildings in the heart of Wall Street psychologically put you in a different mindset. I'm not convinced it would work in a house on Broadway - it just wasn't built for that." How *Morgan* would stand outside New York remains to be seen: En Garde Arts had been in discussion with regional theatre companies before the show's premiere, but any plans which remained following the critical response were subsequently scarpered by Larson's death in 1996. As the global financial system plays a greater role in individual economics and wealth re-concentrates in fewer hands, the real J.P. Morgan's legacy becomes ever-increasingly vital for the average person to understand, lest they again be allowed to fail.

Chapter Seven

Everything is *RENT*

Use your camera to spar!
Use your guitar!

—RENT

A FTER STUDYING VARIOUS opera libretti in the summer of 1989, a young playwright named Billy Aronson set out to write a modern adaptation of Giacomo Puccini's *La Bohème*. Aronson reached out to Ira Weitzman, artistic director at Playwrights Horizons, hoping to find a composer. Weitzman replied with two names: Adam Guettel and Jonathan Larson. Aronson contacted both and ultimately made his way to Larson's tattered loft at 508 Greenwich Street, where the two sat on the composer's roof and brainstormed.

Before working on lyrics, Aronson created a 12-page script based on *La Bohème*'s first act, in which the four male bohemians (here Ralph, Mark, Cornell, and Shaun) complain about being creatively blocked, avoid paying their rent, and celebrate a windfall before leaving Ralph behind to write. He meets Mimi, a boutique embroiderer in search of a light bulb. Larson annotated his copy of Aronson's script, wondering about the bohemians' nature, and told the writer to start drafting lyrics.

In this original draft - and all of Aronson's scripts for the project - the characters and events rarely stray from Puccini (or, more specifically, his librettists Luigi Illica and Giuseppe Giacosa)'s original, but Aronson brings extra '90s sarcasm. In *Boheme,* Mark and Ralph - a painter and playwright respectively - are snobs, looking down on the middle classes they hail from in order to justify their own poverty:

> R: So our playwright and painter deftly avoid their nagging family and thriving peers and devote Christmas eve [sic] to creation!
>
> M: To Truth and Beauty, for which they've slaved!
>
> R: To Art and Meaning for which they've sacrificed.
>
> M: But here's the irony. They're so exhausted from slaving to pay the rent and nervous about another crack addict slithering in through the bars in the window and distracted by the sirens and jarred by the screams and jealous of their peers and angry at their parents and suicidal about their future that they waste the evening brooding!
>
> M: Dark comedy. I like it.[1]

Cornell, true to the university sharing his name, is a philosophy PhD student, incapable of finishing his thesis, indulging in misery and self-doubt. Shaun, the last of the four, is a snarky rock musician who scored a lucky gig (involving a dead dog, this time by accident), straddling the edge of being a rebel and selling out:

---

1. Billy Aronson. *Boheme* (Act 1, pre-lyric draft). Box 10, Folder 1, Jonathan Larson Papers, Music Division, Library of Congress, Washington, D.C., 2.

SHAUN: Chill out! It'll take them a year to evict us. By then you'll have sold a screenplay, you'll have sold a mural, you'll have sold your collected philosophical works, and I'll have sold my soul![2]

Mimi is almost identical to her counterpart in *La Bohème*: submissive, quiet, and stepped upon by life.

Even at this stage, the seeds of *RENT*'s first three songs are there: Ralph and Mark complain about being creatively blocked and paying the rent, Cornell suggests moving to New Mexico to open a restaurant and simplify their lives, and Ralph and Mimi warn each other of their flaws when starting their relationship.

At the end of September 1989, Aronson delivered his first full draft of *Boheme* to Larson, complete with lyrics. In addition to the three songs which survived (albeit in altered forms) to the final version - 'RENT,' 'Santa Fe,' and 'I Should Tell You,' other songs include 'Meat and Vegetables,' where the Bohemians celebrate Shaun's takings, a street song for homeless characters Liar and Schizoid, and a crude song for Suzanne - the prototype for Maureen - to sing at a cafe. All the men are straight, as Cornell, Mark, and Shaun sing:

> To take somebody back
>
> For a pleasing winter evening
>
> Massage her perspiration
>
> Barrage her with saliva
>
> Stare deep into her stare
>
> Mess up her luscious hair
>
> Caress her naked thighs
>
> Her eyelids start to flutter
>
> I need a warm body to lie with tonight[3]

---

2. Ibid., 7.

3. Billy Aronson (Text) & Jonathan Larson (Music). *Boheme* (Draft 22 Sep

By 1990, *Boheme* had a new name. Larson and Aronson fought over the title, with Aronson torn between *Boheme* and waiting for something better, while Larson wanted to call the show *RENT*. The composer loved the term's dual meaning, both in terms of paying but not owning (particularly in regards to housing), as well as the past tense of 'rend,' or to tear apart, particularly in mourning. Aronson's drafts featured less of the latter than Larson's final show would, but Puccini's grand romance inspired the young composer.

The first *RENT*-titled draft advanced Aronson's writing, enhancing a scene where the boys' landlord comes to collect and Ralph's first conversation with Mimi - now a sculptress working with discarded objects. Like the men, Mimi is good enough at her work to get a grant in this edition, but not good enough to make the sales needed to stay out of dire poverty.[4] The songs are finally titled, and one, entitled 'Have a Happy,' is a prototype for Larson's 'Christmas Bells,' but the script still came in at under 60 pages. "20 pages of text can equal hours of opera when set to music," says Aronson, "but in musical theatre, it goes pretty fast, more like in a play. So as Jonathan began writing songs, I started to realize it would need more story. But I can't say we spoke about it much."

After this draft was complete, Larson scored three songs: the opener, 'RENT' (sung on the first demo tape by Larson as Mark and Roger Bart as Ralph), the second number, 'Santa Fe' (Jon Cavaluzzo as Cornell, with Larson and Bart on backup), and Ralph and Mimi's love declaration, 'I Should Tell You' (Bart and Valerie Pettiford). Working in his usual way, Larson took the tracks to Steve Skinner for arrangement and recording, spending almost $600 on the sessions. Aronson had agreed to pay half the bill

1989). Box 10, Folder 3, Jonathan Larson Papers, Music Division, Library of Congress, Washington, D.C., 14.

4. Billy Aronson (Text) & Jonathan Larson (Music). *RENT* (Copyright Date 1990). Box 10, Folder 4, Jonathan Larson Papers, Music Division, Library of Congress, Washington, D.C.

- especially when Larson said he could use sampling to save money over paying live musicians - only to be shocked b Isn't it enough that I'm beautiful and rich? y the final cost. Taken with the tape's quality and passion, he agreed to paid his share.

"After [recording the songs], we were anxious to get a theater involved, so they could give us money and/or guidance to help us develop it," remembers Aronson. "And when no theatre stepped forward, and we didn't really know how to proceed, we put it aside. I wish I could say all that terrific expansion of the story was my work, but it wasn't."

Despite describing Larson as a difficult collaborator, Aronson's complaints reflect Larson's underlying desire for creative control: the composer would refuse to concede on conceptual fights (e.g. tone, location) without significant defence from Aronson, but once such arguments were resolved, Larson was happy to pull back and score what Aronson gave him. While tweaks and revisions were commonplace when Larson scored for collaborators, he set Aronson's lyrics as presented: "He really loved them, especially all the cursing!" remembers Aronson. "He wrote music [for the three songs] without changing a word. The lyrics to those songs changed along the way, but always to reflect story changes and character changes. In fact, I myself wish I could have changed some of the lyrics of mine that he kept!"

With three songs on tape and some experience under his belt, Larson went off to work on *tick, tick... BOOM!* Meanwhile, the AIDS epidemic continued raging through New York City, ACT UP protests became regular fixtures, and ever-increasing numbers of Larson's friends and acquaintances in the theatre were diagnosed HIV+. Though Aronson and Larson agreed that AIDS would take the place of tuberculosis in *RENT*, the disease's presence was minimal until the fourth act, and even then remained in the background and out of the dialogue, only mentioned by name in stage directions. "[Larson's] politics became about health," remembers best friend Matt O'Grady. In 1991, Larson decided to return to *RENT* and asked Aronson's permission to continue the project as sole creator. Aronson agreed, and the two made an agreement that Aronson would be credited for the show's concept and his lyrical contributions.[5]

Between A and B

Throughout 1991, Larson took apart Aronson's script and rebuilt it in his own image. One of his first notes to himself begins by asking himself questions and setting tasks:

> Background -
>
> Billy
>
> AIDS
>
> Murger
>
> Who are Rodolfo and Mimi Today [sic]
>
> [...] Gets stash - shoots up
>
> Seduces - Affirmation Pryr [sic][6]

Following the *Superbia* model, Larson would write pages of notes - often lists of rhymes and themed words - then bring them together into rough songs. Some of those songs, such as 'Another Day' - at first called 'I'll Take the Pain' - and 'Light My Candle,' came together quickly once Larson got a handle on the central lyric. Others, including 'Out Tonight' and 'La Vie Boheme,' had core elements buried under extraneous material and would only take form

---

5. Following Larson's death, Aronson transferred his copyrights to the Larson estate in exchange for a percentage of author's royalties and retained the credit Larson gave him on the final page of every draft.

6. Jonathan Larson. Handwritten note. Box 10, Folder 2, Jonathan Larson Papers, Music Division, Library of Congress, Washington, D.C.

after pages of rewrites were jettisoned. The final group of songs - often cut - were the most frustrating: songs where Larson would write endless page of notes, refine, revise, and fail as characters went in the wrong direction or the song simply refused to gel.[7]

For research, Larson would grab friends (usually Eddie Rosenstein) and go to the East Village, visiting the Life Cafe or other popular haunts. For a middle-class suburbanite, the neighbourhood felt dangerous and scary, far outside his comfort zone - something he wanted to make sure to convey in the piece without detracting from the characters' human core.

The Alphabet City Avant-Garde

In creating *RENT*'s first solo draft, Larson began by reassessing the characters and making his first round of major deviations from *La Bohème*, incorporating lessons from texts by philosopher Susan Sontag, communication with mentor Stephen Sondheim, and his own experiences. Larson kept virtually nothing on paper regarding his early character ideas, making it difficult to place his inspiration, but his own life made two changes easy to spot. Aronson's Suzanne became the bisexual Maureen, and Aronson's Ralph became Rodger - then quickly Roger - the musician.

Larson saved the greatest changes, though, for Cornell and Shaun, turning them into the gay couple Collins and Angel. Collins remained a philosopher, but one more inspired by ACT UP protests to secure funding and research for AIDS treatments. Similarly, Angel remained a musician, albeit one living on the street and with a flair for drag. Once the characters were established, their story remained the only one to stay the same through the entirety of *RENT*'s development: the pair fall in love, stay in love,

---

7. A trio of specific examples are discussed in Appendix B.

and are only split apart by Angel's death, creating a rift throughout the survivors.

Mimi, however, proved a challenge. Aronson had taken the character in a more intellectual direction, from a craft artist to an academic sculptor, but Larson returned her to Puccini's lower-class roots. At first, Mimi works as a coat check girl at a lesbian bar:

> No, I'm not a dyke -
>
> But I work there because I don't get harassed by men.
>
> & the women who hit on me are less threatening.[8]

Larson quickly changed her job to erotic dancer, and the position stuck.

As with Collins and Angel, Roger and Mimi's story arc was largely set once Larson worked out their initial character traits, and remained closely in parallel with *La Bohème*.

Joanne, an original creation combining traits from multiple *Bohème* characters, was more of a plot device than a fully realised character: Maureen orders her to go home and find cables, then flits back and forth between her and Mark. In an outline attached to his first draft, Larson intended for Maureen to spend most of the next year with Mark, returning to Joanne by Thanksgiving, only for them to break up again and Joanne to join Mark and Roger in a song complaining about women.[9] Larson also described Joanne at this stage as a "Boho-wanna-be," and the only hints to her character are the lines:

---

8. Jonathan Larson. Handwritten note. Box 11, Folder 4, Jonathan Larson Papers, Music Division, Library of Congress, Washington, D.C., 27H.

9. Jonathan Larson. *RENT* (July 1992 Draft). Box 11, Folder 5, Jonathan Larson Papers, Music Division, Library of Congress, Washington, D.C., 4-5.

Isn't it enough that I'm beautiful and rich?

Isn't it enough that I pay for all of this?

Isn't it enough that I put up every day with a

Temperamental [sic], selfish, abusive [...][10]

This early draft also featured three homeless characters: Puerto Rican squeegie man Rudy Ramirez, wise African-American bag lady Mrs. Chance, and Dogman, her mentally-ill companion. While Larson did away with the characters by 1994, aspects of Ramirez remained in the Squeegie Man character, and Mrs. Chance went from singing Angel's funeral number to being the 'Seasons of Love' soloist and "Who the fuck do you think you are?" woman in the final show.

In July 1992, Larson completed his draft of the new *RENT*'s first act. Even at this early stage, the song list looks familiar: 'RENT' (albeit with different lyrics), 'Santa Fe,' 'Today 4 U,' an early version of 'One Song Glory,' 'Light My Candle,' 'Out Tonight,' 'Will I...?,' 'Another Day,' Christmas Bells' (both the short versions and the extended number), the first take on 'Over the Moon,' 'La Vie Boheme,' and 'I Should Tell You'. Larson submitted this draft to the New York Theatre Workshop (NYTW), which he stumbled upon while out riding his bike. To help ensure the script got attention, Larson reached out to Naked Angels designer George Xenos, who also worked at NYTW. Xenos passed the script on to associate director Chris Grabowski, who felt the show was interesting enough to bump up the chain to artistic director Jim Nicola.

Along with the script, Larson included a fully produced demo, complete with MIDI-arranged backing sequences and his own

---

10. Ibid., 9. I've removed Maureen's counterpoints (including where she cuts off Joanne's rant with "Sexy") for the sake of clarity.

voice overdubbed on every part. Steve Skinner remembers working on these early tracks:

> When I look back on it, I was perhaps not as open-minded as I could be. He would play something, and I'd be like, "Oh, that's not going to work." His stuff wasn't always what was fashionable at the moment, or in the case of some of the stuff from RENT, I'd think, "Nobody's going to hear [all those parts]," but as it turns out, it was exactly the right amount to keep kids coming back 20 times to hear it all, but still be exciting enough to hear the first time. He started singing 'Seasons of Love,' and I thought, "People aren't gonna want a math lesson." I kept it to myself, and we worked out the song. The basic piano part was there from the beginning, and when he hit on that, he was thrilled.

While Nicola found the script confusing and messy (and too white for the East Village), he found magic in the song 'Light My Candle,' when the frustrated Roger meets Mimi for the first time. He continued listening to the tape and fell for Larson's songwriting. While "[Larson] was not as far along as a playwright, he knew how to write a song for the theatre. I knew he was a rare and gifted person there." Nicola was intrigued enough to schedule a meeting with Larson, and agreed that the Workshop would develop RENT, with a production scheduled for an unknown point in the future. "Jonathan was so smart as a structuralist," says RENT producer McCollum, "loving Fiddler [On the Roof] and West Side Story, and he truly understood the musical form, but he also understood that nobody was going to Broadway because nobody was telling stories about them."

Despite Larson's textual issues, everybody at NYTW loved the music. "When I first read [RENT]," remembers Nicola, "something

I connected to personally - and in some ways was the basis of the relationship between Jonathan and myself - was the original stage directions. There's a band on stage and a Broadway orchestra in the pit, and it seemed to me a very healthy way to look at life, which is, 'I want to be part of a tradition, but I want to make it mine. I want to reinvent it for me and people of my generation, but I want to connect to the Sondheims and the Bernsteins and the Rodgers & Hammersteins. I respect [that tradition], but I want it to go in a new way, and I want to be part of that new life emerging.' He had a similar way of seeing the world as I did."

A reading was planned for summer 1993, and as a show of appreciation and good faith, Larson was also invited to perform *tick, tick... BOOM!* at NYTW's 'O Solo Mio' festival of one-man shows - despite Nicola's ambivalence towards the piece. Larson continued working on *RENT* through the summer and fall of 1992, finishing his first full draft that November. Songs from the first draft of Act Two which made it through the show's development were 'Without You,' 'Contact,' the funeral speeches, 'Goodbye Love,' and most of the Finale.

Before finalising NYTW's commitment to the show, Nicola and a few chosen staff members went to a read-through at Larson's apartment. "It was a mess," according to Nancy Diekmann, then-managing director at NYTW, "but also very engaging. It really pulled you in."

On the Street

RENT was first presented to the public on Thursday, 17 June 1993. A basic reading, the actors stood in front of microphones with scripts in hand and sang to backing music provided on reel-to-reel tape. At this point, *RENT* was anything but finished: the story constantly jumped locations, certain characters were tonally inappropriate, and the show was far too long. In casting the reading, Larson reached out to as many associates as he could: *Sacred Cows* collaborators Bob Golden and Rusty Magee played supporting roles, Naked Angel Beth Blankenship was in the ensemble, and close friend Jon Cavaluzzo returned to play Collins. Larson also tapped two Adelphi colleagues for the reading: Bambi Jones as Mrs. Chance and Clinton Leupp (better known as Miss Coco Peru) as Angel, complete with Coco's signature wig and full drag.

Peru wound up in the cast through pure chance:

> In [*Emote Control*, Larson] wrote a song called 'I Won't Close My Eyes,' and I loved that song. I hadn't heard it in years and years, and I was walking down the street in New York City one night, and the chorus was stuck in my head. I couldn't remember the words, just the music, and it was on repeat in my head, over and over and over. This was before the internet, and reaching out to find someone was difficult. I thought, "I wonder how I can get in touch with Jonathan Larson. I need to hear that song again," and as I'm saying that in my head, I walk past a restaurant on the West Side, down in the Village, and Jonathan Larson is sitting there in the window, eating dinner. I couldn't believe it, and I ran into the restaurant, and I was like, "Jonathan, I'm literally just walking down the street humming [the song,]" and he was like, "I Won't Close My Eyes!" and I'm like, "That's the name of it!"
>
> I was doing my [drag] show at the time, and I told him to come whenever he wanted to see me. He did and brought the sheet music with him and gave it to me. He mentioned that he was doing this

musical, and he thought that I might be right to play a role in it that was a drag queen, and that it would be a backer's audition. So I said sure and reminded him that I don't sing harmony. I'm sure I butchered it, but the nice thing he told me after we did it was that people loved the character Angel so much that he expanded the role and wrote more songs for him. One of the reasons I did drag was because I wanted to be an activist - I wanted to have a voice, to talk about AIDS and other issues that faced the gay community. I didn't want another kid to ever have to go through what I went through. I felt like [RENT] spoke to a lot of that, for me.

While Larson wanted Roger Bart to play his namesake, the actor was unavailable and voiceover artist Tony Hoylen was brought in. Cavaluzzo, also a vocal performer, recalls their first meeting:

We were doing the show, and I heard him singing and said, "Man, you should be singing jingles." Tony replied that it was the one part of his voice he wanted to keep pure. I didn't get it until I turned on the radio the next morning and heard him reading every ad - I hadn't realised he was one of maybe four people doing the majority of voiceovers in New York and spawned an entire industry of guys trying to do his voice.

Karen Oberlin, now a fixture on the New York cabaret scene, was a student at Circle in the Square Theatre School when one of Larson's friends suggested she audition. Oberlin landed the part of Maureen and had to not only learn the score for a rock musical, but an intense solo piece as well. "I think we all realised [at the first rehearsal] as we were singing through it," she remembers, "that this was something very special. We were excited to be in at the ground floor." As for her part: "I thought [playing a radical lesbian perfor-mance artist] was great. I was very downtown back then. The ideas were so new and fresh."

A video from the reading shows a small audience, and the show was politely received, but unlike when *Superbia* got similar responses, Nicola wanted to keep moving forward. Larson began writing what felt to him like a never-ending string of revisions. Says Nicola: "A lot of good discussions about where to go with the script came out of that reading. The first act was more there, the second act needed a lot more reconstruction and restructuring. I think (storytelling) is what he learned in the process of the show. I don't think he understood the structure of narrative - how do you take this state and this group of people and try to dramatise it?"

By January 1994, *RENT's* biggest problem was money. NYTW had never produced a musical, and *RENT* called for a significantly larger cast than their usual productions, plus it required a band and extensive sound design. Larson had applied for the Richard Rodgers grant in January 1992, but was denied. He wanted to apply again in 1994, but there was a catch: shows could only be submitted once. The young composer plead his case, saying that he had made such an overhaul to the show that it was effectively a different piece. The re-submission was allowed, and Larson won the year's studio grant - a cheque for approximately $45,000 made out to NYTW, which would pay for most of the costs associated with doing a two-week workshop production.

While Larson dug in on rewrites, Nicola searched for a direc-tor. He found Michael Greif, a young director who had previously worked at NYTW and was preparing to take over the prestigious La Jolla Playhouse in California. Greif was gay, focused on story-telling, and had an edge to his work - all of which Nicola hoped would provide balance to Larson's straight-male, sentimental views and writing. Greif first listened to *RENT's* score while flying from

La Jolla to New York for his introductory meeting with Larson. Upon landing, the two began going through the script, looking for places to fix the storyline and refine the characters.

Music director Tim Weil was initially hired as an audition pianist. As the stream of untraditional auditioners brought in frequently sub-par materials, such as lyric sheets without any written music, Weil - armed with a knowledge of contemporary pop - would help them prepare. His professionalism and knowledge left a positive impression on Greif and Larson. After two days of auditions, Larson asked Weil if he'd like to take over as music director, as neither he nor Greif liked their initial hire. Weil agreed and began to convert Larson's oft-unreadable printouts into an arranged score for four players. Fortunately, he loved the show:

> I took to [RENT] almost immediately. What I knew was: this was an original voice AND it was steeped in modern, contemporary music theatre. The songs moved plot forward, revealed character, and there were some special material elements to it. Also, it's something that I had always wanted to do in the theatre. When I first got to New York, I was doing a workshop with a really talented man who now plays piano for Patti LuPone - Joe Falcon.[11] Beautiful pianist. We were both assisting on some horrible reading, so we would spend a lot of time and chat, and he said to me, "What would your dream show be?" and I said it would be one with guitars and amps and drums and bass, with a big sound system loaded to the gills, and also be great theatre. We were having this conversation in

---

11. Patti LuPone is known as one of the great divas of Broadway, having been the original Eva in the Broadway production of *Evita* and Fantine in the London production of *Les Misérables*.

> 1987. [...] The thing that I liked about *[RENT]* is,
> we loved pop and rock music as much as we loved
> Sondheim. We found that commonality early on,
> and it helped shape our collaboration."

Weil and Larson decided early on that owing to technical limitations, Angel's big songs, 'Today 4 U' and 'Contact' would be performed against backing tracks. The two songs utilised layered MIDI arrangements which, at the time, would have been impossible to play live, and computers were too unreliable to render through live sequencing. Creatively, Weil also felt the dance-inspired arrangements also gave Angel a unique musical voice in the largely rock-driven score.

Cool/Fool

For the 1994 production, Greif worked with Larson on refining the characters' sexual, gender, and ethnic backgrounds. While Collins was still white at this point, Mimi, Joanne, Angel, Benny, and some ensemble roles were played by performers of colour. Greif also brought in costume designer Angela Wendt and lighting designer Blake Burba (who had previously worked at NYTW), and both stayed with the show for the 1996 off-Broadway run and the Broadway transfer.

"Jonathan called me," remembers Coco Peru,

> and said, "We finally have backers, this thing is
> really gonna happen, we want you to come in and
> audition for it." I remember thinking, "The role
> is for a Latina drag queen that plays drums, and
> that's not what I do." I remember thanking Jon
> and whatnot, and I sort of had this feeling that
> the show was gonna go nowhere. I didn't think it

would explode in the way that it did, that it would have a cute little run. To this day, my mother tells me I should've said yes, but I'm still happy with my decision because I wasn't right for the role and I can't sing harmony!

Patrick Briggs, leader of glam-industrial rock band Psychotica and programmer for drag-rock club night Squeezebox, auditioned alongside New York drag queen Sherry Vine:[12] "I'd moved on from doing theatre as a kid and to rock music and didn't want to look back, but I went to the audition and thought I did a really crappy job of it. Apparently not. I think Jonathan didn't want to use me, but Michael Greif pushed him." Briggs, coming from a rock background, felt the show lacked authenticity, and heard more of the Sondheim and Larson's traditional influences than rock in the score, "But I loved it. They were great songs, and I've never seen anybody pull a show and a cast together like Michael did with us."

Nicola remembers Briggs - who performed at famous punk clubs like the Pyramid - as the most genuine East Village performer in the show, which in turn made the actor a solid gauge of how authentically the show reflected the neighbourhood. "I loved Jonathan," Briggs remembers, "but I found the show too politically correct. On the other hand, so many people say it changed their lives that I may very well have been wrong."

While some of Briggs' fellow cast members hoped to return after the 1994 production, including long-time acquaintance Daphne Rubin-Vega (whom he knew from her days in early '90s pop group Pyjama Party), Briggs himself opted out. "[Greif] said

---

12. In two twists of fate, Squeezebox was across the street from Larson's flat and also where John Cameron Mitchell initially workshopped his musical *Hedwig and the Angry Inch*. Mitchell was asked to audition for *RENT* in 1994, but turned it down on the grounds of "not wanting to play another gay role."

RENT Update Sheet. Box 15, Folder 1, Jonathan Larson Papers, Music Division, Library of Congress, Washington, D.C.

I'd be a good Roger and that he was using the workshop to set me up for it, but he also wanted me to come out to La Jolla to do a production of *Faust* for six months. I'd just been offered a record deal and the opening spot on Lollapalooza, opening for Metallica, and turned him down."

Actress Sarah Knowlton learned the electric cello in a matter of weeks to play it live during 'Over the Moon,' but was also released after the 1994 production. "Sarah and I became buddies during the production," recalls Briggs, "and she was great, but when casting rolled around the following year, they told her she was now too Yale (where Knowlton had studied drama) for the character."[13]

By this point, Act One's storyline was effectively set, though overly reliant upon exposition and lacking material for Joanne.[14] Act Two was beginning to congeal as well, but not as solidly as hoped. "We'd had some ups and downs by that point," remembers Nicola, "because just like any artist, [Larson] was saying, 'Just produce my play,' and I kept trying to say to him, 'You don't get it. You have one shot in front of the *New York Times*, and you have to be prepared. It takes a long time and a lot of effort, and you're gonna be exhausted and feel like it's never gonna end, but that's what it is. You have that one shot, and you have to be the best you can be.'" Larson protested, and Nicola gave the composer permission to pitch the show to other theatres, all of whom rejected it. Larson had learned his first lesson in compromising on *RENT*: "It felt like a parent and adolescent to me," says Nicola. "It ended up coming back to us."

---

13. Larson's backstory for Maureen includes the character being bitter about her best friend getting into Yale Drama School and not her. The character's evolution is covered in more detail in Appendix B. Knowlton would go on to star in the sitcom *Working* for two seasons.

14. Nicola recalls discussions that, if Mark and Joanne had the first act's awkward romance song (initially a new version of 'Over It,' written in 1994 to be between Mark and Maureen, then 'Tango: Maureen'), it would allow Maureen to make a big dramatic entrance, even on a motorcycle.

Despite his anxieties, Tim Weil was getting good feedback from those around him, including one particularly well-positioned associate:

> I called [long-time Broadway actor-turned-direc-
> tor and friend] Lonny Price and said, "The show's
> a big mess, but I'd love to know what you think."
> He's a very smart person, and came down. We
> were standing outside the workshop at intermis-
> sion, and he said to me, "Tim, don't you ever, ever,
> EVER quit this gig." I asked why. He said, "You're
> doing *A Chorus Line*." He saw it.

Patrons at the production - almost exclusively industry invi-
tees and NYTW subscribers - were given a feedback form to fill
out. Greif and Nicola went through the results to get a sense of
audience reactions, and Nicola remembers near-universal praise
for the music. Despite the enthusiastic audiences, "there were a
noticeable group of people who didn't get it," according to Nicola.
"They didn't care about these people - we summed it up as, 'Why
don't they just get a job?' The chairman of our board at the time
felt that way: 'Get a job, stop complaining,' that kind of thing."
Fortunately, her personal opinion was beholden to her respect for
Larson's talent, and the show moved ahead. Thinking back, Nicola
feels, "It was interesting to hear [the 'get a job' comments,] because
it never occurred to me to think about it that way, but as I saw it
emerging, I realised, 'Well, yeah, I guess some people could see it
that way.'" Larson countered such complaints by cutting a voice
mail at the start of the show where Roger is fired for no-showing at
work and adding the drug withdrawal element.

Todd Robinson flew out from LA to support his friend and see
the production:

> I jumped on a plane and flew to NYC and ended
> up in the West Village. NYTW is in the East
> Village. Geographically, that's the widest part of
> Manhattan, and I thought, "How far can it be?" and
> started walking. Then running. And I was look-
> ing at my watch and thinking I was going to miss
> curtain. I had a beard at the time and went right
> by Jonathan, and he didn't recognise me. [Then t]
> here's this black guy in drag, and I'm thinking, "I'm
> a white guy from LA with a family - what the hell
> am I seeing?" I was just completely blown away. I
> was not prepared to see what I was going to see,
> and watched the whole play. Angel died, and I was
> sitting there sobbing, and I realised the brilliance
> of Jonathan Larson. I never got to talk to him
> directly about it, but have thought about it since:
> he walked you into your own bias and made you
> make a judgement about that character. This was
> the '90s, way before transgender issues becoming
> understood or accepted. It was just weird. A drag
> queen was just shocking for an audience who were
> grey-haired ladies. [RENT] forces you to make a
> judgement and then dares you not to grieve that
> loss, because Angel is the embodiment of love
> and compassion and the glue that holds Bohemia
> together, and Bohemia is a metaphor for your own
> life. I was completely swept up in it, but nobody
> understood the power of it in that moment. What
> was there was still uncertain. I was amazed that I
> had been looking at this material over years and

watched it progress, note by note and word by word, and I didn't get it until I saw it, and then it was just overwhelming. And that's when I knew something really special was going on.

Despite the work that lay ahead, the 1994 production succeeded undeniably in one area: securing funding for *RENT*'s future. Jeffrey Seller, still not giving up on Larson's work, brought business partner Kevin McCollum to see a performance early in the run. After the first act, McCollum turned to Larson and asked what he wanted: "A production of the show here." To Larson's amazement, McCollum pulled out a chequebook. "But you haven't seen the second act!" McCollum was already blown away by the energy and, as an actor and writer himself, related to the characters: "I had so many friends who had died in the '80s, and the show affected me deeply. I didn't know what to do with it; I just knew I needed to be a part of it. And then I sat down for the beginning of the second act and I heard 'Seasons of Love.'"

The pair returned the next night with silent partner Allan Gordon. After the 1994 run finished, the three producers agreed to put up 50% of *RENT*'s budget in exchange for right of first refusal on a commercial production. Diekmann and Nicola had concerns about taking so much private money, but were told by NYTW's board that the company had insufficient funds to produce the show on its own. The pair agreed to take the enhancement on the condition that 1) the money be processed as a direct donation to NYTW, not an investment, and 2) all creative feedback for Larson and Greif would be passed through Nicola, who could filter it in a more artist-friendly way. The producers agreed to trust Nicola and his artistic judgements ("We felt we were in safe hands with [him]," says McCollum), and the trio of producers put $150,000 of their own money into the show.

"It was very risky," remembers McCollum. "We went and paid

for a tape of the reading we saw in '94, and it was like $2000.[15] Some of [the cast] couldn't make it, and I grabbed my friend Billy, who sang on it a bit, and I sang on it a bit, to fill out the tenor section. We made these tapes, and I would play it to all my college friends who were still performers or people I knew, and say, 'Hey, listen to this.' I played it for my relatives and put it on in the car or a boombox, and they'd say it was great, but nobody understood it. They thought I was crazy."

Playing Nice

Based on interviews conducted for this book, including creative partners, friends, and Larson's sister Julie, it is rare to hear that Jonathan Larson had particular trouble collaborating: his first 'proper' work, *El Libro del Buen Amor* was a collaboration, and he routinely composed for others' words. Ergo, the stated claim that Larson learned how to collaborate professionally on *RENT* is something of an oversimplification. It would be far more accurate to say that, by allowing too many external influences to shape *Superbia*'s misguided path to non-production, Larson found trouble not in collaborating, but in choosing trustworthy collaborators who shared his artistic vision while providing appropriate counter-arguments, resulting in artistic compromises which enhanced, not weakened, the work. Should a trusted voice, such as Jim Nicola or Michael Greif, offer suggestions and back up their argument accordingly, Larson would write new material and make changes, but he needed to be convinced of the suggestion's validity - and that it was in line with his own creative vision - in advance.

---

15. It was, in fact, almost $6500, based on a fax Larson sent McCollum and Seller.

Jonathan Larson. Fax to Kevin McCollum & Jeffrey Seller, stored as "Sondra Fax" (Microsoft Word File). Contained within disk144.dmg. Jonathan Larson Papers, Music Division, Library of Congress, Washington, D.C.

"Jonathan would go away and think for a long time," remembers Jim Nicola, Artistic Director at the New York Theatre Workshop, "and then he'd just write everything in a flurry." This method echoed an underlying sentiment Nicola presented at Larson's memorial service: "One of the most remarkable things that I observed about Jonathan was that he loved to learn, and nothing could be more exciting to him than to learn something new."[16]

The one collaborator with whom Larson almost never fought on *RENT* was now-retained music director and arranger Tim Weil. "Tim was very powerful in this story," says McCollum. "He understood Jonathan and the passion of the music, and he understood how to carry Jon's vocabulary forward when we lost [him]." Weil remembers:

> For whatever reason, I gained his trust early. He literally would bring songs in and just leave them with me, and there was maybe a certain thing or two he wanted to hear, but other than that, he said, "It's on you, Tim, just go do what you gotta do," which is why I ended up doing most of the vocal arranging. He was so much more instinctively ahead of our collaboration than I was, so I really appreciate that he let me do that.

After the workshop run ended in November 1994, Nicola made the decision that, if NYTW were to commit to producing *RENT*, Larson would need to make "strong and difficult progress on the storytelling," and reiterated his frequent (and frequently rejected) suggestion that Larson hire a scriptwriter to clean up and revise the story. Larson refused: his vision of the show was that of *his* show, and another writer could dilute or change the

---

16. Jonathan Larson Memorial Service. Video. 3 Feb 1996. Privately held by Victoria Leacock Hoffman, Washington, D.C.

purity of his creation. As an alternative, Nicola suggested finding a dramaturge who could function in an editorial role and offer more consistent feedback.[17] As an added incentive, Nicola allowed Larson the final choice over who to hire, while providing a list of potential candidates. Larson went through Nicola's list and came across Lynn Thomson, a drama professor at NYU. While the pair hit it off, Larson initially remained skeptical: "Another friend had been tearing his hair out over having to work with one," remembers dance videographer and friend Amy Reusch. "I remember Jonathan's ambivalence, his feeling that it was a small price to pay to get his work produced... It was a struggle[,] but if that was the condition, he would endure it." Larson and Thomson began working together in December 1994. Meetings with Greif and Nicola were rare, with Larson needing to fly out to La Jolla for extensive discussions, leaving him and Thomson to get down to business.

In terms of Thomson's contributions, here is what the author discerned from Larson's papers:

- Thomson suggested that Larson write biographies and a version of the story from each principal character's point of view.[18]

- Larson did this, extensively re-writing the character histories, getting input from Thomson for the actual script.[19]

- Some of Thomson's suggestions ("Why couldn't [Roger's

---

17. The role of a dramaturge varies from production to production, but is in line with a novel or TV script editor: someone who is available to answer questions, look over material, and make suggestions where problems arise. They are considered work-for-hire contractors and, as such, hold no ownership over their contributions.

18. Lynn Thomson. Fax to *RENT* Creative Team. Box 14, Folder 7, Jonathan Larson Papers, Music Division, Library of Congress, Washington, D.C., 118H.

19. Lynn Thomson. Fax to Jonathan Larson. Box 14, Folder 7, Jonathan Larson Papers, Music Division, Library of Congress, Washington, D.C., 119-121H.

bandmates] replace the drummer and go on with the band? What if this was the guy who was really writing the songs") would be imported into character studies.[20]

• Larson used some of Thomson's wording in lyrics. For example, Thomson described Roger as "the pretty-boy front man" in comments on the character notes, and the phrase appears in the song 'One Song Glory' starting in September 1995.[21]

That said, to accuse Larson of sharing authorship over the last two points - which Thomson did, following *RENT*'s transfer to Broadway - is to display gross ignorance of the relationship between editor and author: it is the former's job to suggest rewrites on the large- and small-scale, to ask questions, and to ensure the author's work is consistent and at its best. For a composer such as Larson to use a suggested line from his dramaturge is perfectly acceptable, and standard practice in creative writing. As Victoria Leacock Hoffman more succinctly puts it:

> One day, Jonathan called me up at home and asked how I'd measure a year. I said, "In cups of coffee." He said, "Thanks," and hung up the phone. Just because he used that as a line in 'Seasons of Love' doesn't mean I own that song.

As it stood, Greif already suggested Larson drop the metaphorical 'Right Brain' in favour of a traditional 'I Want' song. Even

---

20. Ibid., 119H, Jonathan Larson. RENT Outline from La Jolla Meeting. Box 14, Folder 7, Jonathan Larson Papers, Music Division, Library of Congress, Washington, D.C., 112H.

21. Thomson Ibid., 119H, Jonathan Larson. RENT (New Act One Rough, 12 Sep 1995). Box 15, Folder 5, Jonathan Larson Papers, Music Division, Library of Congress, Washington, D.C., 13.

The script in this folder is actually complete, but Larson (presumably) forgot to delete the "Act One" comment from the title page.

before Thomson's September 1995 notes, Larson had reconstructed the song as 'One Song Glory,' albeit with a suicidal Roger:

> "FIND
>
> ONE SONG
>
> ONE ~~MELODY~~ **SWEET REFRAIN**
>
> ONE SONG
>
> THEN PUT OUT THE FIRE
>
> BURNING BURNING BURNING INSIDE"[22]

Larson was also just as willing to reject Thomson's notes as take them. For example, Thomson suggested cutting a reference to Maureen's lesbianism in 'Voice Mail #1,' as it deflates the moment when Mark and Roger tell Benny that her new lover's name is Joanne.[23] Thomson also wanted Larson to cut the second verse of 'Halloween,' where Mark questions how fate brought the group together in Act One, and add Benny to 'What You Own,' as his character is minimised in Act Two.[24] None of these suggestions were implemented, nor do Larson's notes suggest he ever considered them seriously.

---

22. Jonathan Larson. 'One Song Glory' (Draft). Box 15, Folder 3, Jonathan Larson Papers, Music Division, Library of Congress, Washington, D.C., 31H.

The pages are not dated, but this revision is boxed with materials predating Thomson's notes and, following her feedback, Larson rewrote the song again, though the lyrical format goes back to the earlier 'Right Brain,' and the final stanza would remain intact until at least 6 January 1996 (the last dated script with the original lyric), after which the phrase "before you enter the light" became "until the virus takes hold".

23. Lynn Thomson. Feedback Notes for Jonathan Larson. Box 17, Folder 5, Jonathan Larson Papers, Music Division, Library of Congress, Washington, D.C., 5H.

The document is covered in Larson's notes: questions to himself on issues he agreed with, and strikes through entire paragraphs in disagreement.

24. Ibid., 6-7H.

A Year Went By So Fast

NYTW announced *RENT* would open in January 1996, with a private warning to Larson that the show would be held back if it still felt unfinished. Jim Nicola and the producers demanded an overhauled script by July 1995 - a deadline which Larson completely blew by agreeing to work on *J.P. Morgan*. "I saw [*Morgan*]," remembers Nicola. "It gave me a lot of faith in Jonathan's abilities as a composer." However, talent and promise did not equate to a new script. Compounding matters - and without Larson's knowledge - was that NYTW's finances were in dire straits mirroring his own, and *RENT* would make or break the company's future. Nicola felt this information would have put undue strain and responsibility on the jittery Larson and kept it quiet, but was concerned enough to make sure an alternative show could be found to prevent the theatre from taking a wash on the production.

McCollum and Seller were also keeping an eye on their investment: "Jeffrey [Seller] and I are never like, "Call us when you have updates." We're both very passionate, but we didn't get involved in the push between the workshop and the rewrites that were happening. We gave notes on what we needed to see, and one of the big ones was that [the characters] can't be victims." Frustrated though Larson could be, Todd Robinson sided with the producers:

> When somebody is paying you, they're not paying
> you so that you can be left alone to be your cre-
> ative genius doing your opus. They're there for
> business, and they're going to have an opinion, and
> they bought the right to have one. Jonathan was
> in his mid-30s, working in a diner, and living in
> squalor. [He] was a very proud guy, and he wanted
> his parents to be proud of him, and he was getting
> slapped down. After all these years of working to

get *RENT* to this point where it would be work-shopped, all of a sudden there were people with opinions, and he was terrified they were going to wreck it. He was afraid. He felt insecure about it, and he was an emotional person and would react emotionally. That said, the result speaks for itself.

When Larson returned to *RENT* in late summer 1995, he had refined his workflow to a science, now writing an actual scene - often without regard for rhyme or scansion - and subsequently setting it to music. He would then begin converting the dialogue to lyrics and massaging the song into shape, first by swapping out a few words when applicable, then entire lines and stanzas, refining the text to fit the music.

For example, in writing 'Happy New Year,' a lyric which began life as:

BENNY:

YOU JUST DON'T GET IT

CLEARING THE LOT WAS FOR THEIR OWN SAFETY

WE BREAK GROUND AFTER THE HOLIDAY

YOU PEOPLE CAN STAY TIL WE START RENOVATIONS

WHICH ISN'T FOR MONTHS

ROGER:

I WONDERED WHY

YOU'D SPEND NEW YEAR'S DOWNTOWN

WITHOUT YOUR NEW BRIDE AND HER WEALTHY FAMILY[25]

---

25. Jonathan Larson. 'Happy New Year' (Draft). Box 15, Folder 6, Jonathan Larson Papers, Music Division, Library of Congress, Washington, D.C., 131H.

soon became:

BENNY:

CLEARING THE LOT WAS A SAFETY CONCERN

WE BREAK GROUND ~~TOMORROW~~ *THIS WEEK* ~~IF THE~~ **BUT YOU CAN RETURN TIL JULY**

~~YOU PEOPLE CAN STAY TIL WE START RENOVATIONS~~

~~WHICH ISN'T FOR MONTHS~~

MAUREEN:

I WONDERED

~~I WONDERED~~ WHY YOU'D SPEND NEW YEAR'S ~~DOWNTOWN~~ **WITH PEOPLE YOU HATE**

~~WITHOUT YOUR NEW BRIDE AND HER WEALTHY FAMILY~~ ~~**AT HER FAMILY**~~

INSTEAD OF AT YOUR NEW BRIDE'S **COUNTRY ESTATE**[26]

and then:

BENNY:

CLEARING THE LOT WAS A SAFETY CONCERN

WE BREAK GROUND THIS WEEK

BUT YOU CAN RETURN TIL JULY

In this folder, Larson's notes are unusually in reverse-chronological order. It is unknown if this was his doing or a processing error.

26. Ibid., 122H.

Standard strikethrough = crossed out in pencil, bold = pen, bold strike is written in pen and then crossed out in pencil. Italic = written in pencil. Presenting the layers of revision on this page (which is virtually every line) without the benefit of colour does not do Larson's process justice.

MAUREEN:

I WONDERED WHY *YOU'RE HERE*

~~YOU'D SPEND NEW YEAR'S~~ WITH PEOPLE
YOU HATE

INSTEAD OF WITH MUFFY AT MUFFY'S
ESTATE[27]

and finally:

BENNY:

CLEARING THE LOT WAS A SAFETY CONCERN

WE BREAK GROUND THIS MONTH

BUT YOU CAN RETURN

MAUREEN:

THAT'S WHY YOU'RE HERE WITH PEOPLE
YOU HATE

INSTEAD OF WITH MUFFY AT MUFFY'S
ESTATE[28]

Larson's demos for *RENT* reflect this process, with his recordings from September 1995 through January 1996 full of crammed-in syllables, performance flubs, and a general sense of awkwardness on the composer's behalf when performing his new material.

To urge revisions along, New York Theatre Workshop invited

27. Ibid., P125H.

Italics represent a hand-written revision. Strikethrough text is struck out by hand on the original.

28. Jonathan Larson. *RENT* (16 Jan 1996 Draft), stored as "***1/16/96" (Microsoft Word File). Contained within disk57.dmg. Jonathan Larson Papers, Music Division, Library of Congress, Washington, D.C.

This is the last backed-up draft of the show, with one final minor revision saved on Larson's hard drive.

Larson to a writer's retreat at Dartmouth University. During a fren-
zied week away from the city, Larson hammered out a completely
reworked show and delivered his draft in September 1995; the
now-infamous edition which set Act One as a flashback. A read-
through was held to see how the material worked in performance
versus on the page, with a cast including 1994 (and subsequent
1996) ensemble member Gilles Chiasson as Roger. Despite all the
energy and conflict to come, Larson remained self-assured: "He
was very child-like in a way," says Diekmann. "He wasn't self-important, he just really believed in himself. You couldn't get mad at
him, because he had this almost innocent belief that he was gonna
do it. He and I fought about money all the time, and I was the
one who always said no to him, but he wasn't demanding. He kept
pushing because he believed in [the show] from day one."

Larson's new flashback framing device immediately caused
conflict amongst the creative team. Greif hated it, preferring an
upbeat immediacy in the first act, but Nicola and Thomson liked
how it added coherency.[29] Ultimately, Larson caved after even his
friends sided against him: "I told him not to do it," remembers
Victoria Leacock Hoffman, "I just told him flat-out, I hate stories that start at the end." Larson's anger at facing further revisions
manifested in annoyance with his director, and their previously
civil relationship began to get rocky. Nancy Diekmann recalls that,
by the time *RENT* was approaching rehearsals, Larson effectively
focused all of his frustrations on Greif as the person who should
have been - but was just as frequently not - on his side.

---

29. In February and October 2015, the Theatre M-Lab in Amsterdam staged
RENT in a setup similar to the flashback, with 'Mark in 2015' leading his own cast
of eight through the show. Having seen the production, this author is of the opinion that Greif was 100% correct in his assessment: by foreshadowing the second
act's losses so heavily up front, *RENT*'s first act loses the sense of joy and serendipity which sets up the tragedy in the second act. It would be like Tevye's family
packing up to leave or sitting on a boat at the opening of *Fiddler on the Roof.*

Regardless, Nicola was pleased by how far Larson had come: "The things that were missing [were noted], like, 'Here is a song for Maureen and Joanne, here's a song at the end for Mark and Roger,' and those are tentpoles. As he worked on it in this period, the work that came in was really some of the best stuff he wrote for that score. There was a confidence in the new score, and that was reaffirming, that he was growing and thriving."

Larson's close friend Eddie Rosenstein agrees:

> I was so, so pleased with what he was pulling off that [last] year. He understood the drama. Things started to speed up logarithmically, and he could write songs in a day because he figured it out. They took all the cartoony characters and the caricatures and based them in real characters and real people and real backstories and real life and found the real drama. Remember, he won the Pulitzer for drama, not music.

Despite capitulating on the flashback framing, Larson still wanted a reflective moment for Mark and Roger in the first act. Shortly before his famous single-day drafting of Maureen & Joanne's 'Take Me or Leave Me,' Larson dashed off another new song for the show. Built on the echoing guitar riff from 'One Song Glory,' 'Door/Wall' is a split moment between Roger, regretting his actions from 'Another Day,' and Mark, realising that this Christmas Eve is special. The song was short and emotional, but dramatically inert, making the first act feel long when 'Will I?' followed shortly after. 'Door/Wall' remained in *RENT* for the complete run at New York Theatre Workshop, but was removed during the show's transfer to Broadway.[30]

---

30. Larson recorded his own demo of 'Door/Wall' on the same tape as the first two recordings of 'Take Me or Leave Me'. Based on Larson's computer files, 'Door' and 'Take Me' were both introduced between 5 January and 16 January in

Mark's foil, the cheerful Alexi Darling, was a hybrid effort from Larson, Greif, and Thomson: "We talked about the expediency of the phone messages," remembers Nicola, "to get acquainted with different people, to give depth to the personalities of different characters, and also to give a sense of time passing. In 1995 and 1996, those had a currency." One voice mail, however, was cut: a call at the start of Act Two informing Mimi on Halloween that she needs to see her doctor. "Very early on, I was questioning the presence of 'Seasons of Love' and what purpose it was serving," remembers Nicola. Taking the song out of time versus giving it a temporality proved to be the answer.

Finding Maureen's place in the art world provoked constant discussion as well. According to Nicola, "We had to get him to make a decision about, 'Is she a good and interesting performing artist, and is this an act [from] someone who lives in this neighbourhood,' and say, 'That's an outstanding person like Laurie Anderson, or are we making fun of that?'[31] I do remember a lot of the discussion amongst the staff, not so much directly with Jonathan, feeling that some of the political statements were not how they would be articulated by the people in this neighbourhood at the time, that they were an approximation of that." Oberlin remembers the 1993 edition of 'Over the Moon' as "monotonic, but it was cool, and it was fun, and I loved the idea of introducing an outsider performance art thing. That didn't make the final cut, but I loved what [Larson] was saying at the beginning."

Until the September 1995 revision, 'Moon' was more

---

a flurry of last-minute cuts and rewrites. The order on the tape is the first edition 'Take Me or Leave Me' with a different verse for Joanne, 'Door/Wall,' an overhauled 'We're Okay' resembling the final vs. the September 1995 original, and a revised 'Take Me or Leave Me'.

31. This balance would ultimately become confused and muddled as the Broadway run extended, leaning towards being more of a spoof than Larson's initial intentions.

intellectual, textually influenced by environmental philosopher Helen Caldicott, with an oedipal theme: Elsie the Cow blinds herself to see past a desert created by the widespread introduction of cable television, while Ferdinand the Bull says everything will come back if everybody just tunes in and zones out. Topical references were updated from 1993 to 1994, and Larson shaped the piece's narrative more clearly, making the monologue funnier without turning it into a joke. That said, 'Moon' was still on a different linguistic and verbal level from the rest of the show, breaking consistency with the piece as a whole.

According to the 1997 *RENT* collector book, Greif's response was to consider casting a performance artist as Maureen, but Larson refused: most performance artists lacked the musical or acting skill to perform the rest of the part. Their compromise was to simplify 'Over the Moon' and make it easier to perform.[32] Unfortunately, Greif and Larson also had diametrically opposed views of the content. As quoted in 1997, Greif felt, "It was very important to Jonathan that she had something to say. It was very important to me that it seemed like bad performance, but with all the best intentions. She hasn't found out who she is as a performer yet."[33] As *RENT* entered rehearsal, Larson rewrote the piece to fit Idina Menzel's strengths, and recruited her for ideas and contributions, making the piece her own. Despite the new direction, Larson still wanted to push buttons, such as with this soon-to-be excised segment:

> They're building walls with rules here, like 'no rusty cars' or 'no basketball hoops over the garage door' and 'no sugar-lending to neighbors'. 'What do they allow here', I asked. 'Guns'.[34]

32. Giel, 44.

33. Ibid., 44.

34. Jonathan Larson. RENT (15 Dec 1995 Draft). Box 16, Folder 7,

Larson would simplify the piece even further, and additional revisions would be made posthumously, such as removing references to virtual lap dances and a homeless person interrupting the performance. Greif, however, remained unconvinced and found himself unable to get a grasp of the piece, ultimately instructing Menzel and choreographer Marlies Yearby to sort it out between them. As Yearby remembers:

> Idina just had the quirkiest sense in her body. I understood performance, and it was just a thing of watching her initially, and collecting little gestures that I thought would work with her, and then helping to connect them to the performance piece. [...] It started off with this little simple rolling hands gesture that came out of something she did, and I started playing with it, and then I started evolving that this principle - this little gesture is going to be your chorus. It began to enlighten the story, it began to bring humour because it was so off-beat. And she just had this sense of wonderment in how she addressed everything, that it was almost like she was laughing at herself as she was doing it, and there's something about that which is endearing to an audience, and I did not take that away, I encouraged it. Her performance very much became about her enjoying herself, not understanding what she's doing.
>
> And then later, it shifted, and suddenly I was not feeling it anymore. It started doing something else, and the character changed. For me, now, a lot of the Maureens are directed sexually in that moment,

Jonathan Larson Papers, Music Division, Library of Congress, Washington, D.C., 16-17.

and there's sort of like an uncontained sexuality about her that was very different when Idina was there. Idina just naturally had some things about her that were that way, but it wasn't what [she] was trying to feature. It was just her ability to own completely her not knowing what it was and enjoying that she's not knowing. It was masterful. That on the stage endeared her to the audience. That's much better than to put on this air of, "I'm gonna act like I'm not knowing," or that, "I'm going to rely on my sexual being that's gonna get me through," and neither one of those were [there]... it was just so pure and endearing because it was honest.

As Maureen's counterpoint, Joanne also needed fleshing out. Despite always being described as financially well-off and successful, the character was barely a supporting role through the 1994 workshop, only appearing alongside Maureen and wrapped around her finger. Adding 'Tango: Maureen' helped, with Mark clueing the helplessly head-over-heals uptown girl in on what she was up against, but something was still missing. For the same September 1995 draft, Larson wrote the first version of 'We're Okay,' Joanne's solo number. The character was able to vent her frustrations, such as Maureen's habitual infidelity, with lyrics like:

> No baby talk - tell me...
>
> ...three times...
>
> ...a year...
>
> ...on average...
>
> I'm not
>
> Not sad
>
> Just curious

We're okay

You're wrong

Not mad

(I'm furious)

We're okay[35]

While Larson's collaborators impressed on him the need to define the character further, drafts like this kept Joanne lyrically running in neutral despite consistent improvements musically. In fact, it took until Larson's final revisions in January 1996 to revise 'We're Okay' into its current form, showing Joanne as a successful woman in her own right as she takes charge of her office subordinates and maturely handles her family despite Maureen's chaos unfolding around her. 'Take Me or Leave Me' would refine that further, with Joanne dumping Maureen not once, but twice, during the show (the first time at the start of 'La Vie Boheme B'). In the first edition of 'Take Me or Leave Me,' sung only by Maureen, Joanne even rebuts with "I guess I'll leave you. But it's my house. You're out."[36] Maureen responds with shock.

Following the September 1995 table reading, Greif and Larson had a meeting to discuss the show's other problem character: Benny. Greif felt the landlord was still too much of a caricature and not enough of a real person.[37] The director suggested keeping Benny's business in the family - hence the Blockbuster Video

---

35. Jonathan Larson. *RENT* (New Act One Rough, 12 Sep 1995). Box 15, Folder 3, Jonathan Larson Papers, Music Division, Library of Congress, Washington, D.C., 31-32.

This version includes the complete first two verses of the finished song and the bridge before repeating the chorus and Joanne replying.

36. Jonathan Larson. 'Take Me or Leave Me' (Annotated Draft, 3 Jan 1996). Box 16, Folder 8, Jonathan Larson Papers, Music Division, Library of Congress, Washington, D.C., 78.

37. Jonathan Larson. Handwritten notes. Box 16, Folder 3, Jonathan Larson Papers, Music Division, Library of Congress, Washington, D.C., 45H.

representative becoming Benny's father-in-law - but also to reexamine the landlord's role amongst his group of friends.[38] Larson had to ask himself: "[What is the] nature of Benny's Villainy[?]"[39] Conferring with his dramaturge, Larson finally found the character's trajectory: Benny believes he's doing what is right in giving his friends the opportunities he'd so far had to renege on. However, he uses unpleasant tactics (such as extorting Mark and Roger with the full year's rent demand), and it backfires. Benny tries to save face, but it's too late and he undermines his own actions, losing his friends and jeopardising his marriage in the process.[40]

The producers did what they could from a distance to encourage Larson to make necessary changes. Says McCollum: "Part of our contribution was to make sure that good producing is never your idea. Good producing is creating an environment where people can do their best work and creating opportunities to nudge it forward and finding the right people." Michael Greif recalled at Larson's memorial service:

> Jim, and Jonathan, and I had a conversation about the possibility [in November 1995] of postponing *RENT*. I said to [him], "Look, if you have to postpone this play, just do it without me. You've waited a year for me, and my schedule's really impossible. Just do it, and good luck to you." and then Jonathan started crying. And I thought, "Oh that baby! And he's upset about the postponement!" And then he said to me, "How could you just walk away from this?"[41]

---

38. Ibid. 45H

39. Ibid., 46H.

"Benny's villainy" is written with a large box around it.

40. Ibid., P58-61

41. Jonathan Larson Memorial Service. Video. 3 Feb 1996. Privately held by

Amongst the cast from 1994, Anthony Rapp was guaranteed his role as Mark when the show went to production in 1996, but others in the 1994 workshop weren't so lucky. Daphne Rubin-Vega had only played Mimi due to influence from Jim Nicola and Michael Greif. Larson had considered Karmine Alers, a singer he had worked with on 'With Open Eyes,' one of his pop songs, but selected Rubin-Vega on the condition that she take voice lessons and re-audition for the actual production. Ensemble member Gilles Chiasson auditioned for the role of Mark, but took the ensemble role of Squeegie Man to continue acting at home in New York versus going on tour. Likewise, the creative team decided to cast Wilson Jermaine Heredia - a Hispanic actor - as Angel to the dismay of 1994's Mark Setlock, who would understudy the part on Broadway.

Joining the creative team at this point was choreographer Marlies Yearby, a contemporary practitioner working mostly in New York's performance art scene. Larson - along with Greif - selected Yearby after the pair watched a video of the choreographer's work for En Garde Arts' *Vanquished by Voodoo*, with text by Laurie Carlos and music by Don Meissner. Yearby recalls that Larson

> said was that, when he was looking at my work, the one thing [he and Greif] found really fasci-nating was how human the performers looked, the feelings really transferred to them as audi-ence members as believable, like they lived on the stage versus performed or acted, so he said that he really loved that feeling on stage - something that transcends the acting and feels more connected to human emotions, feelings, physicality.

Victoria Leacock Hoffman, Washington, D.C.

Yearby's style, based primarily in gesture and the aspects of the performer, differed from standard choreographic practice:

> A lot of times, dance has a vocabulary that can be very specific and familiar, and when you look at my work over the years, whether it be on *RENT* or another theatrical production, or even on my company during the years, you'll note that the vocabulary really shifts. I have my -isms, but it really finds itself based on the story - whether nonlinear or linear - that's being told, based on the music that's present, based on the images, if that's what's driving it. I like to watch people, and part of my work is to watch bodies in the space, be it actor bodies or dancer bodies or human beings walking down the streets. Often times, in the body of the work, I'm moving from an emotional place based on a particular beat in that moment, and I'm incorporating from that the base vocabulary - it comes oftentimes from the bodies I'm looking at and the way that they naturally move in the space, as they're embodying the character and as they're embodying themsel [sic]. It's a process that evolves out of gestures that I've worked with. I call it gesture dances. I think of my work more as gesture dances than I think of it as the technical language associated with dance and the technical phrases. I'm evolving that language out of what I'm imagining. Much like a writer would choose words, choose phrases, to choose their route to get to the story, as a choreographer, I am choosing the base language and evolving it from there into its own language for each story or piece.

Even as *RENT* came together, Larson was planning new projects and staying looped into the theatre scene. During his last conversation with Bob Golden, the two discussed another show preparing to open off-Broadway at the same time:

> We had another mutual friend, Adam Guettel, who had a show [opening] called *Floyd Collins*. I asked [Jonathan] if [he] was afraid if the publicity for that [due to Guettel's family, might start] eclipsing *RENT* in any way, and he said, "No way, this is our era of musical theatre, and I hope Adam's show goes really, really well." And he was just so gracious about it.[42]

As Nicola recalls,

> By the time we were in rehearsals, we were pretty [much] on board. The atmosphere was more [standard disagreements]. I heard a lot of anxiety about the high stakes he was dealing with at that point, but I thought he was young, and the next time it wouldn't be that bad. My general rule is, once they're in rehearsal, hang back and let the artists get to work. My moment of reckoning with where it was, was at the dress rehearsal. We were all pretty pleased with where we were, and we were over the hump, and there was a lot of work to be done, but it'll all hang together. Things like, "is that a verse too long," things you want to be asking at that point. We all felt humbled that there was a show, but we had a lot of work to do, and there wasn't a lot of time.

---

42. Vicky's Larson Evening, Tape #1. Video. February 1996. Privately held by Victoria Leacock Hoffman, Washington, D.C.

But, for Larson, time had run out. On 25 January 1996, following a week of chest pains and two emergency room misdiagnoses, Jonathan Larson died of an aortic aneurism caused by Marfan's Syndrome. He had seen *RENT* through to its dress rehearsal, taken an interview with Anthony Tommasini, an opera critic from the *New York Times*, and collapsed while making a late night cup of tea. He was 35 years old, a mere week away from turning 36. Amidst the heartache and confusion, Larson's family made the decision that the show must go on.

We Were the Lucky Ones

RENT had two weeks of preview performances before the press came, during which time the team at NYTW had to try and make adjustments without the show's key creative voice. Nicola remembers:

> The vivid memory is a meeting [in my office] of the four of us [Nicola, Greif, Thomson, Weil] that day, and my question was, do we proceed, or do we stop - and if we proceed, what is the ethical way to do so? I said, "Is it more ethical to involve someone that's more an expert in the things that need to be done than we are, or not?" We decided it was not the right way to go ahead, and we made a pact of consensus amongst us that changes would only be made with the approval of all of us, and we would defer to the expert in a particular area, like Tim for the music. There were a lot of little polishing things to be done. In one of those conversations, Tim was asking us to cut a bar out of a transition, which was a detail past my expertise, but if he wanted to do it, I thought it made sense. We proceeded down that

road and got to where we felt we'd gone as far as we
could in his absence.

Most of *RENT*'s posthumous changes were made during previews at NYTW, such as having Mark read stage directions as narration, varying the time signatures in the opening 'Tune Up' section (Larson wrote it all in 4/4), cutting verses and a bridge from
'Tango: Maureen' and 'What You Own,' respectively, and finding
the best location for 'We're Okay'.

The new narration - built from the standard practice in readings
and workshop performances - reinforced the figurative, exposed,
Brechtian world of Greif's direction versus the larger, more literal,
and expensive staging Larson imagined. Lighting cables were visible, actors would be given a handheld microphone if their wireless
battery pack died, and the cast handled all the scene changes.

Greif also came up with the idea of using a mix of handheld
and stand microphones to get around a technical limitation: the
sound system at New York Theatre Workshop was incapable of handling 15 wireless channels (one for each cast member). A decision
was made to only put the principal characters on wireless headset
microphones, with the ensemble sharing a spare headset for scenes
where a wired microphone would be too impractical. Otherwise, in
a feat of choreography lost when the show transferred to Broadway,
the cast passed around wired hand microphones, creating spaces for
scenes to take place, and even building small character moments,
such as when one of the homeless people sets himself up as The
Man's assistant, holding up the microphone on "And it's beginning
to snow" in 'Christmas Bells.' If the Broadway production's staging
was defined by its shifting metal tables, the movements required to
make *RENT*'s sound work at the Workshop deserve equal credit,
warts and all. As Weil recalls:

We had a sound designer who, by his own admission, wasn't a rock-and-roll guy, so we had a lot of difficulty starting out. Also, we were running too much volume on stage. The actors wanted to have that club experience, to hear themselves in the monitors, but in the theatre, it's just not practical, because the sound from the monitors feeds into the mics, and you get an echo chamber. It took a lot of time and another sound designer or two to sort all that out.

In terms of the band, we were all musicians in the younger part of our prime, and we had all played in rock bands. It wasn't a Broadway orchestra at all. We knew what that sound was, and we made that sound live on stage, and the band part took pretty good care of itself. [The challenge] was balancing what was on stage and what could be understood by the audience, and still keeping the actors happy. We had to slowly ween them off of being able to listen and hear for themselves. I had to keep pounding it into them, just breathe and sing and trust. This is not to say we didn't get a lot of complaints, but at the time, there was no such thing as a Broadway show that runs at 100db.[43] That's just insane. The average Broadway show runs at 75-80, and we just blew that out of the water. There was a little bit of shock value, which we liked and was part of the gestalt of the show, and the people that were gonna leave were gonna leave anyway.

---

43. The sound threshold for damaging human hearing is 120db. A Boeing 737 airplane taking off creates about 80db, and a lawn mower approximately 100db.

For the Broadway transfer, Larson's long-time producer and *RENT*'s early arranger, Steve Skinner, would stop by to offer advice on perfecting the rock-and-roll sound Larson wanted, one where the band and vocals retained the necessary conflict at the essence of rock:

> The standard Broadway thing to do [on the song 'Out Tonight' is have] one fader for the band and one fader for Daphne [Rubin-Vega as Mimi], and when Daphne came on singing, [the board op] would lower the fader for the band, so everything came down to make room. I said, "Why don't you make two faders? Have the guitars on this fader and the rest of the band here, and just lower the guitars, since that's where the voice is?" They went, "Okay, okay," and did, and it had more of [a rock] effect - with mixing, you always have to trick the ear into thinking [the vocals and band are] still fighting, but at the same time, the guitars are kinda giving up, which is why the vocal wins there.

Meanwhile, Tim Weil took Skinner's MIDI sequences from Larson's ongoing demo tapes and reworked them for a live band - a challenge, as musical trends were changing in the mid-'90s:

> "I custom-tailored the band to what we were trying to do. One of my good friends who I'd worked with quite a long time was Dan Weiss, who's a great musician. He plays every instrument, but he's an especially great guitar and keyboard player, and he's a great Hammond player. We only used four people in the '94 version, and then we added the second guitar and organ chair. If you really got inside that bandstand and really heard what was

going on with the guitars, it still had a pretty good element of grunge, but you have to remember, we were starting to pull out of the early R.E.M. and the Seattle and the grunge. The closest we got to that alt-thing was 'What You Own'. Music was evolving a bit at that time, and we had a better sonic palette to work with in the band, and we had to make it a little bit more theatre-friendly. The intent was always the same, that it wasn't, "Let's play a tango," it was, "[How] would this band, with this personnel, with these instruments, play a tango?"

Viva La Vie Boheme

At the time of Larson's death, *RENT* may have finally come together creatively, but the finances were less encouraging: advance ticket sales were soft, as is common during winter months, and NYTW faced a cash flow crisis to the extent of questioning if employees could be paid. "We needed it to be a hit," remembers Diekmann. Audiences at the first performances were packed with Larson's friends, invited to visit for free and sit on the theatre's steps, but word of mouth and rave reviews, along with the press jumping on Larson's tragic story, set the box office on fire. The run sold out, extended, and the question was: what next?

The producers took up the task of running the show at this point. "I remember when we opened," says McCollum. "We got a call from a very, very powerful London entity who wanted to fly us over and talk about the show, because he was sure he could fix it." Feeling there was nothing for an outsider to fix, the producers refused the meeting. Larson had left behind enough material in his revisions for clean-up work to be made, and Weil possessed copies of Larson's master composition data. For the cast, the show went on as usual: rehearsing, implementing changes from Greif, Nicola, Thomson, and Weil, and performing at night. The show had ceased to be just a job, but a mission and a calling.

Initial ideas for a transfer, discussed while Larson was still alive, would have resembled the staging used for 2013's *Murder Ballad*, with the show performed not in a theatre, but a rock club with drinks on hand, tables throughout, and a standing section. McCollum remembers how a more traditional off-Broadway transfer was also considered following Larson's death:

> I thought, we'll put it in a 400-seater, it'll be like *Forever Plaid*. I hadn't really understood this show is way too big for 400 seats. People said, "You can't go to Broadway." I said, "We can't afford NOT to go to Broadway. It's the only place where theatres are big enough in this town." We also thought it was epic enough [to play to a large house.] But Jeffrey and I weren't really thinking business at that point. Yes, we got good reviews, but the experts were like, "Be careful, it's a downtown show" and I was like, "What does that mean? It's inspired by *Bohème* and it's some of the greatest music I've ever heard."

Following a bidding war for the hottest show in a decade, the Nederlander Organization spent eight weeks rapidly repairing their namesake theatre, fixing a leaky roof, and reinstalling the entire electrical grid to accommodate *RENT*, their tenant for the next 12 years. Says McCollum:

> Jeff and I took a walk around Bryant Park, and we were weeping, and he asked what we were going to do, and I told him we were going to do the show. Our job was to make sure everyone remembered

[Larson]'s name, and it gave us great clarity and purpose.

One edit, however, was made involuntarily after Larson's death. From 1993 on, Benny entered singing the chorus from Band Aid's charity single 'Do They Know it's Christmas?'[44] In early drafts, the line was a throwaway joke for Larson to riff on self-important yuppies who think buying a record makes a significant impact on global poverty. As Larson refined Benny's character, though, the line gained additional depth by highlighting the schism between Benny's impoverished background, his time as a Bohemian, his belief that gentrification truly will improve the area, and the roughshod way he's trampling on the homeless and his friends along the way. Unfortunately, the song's publishers refused to grant *RENT*'s producers a license to include the segment in the Broadway edition, and the line was changed to the royalty-free 'Joy to the World' during the show's first weeks post-transfer.

Moving to Broadway also meant restaging and relighting the entire show. Despite only seating 200 patrons (then 150), the New York Theatre Workshop's stage is as large as in many Broadway theatres, and was actually wider than the Nederlander's. In contrast, *RENT*'s Broadway stage was deeper and had a higher ceiling. At NYTW, *RENT* went up to the walls in all three dimensions, pulling the audience into the show's claustrophobic world of tightly packed apartments and crowds, whereas everything at the Nederlander had to be hung from adjustable batons, and a fake wall (painted to look like the NYTW's brick backing wall, complete with cutaway) and curtains were utilised to create a playing space which mimicked the original venue. As a bonus, the Nederlander also offered of wing space for costume changes and a trap door for the junkies' entry during 'Christmas Bells'. When rehearsal for

---

44. The specific line is "Feed the world / Let them know it's Christmas Time." The original Band Aid single has been rerecorded multiple times.

the transfer started, the cast would learn the new staging during the day and perform the old staging at the Workshop that night, before immediately moving into the venue for technical rehearsals after closing at NYTW. *RENT* opened for previews at Broadway's Nederlander Theater on 16 April 1996, with its press night on 29 April 1996.

The first national tour - nicknamed the Angel tour - opened six months later in Boston. The Benny tour opened six months after that at Michael Greif's home base, La Jolla Playhouse, before an extended run in Los Angeles and going on the road. Neil Patrick Harris, known at the time solely as the child actor from *Doogie Howser M.D.* (a primetime TV drama about a teenage doctor), played Mark for the La Jolla and LA runs. Harris' performance was seen as a revelation, and *RENT* relaunched his career.

For *RENT*'s first year, the producers kept a close eye on the show, before stepping back to handle the show's global strategy and finances. Says McCollum: "The first negotiations after the [initial six month contracts] term were ugly, as [members of the cast] decided what they were worth and we [the producers] really had to turn the show into a business."

"The producers flew us [up to Boston] to see [the Angel tour]," remembers Chiasson,

> and partly, sure, it was to get them press - which was great - but it also gave us an opportunity to experience the show, and it deals with mortality and all these weighty issues. From the moment Jonathan passed away, my only experience from the show was on stage as a performer - there was no time, and I had sung the show almost every day, except for my days off, from the day Jonathan died until this Monday, when we flew up to Boston, and

suddenly we were sitting in the audience, experiencing the show. We weren't performing, and we didn't have to maintain anything, we could just experience it. I just fell apart. It was extraordinarily cathartic to finally hear the music and not have to be on stage holding it together. There was a never a time when we did the show and it was casual.

Now, 20 years after *RENT* opened, the show maintains its hold and power. Productions are consistently going up around the world, and the show is touching a new generation. Todd Robinson feels this has to do with Larson's ability to tap universal truths: "The thing that's so powerful about *RENT* is that, even though *RENT* was about AIDS, it was really *La Bohème* combined with popular music. [...] He was writing about things in terms of his point of view and his politics and his heart. He was writing about things that were true because they really happened to him. Jonathan sucked everything in, and you can see it in his work."

Eddie Rosenstein agrees:

Jonathan was already interested in pegging this to contemporary issues, the biggest issues being fear vs. love or just issues of spirit and love and community. He was looking for stuff that's universal, and that's, "How do you deal with those choices, and what do you do when you don't have all the time you want, how do you make choices? What do you with feelings you're not sure how to resolve, what do you do with people who might be dying? What do you do with your own mortality? When do you say this is real and this matters, and how do I get rid of the artifice?" And that cutting through the bullshit, the false ideologies, the shit we buy into oftentimes without questioning because it's

just what we do. That bullshit is what any artist
spends his entire life trying to cut through.

As *RENT*'s popularity exploded in the wake of Larson's death, his story spread through the press and into *RENT*'s early-internet-enabled fandom, leading to feelings amongst his friends that the departed had been co-opted by the media storm and total strangers who saw him only through the show's prism. As Lin-Manuel Miranda, Larson's clearest spiritual successor, would write 20 years later: "You have no control: Who lives, who dies, who tells your story?"[1] As the media machine grew, some friends got shunted to the side, egos flared, and the combined drama on- and off-stage fed the story, creating the now-standard myth of Jonathan Larson.

---

1. Lin-Manuel Miranda and Jeremy McCarter, *Hamilton: The Revolution* (New York, NY: Grand Central Publishing, 2016), 280.

A Half-Empty House

Once upon a time
I forgot the date
There was a famous apple orchard
The Dustin Estate

—1/2 MT House Intro

WHEN JONATHAN LARSON died on 25 January 1996, he left behind a Pandora's box of questions regarding his work: not only did *RENT* need to be put in order and opened in his absence, but what was to be done with his remaining output?[2] As the past seven chapters have shown, Larson wrote far more than three musicals, and in early 1996, most of them had been filed away and abandoned. Initially, the sole priority was ensuring nothing got lost: Jonathan Burkhart spearheaded the process of clearing out Larson's flat, and every paper and recording was kept for archive. Some items, such as Larson's journals, would

---

2. When he died, Larson had also been commissioned to write an opera for the Adirondack Theatre Festival in Glens Falls, NY. He had yet to begin work on the show, and nobody interviewed knew what he was planning to write for it. However, Larson had told Matt O'Grady that he wanted return to more overtly political work. O'Grady believes Larson would have been fascinated by the Clinton impeachment scandal in 1998, and eventually written a show about that.

be sent to California and held privately by Larson's family, but the majority of materials stayed in New York.

At first, *RENT*'s producers held an option on the rest of Larson's work. As Kevin McCollum states: "We felt we sudden[ly] became wards. We had a job to protect the integrity of Jonathan's work, as producers with artist's hearts. The family gave us permission to do what we had to do to get as many people to see *RENT* as possible. Even in shock, even not knowing the process - and we didn't know how big this would be."

As *RENT*'s financial success grew, Larson's estate founded the Jonathan Larson Performing Arts Foundation. Todd Robinson, being on the West Coast near Larson's family, was able to assist with the initial startup, and encouraged Allan Larson to help up-and-coming artists.

In addition to presenting grants to deserving individuals and organisations, the Foundation also managed Larson's intellectual property. His papers and tapes found their way to the organisation's office in New York, but at first, nobody was even sure of what they had, let alone how the work could - or should - be released. Despite initially rejecting advances from the Library of Congress, which asked to take responsibility for the materials, the estate accepted the Library's introduction to archivist Amy Asch, who had previously catalogued legendary composer Oscar Hammerstein's papers. For the next two years, it was Asch's responsibility, along with a small team of assistants, to go through every item recovered from Larson's apartment, catalogue it, interview any collaborators, and create a database for the Foundation's reference.

In 1999, a small reading was held for a new musical built around the Jonathan Larson songbook at Manhattan Theatre Club. This is the story of how one of Larson's abandoned concepts from 1991 became that show.

Following *Superbia*'s stall-out at the end of 1989, Larson began writing *30/90* and turning it into *Boho Days*, but knew he wanted to work on something larger and more political. *RENT* had temporarily fizzled out due to collaborative disagreements, and Larson - ever-motivated by America's decline from JFK-era idealism - set out instead to write his epic: a cross-generational *Hair* about the US on the edge of implosion. In a flurry of notes and conceptualisations written between March and June 1991, he created not one, but two unique plots and sets of characters for his show. The name? *1/2 MT House (or Deform Follows Disfunction)* [sic].[3]

In the initial outline for the show, dated 14 March 1991, the setup is as follows: an early settler named Wiley Jack Cross tricked a group of Native Americans out of their land and set up a massive apple orchard, which quickly became renowned for its quality. Shares were sold, and everybody was happy until Cross's descendants decided to discard the apples and only process the seeds to create cyanide. Now leaders in the poison business, they dispatched dissenting shareholders with the product and placated the rest with the world's largest satellite dish. However, the dish blocked out the sun and the orchard died, sending the estate and its central residence into disrepair. In order to prop up the perceived value, what's left of the dysfunctional Cross family hire a young, idealistic woman to run what they hope will be a failed campaign to save the orchard and sell it off to developers in the wake of good publicity. However, she sticks to her ideals and fights the family to try and actually succeed.

The Cross family, as can be imagined, are quite loathsome, and

---

3. Jonathan Larson. Folder '* 1/2 MT House'. Contained within disk12.img. Jonathan Larson Papers, Music Division, Library of Congress, Washington, D.C.

These dates are taken from the 'Created On' and 'Last Edited On' dates on Larson's computer files. The hard copies are undated, and these dates, which remain consistent across copies on different floppy disks, are the best available source.

the character biographies are filled with references to incestuous sexual abuse, fraudulent evangelism, closeted AIDS patients, and racists. The upper-class white men are blatantly evil, and the wise minority women aim to save the day.

The second version is more confused (and confusing): The 1990s are a post-apocalyptic era without oil, and the show is now about the Hope and Paine families. Amongst the Hopes are Daisy and Penny, a pair of New-Age idealists who escaped their urban ghetto, Oliver Wendell, a toddler, and Spike, the angry brother they left behind. Patriarch Earnest is an army General and (first) Gulf War hero. The Paines are a political family, and sound-bite-spewing patriarch Tom-Tom is the US president.[4] Angel, the president's daughter, is a Mimi prototype (skinhead heroin-addict singer, into S&M, raped by her father), and her boyfriend Jeremy has the same plot device as early drafts of *RENT*'s Roger (old car he never drives but wants to use to escape). On the perimeter are the head of the Broadway landlord Shubert family (he likes that Penny runs support groups at his old theatre), Reverend Whitey Cross (a closeted evangelist), and *Newhart* parodies Bob and Shirley Hart, an ageing couple gone paranoid from their world's decline. Larson built these characters out of archetypes ("Soldier - Black Man," "Sad Skinny Girl") and based them upon the friends he wanted to play each role.[5]

Larson spent more time working on the first version, and his handwritten notes remain in the archive. At first, he thought of naming the show or setting after an anagram of 'America' before working out 'Dustin Estate' as an anagram of 'United States'.[6]

4. Jonathan Larson. *1/2 MT House - or "deform follows disfunction"*. Box 1, Folder 1, Jonathan Larson Papers, Music Division, Library of Congress, Washington, D.C., 1H.

5. Jonathan Larson. Characters (*1/2 MT House*). Box 1, Folder 1, Jonathan Larson Papers, Music Division, Library of Congress, Washington, D.C., 8H.

6. Jonathan Larson. Handwritten Note. Box 1, Folder 1, Jonathan Larson

The house would be as much a character as the inhabitants, each scene taking place in a different room and symbolising a different aspect of American life. A key theme was to be "isolation and community," as one note states: "We're living under the same roof but we don't see each other - we're afraid to connect."[7]

After sending some early notes to his 'Uncle' Dave, Larson was greeted with the sort of response an idealist would hope for:

> [Y]ou're doodling with an idea that is, potentially, much bigger and more important than SUPERBIA. […] Just about every day one reported act of idiocy or irresponsibility or cheating or violence or deception or another leads me to, literally, scream out loud, in frustration and despair, not only about the present but the future, which belongs to your generation and the generation of our grandchildren.
>
> As a nation, we still pay lip service to our democratic history, but the bottom truth is: We've lost it. Most, if not all, of it.[8]

While Larson had themes and a message, he had trouble finding the plot. He knew he wanted Penny the idealist to blow up the Cross family's satellite dish (they told her she couldn't enact her rescue plan without sleeping with her boss), but no other details for the story ever came together. Despite not having a script, this edition's character relationships were so complicated that Larson himself needed a diagram with multiple lines looping back and

---

Papers, Music Division, Library of Congress, Washington, D.C., 29-30H.

7. Ibid., 54H. Underline in original.

8. David Maness. Letter to Jonathan Larson. Box 1, Folder 1, Jonathan Larson Papers, Music Division, Library of Congress, Washington, D.C.

forth to keep track of his cast.[9] At one point, he went so far as to ignore actual characters and just go for types, such as "the psychos" or "the lovers" before asking "who's in the room/past/present/future?[10]

Larson did work out a rough song list, which included the entirety of *Presidential Politics*, 'Valentine's Day,' 'Open Road,' and nine new (incomplete) songs. A demo exists for the planned opening - a rhythmic hip-hop track proclaiming the legend of Wiley Jack Cross - but the remaining songs never made it past their first drafts, with only lyrics ever written. One exception, 'Love the Pain,' would be rewritten into the first all-Larson edition of *RENT*. Still, a musical is not songs alone, and the story continued to prove elusive. While Uncle Dave may have loved the idea of blowing apart the issues CNN happily glossed over, he was only able to offer suggestions for how to line up the show's underlying messages, as well as a tip from his own experience as a literary editor: "Never use [a pun] in a title, whether it's for a show or a song."[11]

By June 1991, Larson was reworking his ideas, but time had gotten away from him: May and June were spent performing with Roger Bart in *Billy Bishop Goes to War* in New Jersey, along with underscoring the New Jersey Shakespeare Festival's *A Midsummer Night's Dream. tick, tick... BOOM!* was going to the Village Gate, and Larson was trying his hand at screenwriting, adapting *Superbia* as a film and sending off a spec script for TV history drama *The Wonder Years* in the hope of getting attention during a writer's strike. The house of Larson's schedule had gone from half-empty

---

9. Jonathan Larson. Handwritten Note. Box 1, Folder 1, Jonathan Larson Papers, Music Division, Library of Congress, Washington, D.C., 42H.

10. Ibid., 43H. Questions amalgamated for brevity.

11. David Maness. Letter to Jonathan Larson. Box 1, Folder 1, Jonathan Larson Papers, Music Division, Library of Congress, Washington, D.C.

to overflowing, and word was soon to come that his friends were falling ill. Another issue gained higher priority.

You Can't Go Home Again

After Larson's material was initially catalogued, Victoria Leacock Hoffman and producer Robyn Goodman began discussing the possibility of building a show from catalogue highlights. Goodman had helped Larson get *Boho Days* off the ground at Second Stage in 1990 and was now producing for the non-profit Manhattan Theatre Club. Leacock Hoffman, also a founding board member at the Jonathan Larson Performing Arts Foundation, had access to the materials and found Larson's outlines for *1/2 MT House*. It seemed like a match made in heaven.

At first, the pair considered following the simplest of Larson's ideas - a song set in each room of a house. Leacock Hoffman reached out to fellow Adelphi alumnus and Larson collaborator David G. Armstrong for help, and a small table reading was organised to test the concept. For the next six months, from September 1998 through March 1999, Armstrong and Leacock Hoffman went through Larson's musical output, trying to pick the best songs possible. Some material, however, was off limits: *Superbia* had been optioned for a film adaptation, and contractual obligations meant none of the songs from *J.P. Morgan Saves the Nation* could be repurposed. As a sign of respect, *tick, tick... BOOM!* was omitted as well, the work being too personal and wounds left by Larson's death too raw to approach so soon. Everything else - including all of Larson's collaborative work going back to his time at Adelphi - was fair game.

After the initial reading - one which presented the show as a concert or revue - Leacock Hoffman and Goodman decided to push the show in a different direction, one which attempted to

do for *1/2 MT House* what *I Made Me a Promise* did for *Blocks*: turning a conceptual revue into a traditional musical with more well-defined characters. Armstrong was not amused: "It was very sudden, and out of nowhere, I got this message that what we'd spent the last six months working on wasn't the idea for the show anymore." Out of loyalty to his deceased friend, he stuck with the project as Leacock Hoffman and Goodman hired another ex-Larson collaborator, *tick, tick... BOOM!* director and Naked Angel Pippin Parker to write a script.

Before songs could be re-selected, Parker needed to decide how to execute Larson's concepts. Eschewing a linear plot, he focused on Larson's idea of a collage built upon the residents of an old house split into different apartments. The characters would interact, but stay largely restricted to their own smaller worlds and stories. "We tried to remain loyal to some sketchy information that we had from Jonathan," Parker recalls. On paper, Parker's *1/2 MT House* read like a Naked Angels show, full of monologues from unhappy people revealing edgy backstories. In practice, making the show work would be far more difficult.

As Parker built up his characters, Armstrong focused on selecting songs to fit the situations and graded 90 options from 0-3 in terms of how good the song was and how well it could fit the show. Leacock and Parker composed similar lists, and the group compromised as best they could, based on what could be done without altering the music. The final setlist came from Larson's various Adelphi cabarets, *Blocks*, *Away We Go*, and a handful of pop songs and one-off contributions to larger projects. Parker took some characters from Larson's *1/2 MT* outlines and reworked others from earlier works - at one point, even Velma from Larson and Armstrong's *Pageantry* makes an appearance. Some of the characters know each other, some don't, and the script makes no reference about any sort of time or place.

In most cases, songs would be integrated with few-to-no lyrical revisions. Others, however, were rewritten from the ground up: Armstrong rewrote the three 'Moment of Silence' tracks from *Saved!* to be about uncomfortable nursing home visits (versus the originals about school prayer) and environmental hymn 'Pura Vida' became 'Empty Spaces,' a makeshift introduction. With home internet penetration growing, Alicia Stone was tapped to update the lyrics to 'Atarii Videoland' to discuss the early days of online gaming. Unfortunately, none of these rewrites actually improved upon the originals.

Complicating matters further was the lack of a musicologist on the team. While Kimberly Grigsby, an up-and-coming music director later known for her animated, barefoot conducting on Broadway, worked as the musical director for *1/2 MT*'s backer's reading, the core trio of Armstrong, Parker, and Leacock Hoffman were forced to play the composer's role despite none of them having a music background. "There wasn't, compositionally speaking, a proxy for Jonathan," remembers Parker. "If you change a lyric to help this song [or] narrative moment, that's dicey. We didn't have someone to do that. We didn't figure that out ahead of time. We put it together without a huge power strategy." Problems began popping up as songs stopped working (if they ever had), and the team found it increasingly difficult to work together. The conflicts off-stage began trumping those on-stage as styles consistently clashed: "Pippin's writing tends to be very subtle," explains Leacock Hoffman, "and David wasn't."

Parker's writing also clashed with Larson's music. The new script leaned toward the morose, full of characters exposing self-pity and lower-middle-class misery. As Parker recalls: "The source material that related directly to *1/2 MT House*... there was a certain kind of a darkness there, and I think we plucked out material that was more of a dark nature as we started to thread the pieces of the story together. I don't think we imposed anything on [it]." As the characters spoke of peeping on neighbours, running into unpleasant exes, and visiting dying relatives, the related songs could be appropriate, split to unrelated characters, or clash entirely: one character reaches a breaking point with his controlling, shut-in parent, only to follow up his outburst with Larson and Kagan's jaunty tune 'I Told My Mother I Hate Her'. A generous person could call this an attempt at Brechtian alienation, wherein the audience is deliberately distanced to remind them they are watching a show and need to focus on the larger issues being discussed, but a realist would be more direct: the song was tonally discordant and a poor fit for such a lachrymose, depressing piece.

The depressing tone was – as Armstrong (and the author) believe - ultimately the show's biggest problem: at a time when the mourning process had been extended by *RENT*'s runaway success and the subsequent media circus, a show about people at their emotional nadir may have been an inappropriate way to celebrate the composer's untapped legacy.

Despite the problems behind the scenes, the *1/2 MT House* reading boasted a rock-solid cast including *RENT* alumnus Rodney Hicks, then-unknown actress Natascia Diaz, and *Star Search* champion Sam Harris, who was coming off an acclaimed run in Tony-Award-nominated musical *The Life*. A video was shot during one of the last rehearsals, and the script's problems were only magnified in performance: murky storylines, fuzzy relationships, and a leaden story holding down 15 songs which could have stood on their own. Money was not raised, the house was fully emptied, and Leacock and Goodman focused their energies more productively in the aftermath to revive *tick, tick... BOOM!*

Leacock ultimately ascribes the show's problems to "three people who each wanted it to be something different." Parker, however, is more poetic: "There were three people trying to make something that, in the end, belonged to someone who was absent and couldn't respond and help us."

Regardless of *1/2 MT House*'s legacy, something joyous and smart is waiting to be created from Larson's deeper cuts. One day, that show might be found.

Appendix A

Additional Works

I N ADDITION TO his major works, Larson wrote pop and cabaret
songs, dabbled in screenwriting, and scored dance pieces.
Smaller works with an interesting story that fall outside the
main arc of Larson's development are discussed here.

Jonathan Burkhart on Larson's Working Methods

> At [Larson]'s desk, where he worked in his apart-
> ment, he had little sayings up there for years and
> drove them into my head. Some of them, which
> he recited to me daily, were: "Actions speak louder
> than words," which was said the most, either in
> times of crisis and people not being dependable,
> or people being dependable and loving and caring;
> "Argue for your limitations, and sure enough,
> they're yours" (Richard Bach); and, "Simplify, sim-
> plify, simplify."[1]

> Steve [Skinner] was Jonathan's engineer, arranger,
> technical master for a little over 10 years.
> Everything Jonathan wrote went to Steve's studio

---

1. Jonathan Larson Memorial Service. Video. 3 Feb 1996. Privately held by
Victoria Leacock Hoffman, Washington, D.C.

in midtown, where it was recorded, and Steve was responsible for showing Jonathan new directions in electronic music, how to produce things, and deserves a great deal of credit for those recordings Jonathan put out.[2]

Steve Skinner on working with Larson in studio

Jonathan was one of the very first people that I worked with as a demo producer. I had just gotten an early system - it was actually called 'The System,' made by Oberheim. This was pre-MIDI. It was a box that was a sequencer, a synthesiser that could play two different sounds, and a drum machine. I think I had it hooked up to a Yamaha DX-7. Somehow, he heard about me and came to my apartment to do a demo - I think the first one was [Mowgli]. I had a little 4-track cassette recorder, sounded horrible. We used a headphone [as a microphone]. We programmed the track on this thing and laid that down on two tracks of the four-track and then did the vocals on the others, and he was happy.

We had a relationship that went on a long time, and he would come by every few months with a new song. I got more gear, and my career started doing better. We really were working in parallel - he was afraid that I'd get to be too famous to work with him. He was one of the easiest people to work with. He'd have these great ideas, and he appreciated what I did. I really had no complaints there.

---

2. Ibid.

[He would say,] "I want it to sound like this - and I trust you." And, not but.

His writing got more sophisticated [as time went on]. Some of his stylistic things stayed the same all the way through. He was very attached to the interval of the open fifth. You can hear that in all of his writing; even the chords of 'Seasons of Love' are based on open fifths. In *Superbia*, they're all over the place. He did bring in other influences as he developed, and he would see what I did and then try to use that in what he wrote.

Larson's home system evolved as well, thanks to gifts from his friends: a Yamaha DX-7 - then the studio standard for digital synthesisers - replaced his Casio keyboard one birthday. To go with it, Traci Robinson persuaded her bosses at Opcode to send Larson a copy of their groundbreaking Studio Vision MIDI sequencing software for the Macintosh. After a robbery left him without a computer or keyboard, the insurance money covered a new Roland keyboard and Mark of the Unicorn's Digital Producer software, bringing Larson's home studio in line software-wise with Skinner's and allowing easier interoperability between the two.

Eddie Rosenstein on creating alongside Larson

We were all young and hungry artists. New York was living on passion and dreams. It felt like it had a locus, like there was actually a way to be in the centre of it. Maybe it was just the naiveté of not having a cell phone and social media and so many options at the time. There were certain places where you went and a few places where everybody you knew would be, and you made plans and went

THERE. It all felt more achievable and attainable. Everybody I knew at that time wanted to make art and to say something. Back then, Larson specifically, myself, a bunch of us, we had no money. We were bonded by our desperation and passion to succeed, and it always felt for [guys like us] like, "Will we ever get there?" We could be honest about that with each other. We talked daily, partly about keeping that fear at bay.

He didn't feel like his world was limited. He was a voracious researcher, which is just as effective. He read the [New York] Times cover to cover. He was a news junkie, totally a free thinker. He was very political and in it from a real social standpoint. Those were passionate conversations. We were exploring the world in huge ways. We could talk about an article in the paper or some issue going on. He was defined by his curiosity and his passion as much as his work. A conversation with Jonathan was always an hour. He was a great conversationalist, and he was absolutely curious and generous of spirit. He'd have wanted to know a lot about you, and he'd have heard, and he was the first person who'd come through for his friends. He was always there for his friends, 100%, and that was as much a priority as his work. If I needed one person I could trust, it would be him. [... H]e was a huge and generous spirit to the people he loved. He wasn't just presenting that to an audience; it's how he saw the world: we are a community.

J. Glitz

After graduating from university, Larson left his Adelphi compatri-
ots and journeyed to the wilds of Michigan, earning his American
Actor's Equity membership by doing summer repertory theatre.
During the 1982 season, Larson met Michigan locals Scott Burkell
and Marin Mazzie, who subsequently became a leading lady on
Broadway. In addition to appearing in the company's main season,
Larson would play piano in the bar afterwards as part of after-show
concerts, Burkell taking vocals.

For the sheltered, midwestern Burkell, meeting Jonathan
Larson was an eye-opener: "I'd never met anyone like him. I was
fascinated by him." At the time, Larson was just starting out as a
writer, but the passion was already there: "I remember we went
and sat on a swing set at a nearby playground," says Burkell, "and
Jonathan sat there and said, 'I'm gonna change the face of musical
theatre' with a totally straight face."

Following that summer, the three friends moved to New York
City, with Larson eventually settling into his now-infamous flat in
the West Village. While the young composer increasingly focused
on his writing, the performance bug remained with him, and
Larson joined Burkell and Mazzie to form the cabaret trio J. Glitz
(the period is pronounced). Playing anywhere they could - from
open mic nights to dive bars - the three friends were ready to conquer the world.

As with much of Larson's early work, the world wasn't ready
for what he had to offer. "We were an odd trio. Nobody knew
what to make of us," says Burkell. "We'd do a mix of covers and
new stuff, and Jonathan arranged everything. He'd string together
a song like 'Tea for Two' and give it new lyrics and put it with
something else. It was all over the map. One time we booked a
gig, and Jonathan's parents were the only people who turned up.

262 | J. Collis

We did the whole show for them anyways." The three performers would also drift in and out of character, with Larson, Burkell, and Mazzie sometimes playing themselves and other times the fictional Joan Glitz (Mazzie), Elwood Fritz (Burkell), and Marv (Larson). Skits would mock fan clubs, posh New York life, and infomercials.

Despite reality falling short of his dreams, Larson continued to set his sights high for the group, handling all booking and publicity (limited as both were) and sending a stream of letters to get the group on *Late Night with David Letterman* (then the hottest show on TV), recording demos, and finding any gig he could. For Burkell and Mazzie, the stars quickly fell from their eyes, even in pursuing minimal comfort during rehearsals: "Jonathan's apartment was always freezing. He loved the place, but we hated it and used to beg him to let us rehearse at Marin's, because she had heat."

Larson's lack of technical knowledge also made for interesting rehearsals. "He didn't know how to notate music back then," says Burkell. "He'd give us a lyrics sheet with arrows going up and down or a note like 'Hold.' He had an unstoppable gift for writing catchy melodies. He created easy to latch onto, ear-friendly melodies - they had to be accessible right off the bat." Original Larson songs in J. Glitz's 1984 setlist included 'Atarii Videoland,' 'Crime Don't Pay' from *The Steak Tartare Caper*, and 'After the Revolution' from *1984*. Covers ranged from Dan Fogelberg's 'The Reach' to 'Somewhere Over the Rainbow' and the group's infamous medley of 'On Broadway,' Petula Clark's 'Downtown,' and the title song from *Fame*.

Even as J. Glitz wound down throughout 1984 and Larson exclusively focused on his writing projects, he remained close with Burkell and Mazzie through the mid-1980s, utilising their talents on his demos for *1984, Mowgli*, and early editions of *Superbia*.

Dance Scores

In the late 1980s, Larson dated Brenda Daniels, a Merce Cunningham dancer establishing her own company in New York, and scored three of her dance concerts during their time together: *Garden Party*, *Venus and Other Myths*, and *Damage*. While much of Daniels' character manifested in *RENT* as Maureen (leaving the author-insert character for a woman, being an avant-garde performance artist), Collins' line in 'La Vie Boheme' about Mimi being 'clad only in bubble wrap, [performing] her famous lawn-chair handcuff dance to the sounds of iced tea being stirred' are direct references to *Venus* (wherein Daniels wore a revealing bubble wrap dress) and *Garden Party* (which opens with three women in lawn chairs, complete with a sequence of comedic mechanical malfunctions to, indeed, the sounds of iced tea being stirred in a pitcher). Larson's compositions were part-sound collage and part-minimalist work inspired by Cunningham's partner and composer of choice, the minimalist icon John Cage.[3]

For all of his dance scores, Larson worked in composition notebooks versus his preferred loose-leaf paper, pasting in clippings from commissions and relevant notes, such as the Cunningham dance philosophy. Runtimes would be approximated, and the material composed and dropped to tape for performance use.

In 1987, Larson scored *Garden Party*, a two-act dance comprised of 'Cartoon Artificial,' a satire on suburban afternoons, and 'Ideal Landscape,' set in the Garden of Eden before the fall of man.[4]

---

3. Cunningham built his technique while at Black Mountain University in 1953. Cunningham-style dance is avant-garde, primarily focused on separating (mostly) minimalistic music from abstract dance - in some of his pieces, the performers would only hear the score for the first time when performing - and on creating works which use ballet moves with non-ballet meanings.

4. Daniels was gracious enough to supply a DVD of *Garden Party* for viewing.

For dance novices, 'Cartoon Artificial' is the highlight: a tongue-in-cheek spoof mocking idealistic Americana. Three women sit in their backyard and fumble with the lawn furniture before their children enter and play with inflatable dinosaurs. The children leave, and the husbands (the same three male dancers) enter, with one seducing one of the women. The men then chase dollar bills hanging off their heads on wires, and the seducer builds his wife a tower made of household goods such as laundry detergent boxes. The act ends with her destroying the tower. The piece is light and comedic, easy to follow, and never outstays its welcome.

'Ideal Landscape' is, in Daniels' words, "showing an idyllic and supportive pure-dance 'Eden.'" The lights are low, the choreography fluid and abstract. For those not versed in dance linguistics and the inherent meanings in the movements, 'Landscape' can be difficult to follow: a dreamy haze of repetitive motion expressed through pure Cunningham - dance about dance, moving independently of the traditional languages of ballet and the score.

Saying Larson scored *Garden Party* is something of a misnomer, as 'Cartoon Artificial' features a sound collage, rather than music. The score for 'Ideal Landscape' is John Cage-inspired minimalism, ethereal and spacey, building upon a synthesiser drone and crashing waves before culminating in a symphony of strings, scratching pencils, and finally, a distant, female voice reading key lines from W.B. Yeats' *Her Anxiety*.

Larson clearly desired to create a work in the Cunningham-Cage model for Daniels, as his notes for *Garden Party* as well as *Venus and Other Myths* both contain the same quotes which Larson attributes to Cage:

The function of music is to sober and quiet the mind, thus rendering it susceptible to divine influences.[5]

Art shouldn't be concerned with entertainment and communication or symbolic expression of the artist's ideas and tastes, but should help men and women attain a more intense awareness of their own life.[6]

Larson's work on Daniels' dance scores netted him his first review in the *New York Times* for *Damage*, with critic Jack Anderson stating: "[Daniels] made her thematic points to a recorded accompaniment that combined an original score by Jonathan Larson with old pop songs. The ferocity of the choreography and the clamor of Mr. Larson's music prevented those songs from inducing nostalgia."[7] Janet Charleston - Larson's soon-to-be girlfriend - performed in *Damage* as well, dancing a solo.

Larson also composed a score for *Roam*, choreographed by William Douglas. *Roam*'s music starts out based on heavy percussion, with synthesised flutes and keys above a ticking clock and hefty drum beat. Orchestrally, this section is similar to the opening credits on *Away We Go*, though melodically unrelated. The second section calls to mind science fiction, boasting ethereally echoing synths and howling wolves. The last section is gentle, featuring an acoustic guitar playing a simple melody as the ticking clock and wolves fade in and out alongside a blowing wind and passing train.

5. Jonathan Larson. Garden Party (Notebook). Box 4, Folder 15, Jonathan Larson Papers, Music Division, Library of Congress, Washington, D.C.

Jonathan Larson. Venus & Other Myths (Notebook). Box 35, Folder 7, Jonathan Larson Papers, Music Division, Library of Congress, Washington, D.C.

6. Ibid.

7. Jack Anderson. 'Reviews/Dance; Aggression and Passion in Many Guises.' *New York Times*. 08 Jan 1990. Accessed 26 Jan 2016: http://www.nytimes.com/1990/01/08/arts/reviews-dance-aggression-and-passion-in-many-guises.html.

Miscellaneous Songs

Larson wrote over 20 pop songs, hoping to either get a record deal for himself, sell the songs to performers such as Bette Midler, or both.

Jonathan Burkhart (on cleaning out Larson's flat and arranging his tapes)

> The amazing thing was that I'd come across these pop songs. He'd say, "Oh, I'm gonna go and do the pop song thing for a while," and he'd write like 10 pop songs and record them at Steve Skinner's, and they worked and they were really good, and then he'd shelve them.[8] He did that over and over again, so I found like pop songs here, pop songs there. They were catchy! They were so fuckin' catchy! And he knew the Taylor Dane/Mariah Carey syndrome, how to make a song sound that way.[9]

Some highlights follow, arranged in rough chronological order.

Kip Hubbard Collaborations

Via Larson's friend Todd Robinson:

---

8. In the early days after Larson's death, the volume of his output was over-estimated based on the volume of raw material in his archives, not considering the multiple drafts of different lyrics or alternative recordings of songs (e.g. just background music, duplicates across formats, etc.). In reality, the "10 pop songs" at a time mentioned here was more like two or three.

9. *RENT* to Broadway. Video. February 1996. Privately held by Victoria Leacock Hoffman, Washington, D.C.

Kip [Hubbard] is one of my best buddies. We met because my childhood girlfriend and his girlfriend at the time had been roommates as actresses at Point Park. Kip was in advertising, a total button-down white collar dude working for a big ad agency. At that point, I was looking for something entrepreneurial where I could do a one-man show or some way I could showcase myself as an actor. His girlfriend said he was a writer. I'd found a book on Billy the Kid and the Lincoln County War, and I became sort of infatuated with that piece, and I met with Kip and said maybe we could do a play, and started to write the thing together. It didn't get to a performance, but 10 years later, I made a documentary about it and won an Emmy Award. But Kip was this guy who was sort of a poet, and Jonathan was always looking for material, and I brought them together. Those songs were written on a junky upright Spinet piano that we hauled into an apartment we shared on West End Avenue. They would come together with an idea, and Kip would write to the music, or Jonathan would compose to the lyrics.

Hubbard, who now lives in the mountains and teaches drum circles, describes his relationship with Larson in simpler terms: "Jon and I were friends, and he put my few goofy poems to music. I wouldn't characterize our relationship as musically collaborative. In fact, until I received [a] packet from Amy Asch in around 2000, I don't think I realized Jon had even recorded [them]."[10]

---

10. Amy Asch was the Larson Family's official archivist, compiling backstories and organising Larson's mountain of tapes and papers for the family's records before sending the majority of the material on to the Library of Congress. When the Jonathan Larson Performing Arts Foundation closed its office in 2009, Asch's

268 | J. Collis

'Barroom Conversation' is a highlight amongst Larson's non-theatrical songs, and the demo is passionate despite Larson flubbing the words. In the lyrics, the singer talks about the average man's longing helplessness, hiding in small talk as the world approaches its own self-destruction:

> We pass barroom conversation,
>
> Nothing more than meets the eye.
>
> And when we turn to tell another joke,
>
> We find that life has passed us by.
>
> […]We find little animation,
>
> In our catatonic state.
>
> But simply sketch a path to emptiness,
>
> While our minds we abdicate.[11]

'Building Castles' is similarly melancholic, about the passage of time and facing the disappointment of crumbling dreams and aspirations. 'Giznoid Claptrap' is a reggae pastiche about an office janitor who dreams of rising to the top of his father's firm - except his father is only a middle manager and the son is merely "heir to the company car."[12] Despite that, he lives a flashy, wealth-driven lifestyle. "Weird Al" Yankovic would cover similar ground a year later in the song 'Buy Me A Condo,' where a Jamaican immigrant dreams of a comfortable, trendy suburban life.

---

database and documents went into storage. As such, they are currently unavailable for reference.

11. Kip Hubbard (Text) & Jonathan Larson (Music). 'Barroom Conversation'. Box 8, Folder 9, Jonathan Larson Papers, Music Division, Library of Congress, Washington, D.C.

12. Kip Hubbard (Text) & Jonathan Larson (Music). 'Giznoid Claptrap'. Box 8, Folder 9, Jonathan Larson Papers, Music Division, Library of Congress, Washington, D.C.

'Flame'

via Todd Robinson: "'Flame' was a Jonathan Larson song that was interesting because it was based on a high school girlfriend, very pretty. We might have performed it in our trio. It's basically a heartbreak song."

'Yerikerligah'

With its unpronounceable title (think "you're a curly guy"), 'Yerikerligah' combined the verse music from 'Barroom Conversation' and the chorus from the epilogue of Larson's then-current musical, *1984*. The lyrics are Harry Chapin politics mixed with a Billy Joel tune about a wanderer encountering a young boy, a soldier, a doctor, and finally, an old man, who encourage him to live his life and speak up for what is right.

'Sushirama'/'Casual Sex and Pizza and Beer'[13]

If Jonathan Larson had written the *American Psycho* musical back in 1985, its opening number would have been 'Sushirama'. The song is written from the perspective of a woman who goes on a blind date at a trendy restaurant, parties at a fancy club, and goes home with the man, only to leave before he wakes up, claiming she "hate[s] melodrama - See you tonight at the Enchiladarama."[14] 'Casual Sex and Pizza and Beer' is a drinking waltz in honour of the titular material.

---

13. Songs which were written together/archived to the same tape are presented as one listing.

14. 'Sushirama'/'Casual Sex and Pizza and Beer'. MAVIS 186838-3-1. Jonathan Larson Recordings, Recorded Sound Division, Library of Congress, Washington, D.C.

'It Only Takes A Few'/'All I Know'

Larson wrote 'It Only Takes A Few' about the summer he met Jonathan Burkhart (who contributed to the lyrics) on Nantucket and the house they and their friends shared. The song is catchy and upbeat, talking about friends enjoying the sun and each other's company - the kind of once-in-a-lifetime summer Hollywood idealises - professing that "It only takes a few good friends to be first class / First class only takes a few."[15]

At roughly the same time, Larson wrote and mastered 'All I Know,' a Police-esque love song. The track appears with further notes on the *Jonathan Sings Larson* CD.

Mark O'Donnell Collaborations

When people talk about a friend of a friend, they usually mean it in a gossipy way. In this case, it led to five songs.

Victoria Leacock, through her own connections, knew Paul Shaffer - leader of the *Late Night with David Letterman* band, and invited him to see Larson and Armstrong's *Saved!* in 1983.[16] Shaffer liked the show and suggested to Leacock that Larson get in touch with Steve O'Donnell, one of Letterman's writers. Larson dashed off a letter, and while Steve O'Donnell was uninterested, he introduced the composer to his twin brother (and musical theatre fan) Mark.[17] The pair would write five songs, including New Wave pop

15. *Mowgli* Demos/'It Only Takes A Few'/'All I Know'. MAVIS 186211-3-3. Jonathan Larson Recordings, Recorded Sound Division, Library of Congress, Washington, D.C.

16. At the time, Letterman was in his ascendency, being broadcast after *The Tonight Show*, at around 1AM. Letterman would feature younger, more up-and-coming bands and edgier comics amongst his guests, as Johnny Carson's *Tonight Show* was aimed at an older demographic.

17. A draft of Larson's letter to Steve O'Donnell is in Larson's papers, but the exact details of how Larson got from one O'Donnell to the other are obscured.

tune 'The Earth is Turning,' novelty songs 'You Owe Me A Dollar' and 'Suffers from the Heat,' the hypnotic 'Remember Me,' and 'All For Now,' a mournful torch song. Arranged demos were recorded for all five numbers, with Larson on vocals.

'Genre in a Drum'/'Out of My Dreams'

Two songs, one backing track. 'Genre in a Drum' was written during Larson's Area days, created more as the music for a satirical video project than an actual song. An avid reader of *Details*, Victoria Leacock found an article by clubbing guru Stephen Saban about a nasty run of nights: dinners not being served, boring near-identical parties, and crowds refusing to move out of the way and let people pass. Leacock and Larson pulled a handful of highlights, got Leacock's friend, up-and-coming comedian Ben Stiller, to narrate, and Larson scored a seven-and-a-half minute epic of drum machines and passive-aggressive synths beneath a cheerful female chorus singing, "It's times like these, I wish I were licensed to kill…"[18] Leacock took the tape to Paul Shaffer, hoping to get it produced as a video to play at clubs across town, but the project never moved forward.

In 1991, Larson would reuse 'Genre in a Drum''s backing track for a segment in Brenda Daniels' *Venus and Other Myths*. 1991 also saw Larson write 'Genre in a Drum' a new lyric and relaunch the song as 'Out of My Dreams,' a sultry breakup song about being unable to leave everything behind:

Nasty words

This is the most likely scenario. Mark O'Donnell passed away in August 2012 and is most fondly remembered among musical theatre enthusiasts as a co-author on the 2002 stage adaptation of John Waters' *Hairspray*.

18. Saban himself posted the song online for a bit at the World of Wonder Productions blog, but the link is now dead.

on the telephone

alarm goes off

I'm in bed alone

You left my life

stay out of my dreams.[19]

The new, female vocal provided a mix of spoken and sung stanzas with a varied echoes and a vocal line *a la* turn-of-the-decade pop artists such as Paula Abdul.

'Hosing the Furniture'

The American Music Theatre Festival, now renamed the Prince Music Theatre (after legendary Broadway director and producer Harold Prince), was founded in 1984 to develop and premiere new American musicals. Each year, a gala would be held to present awards and grants managed by the festival's staff, as well as to preview a show in development. In 1989, David Thompson, Michael Barrett, and R. J. Cutler presented their ambitious collaboration, *Sitting on the Edge of the Future*. The show looked at how past, present, and future interact by building scenes around a family visiting the 1939 World's Fair. The Fair - held 50 years earlier when such things still garnered international attention - was a grand display where nations would send cutting edge works of art, industry, and science to showcase themselves on a global stage. Amongst the composers on the project were Michael John LaChiusa (*The Wild Party, See What I Wanna See*), Scott Frankel (*Grey Gardens*), and Jonathan Larson.

Future's pitch asked the composers to create songs based on different exhibitions and to look at the "perfect world created

---

19. Jonathan Larson. 'Out of My Dreams'. Box 36, Folder 5, Jonathan Larson Papers, Music Division, Library of Congress, Washington, D.C.

by man and machine. [...] What would happen if a young boy attending the fair with his family actually found himself magically transported into 'The World of Tomorrow?'"[20] Participants were given a rough outline of the story, along with excerpts from period publicity materials and articles. Larson took particular interest in a scene from the second act, wherein a futuristic housewife cleans not with a dust rag and vacuum, but a garden hose. Her entire home is filled with streamlined curves, and everything - from the books to the sofa - is made from waterproof material. All she has to do is rinse it off.

Larson knew the song would be seen by a veritable who's who of attendees, including Sondheim, and worked feverishly to perfect it. Taking a page from the master, he aimed to write a "disjointed, spacy [sic]" song similar to 'Putting It Together' from Sondheim's *Sunday in the Park with George*.[21] Sold on the concept of spray cleaning, he fished for his angle: 1939's future woman would still be a housewife - what were her daily goals? Did they make her happy? Larson scratched out lyric after lyric, trying to capture his subjugated subject.

The struggle was worth it: 'Hosing the Furniture' is a jumpy, laugh-out-loud roller coaster as a seemingly sublime housewife revels in her compulsion for cleanliness, subsequently exasperating her own fears about ageing and her loveless marriage, tragically leading to a full breakdown:

MY HAIR! MY GOD! A GREY HAIR (OUCH)

TOM LIKES COCKTAIL ONIONS

TOM NODDED OFF AGAIN LAST NIGHT

---

20. David Thompson, Michael Barrett, & R.J. Cutler. 'From the Artistic Team' in *Sitting on the Edge of the Future* Programme. Box 21a, Folder 5, Jonathan Larson Papers, Music Division, Library of Congress, Washington, D.C., 1.

21. Jonathan Larson. Handwritten Note. Box 21a, Folder 5, Jonathan Larson Papers, Music Division, Library of Congress, Washington, D.C., 68H.

WAS IT ME? WAS IT--?

I GET TREATED LIKE DIRT-

OH, DIRT, DIRT- HERE'S A SQUIRT!

WHAT A GLOW![22]

The song consistently builds in tempo, making it one of Larson's most difficult works to perform, with Mrs. Modern required to deliver dense lyrics while falling apart at the crescendo. Because the number offers so many stumbling blocks (phrases are repeated and the song follows a standard pop formula, albeit with subtle variations each time), 'Hosing the Furniture' can be sublime when performed well, as by original singer Judy Kaye at AMTF, or Natascia Diaz at the 2006 Jonathan Larson Tribute Concert at the Library of Congress, but any actress attempting to perform it skirts the edge of disaster.

'Iron Mike'/'Gotta Get Extreme'

These two songs were written at roughly the same time as 'White Male World' for Maggie Lally's cabarets at the New York Repertory Theatre Company, but Amy Asch's catalogue of Larson's work never pinpoints their exact use. 'Iron Mike' is lyrically dated but the better of the two numbers: a seafaring ballad about the Exxon Valdez oil spill, combining searing lyrics with gentle music. 'Gotta Get Extreme' is a comedic song about doing what it takes to get attention, be it in art or politics.

---

22. Jonathan Larson. 'Hosing the Furniture', stored as 'HOSING THE FURNITURE' (Microsoft Word File). Contained within disk29.dmg. Jonathan Larson Papers, Music Division, Library of Congress, Washington, D.C.

'Pura Vida'

Larson wrote 'Pura Vida' (Pure Life) in September 1991, his files for the song kept with materials from *tick, tick… BOOM!* Larson's initial notes ask: "What if the world ran like a river?" and suggest "environmental focus," "rainforest festival," "co-operative global environment or community through competition".[23] The song is a harmonic tribute to innocence and nature:

> We are the people who float on the river
>
> […] Birds laugh and the sun she smiles
>
> and the trees, they dance in the wind
>
> Can this race endure?[24]

as well as the threats they face:

> Must there be finish lines?
>
> The rivers will dry - and the birds will die[25]

'We Can't Go On This Way'/'You Called My Name'

These two songs were Larson's 1991 attempt to break into the world of adult contemporary. 'We Can't Go On This Way' is a solo breakup ballad. 'You Called My Name' is smooth jazz, about a couple finding love: "I knew I'd never be lonely again / When you called my name." Idina Menzel and Taye Diggs sang the song together (then at the start of their relationship) at the 1997 Today 4 U benefit concert. Roger Bart sang on the demo for both songs, though the female singer on ''Name' is unknown.

23. Jonathan Larson. Handwritten Note. Box 34, Folder 4, Jonathan Larson Papers, Music Division, Library of Congress, Washington, D.C.

24. Jonathan Larson. 'Pura Vida' (Lyrics & Chords). Box 34, Folder 4, Jonathan Larson Papers, Music Division, Library of Congress, Washington, D.C. 1-2H

25. Ibid., 3H

'Love Heals'[26]

Alison Gertz was far from being a stereotypical AIDS patient. Upper middle class, well-educated, and infected at 16 by her boyfriend during their sole sexual encounter, Gertz became a poster child for HIV's widespread reach by the time her first symptoms manifested at 22. She would spend the last three years of her life as an activist, speaking up about AIDS' mainstream impact and the importance of teaching young people about safer sex practices. A new face of the disease - one outside the easy-to-shame zones of gay life and inner-city drug users - Gertz was courted by the media and used every possible outlet to make it clear that AIDS was a disease which affected everybody. Love Heals, the Alison Gertz Foundation for AIDS Education, was conceived and named by Ali. Following her death at the age of 26 in 1992, her three best friends - Victoria Leacock, Dini von Mueffling, and Stefani Greenfield - co-founded the organisation along with Gertz's parents, to honour her memory.

To promote the organisation, Leacock asked Larson, who had also befriended Gertz, to write a charity single, in the hopes of getting a celebrity to sing the track and raise funds for the organisation. Larson interviewed the three friends about how the Ali had affected them, turning their answers into a gospel-driven ballad about finding love in hopelessness - something fit for a diva and living up to the name 'Love Heals'. While the project was shelved by 1994, the song was recorded as a bonus for the 2008 *RENT* film's soundtrack album. Gertz would also be memorialised in *RENT* as 'Ali' in the 'Life Support' scene.

---

26. Additional contributions in this section are courtesy of Victoria Leacock Hoffman.

'With Open Eyes'

Larson first became aware of Nan Knighton during *Sacred Cows*. Producer Jeremy Roberts worked (and continues to work) regularly with composer Frank Wildhorn and produced the concept album for Wildhorn's second musical, a collaboration with book and lyrics written by Knighton: *The Scarlet Pimpernel*. After hearing the recording, Larson reached out to Knighton about collaborating on a song or future show. Knighton agreed to meet up, and Larson visited her flat, telling her about *RENT* and discussing other ideas. She was pleased with the meeting and liked that Larson would let her write the words first - Wildhorn prefers to write music and hand it off to lyricists.

Knighton's contribution, 'With Open Eyes,' is about a prostitute seeking a client. The lyrics are explicit and gritty, but also sensual and empowered:

> Does your breath rise
>
> Seeing me smile through a back-alley breeze?
>
> With open eyes
>
> I pull you into my afternoon tease
>
> Imagine me
>
> Backing you into the wall
>
> Fevered and doing it all
>
> With open eyes[27]

These days, Knighton feels the song is "too 'out there' - [now I'd have] made it MUCH more subtle." Larson liked the lyric and composed the music, driven by a silky, Latin-influenced beat.

Similar to Larson's ASCAP workshop days, Knighton was

---

27. Nan Knighton (Text) & Jonathan Larson (Music). 'With Open Eyes'. Box 36, Folder 7, Jonathan Larson Papers, Music Division, Library of Congress, Washington, D.C.

invited to present a concert of her songs at the Donnell Library Center, part of the New York Public Library.[28] Jeremy Roberts played piano, a parade of actors sang, and between numbers, Knighton and the moderator would discuss the songs. Knighton recalls:

> I was truly embarrassed after 'With Open Eyes' when the moderator asked me with a leer, "So what was going on in your life when you wrote that song?" Yuk-yuk. [The] audience laughed, too.

Larson recorded a demo featuring Karmine Alers, and Farah Alvin sang the song at Knighton's *Storybook* cabaret series in 2000.

'Let Go The Line' (For White Squall)

via Todd Robinson, scriptwriter for *White Squall*:

> My career took off long before Jonathan's did. Everything sort of came together for me, and when I discovered writing, I was good at it right away. It was making him crazy. [Larson and Eddie Rosenstein] called me, because they had an idea for this shipwreck, and it was a period piece.[29] Some time later, I was in Hawaii on a family vacation, and my sister brought this [50-year old] guy. After being there for a week, my sister had him tell me a story about a sailboat, and he presented me with

---

28. The Donnell was closed at the end of August 2008, as its building was sold for redevelopment. Plans were delayed three years due to the financial crisis, and after the land changed hands, it was demolished in October 2011. Designs have been approved for a new high-rise building, which will include a library on the lower levels.

29. Larson and Rosenstein collaborated on adapting a screenplay based on Gustave Wrathe's book *The Wreck of the Baroque Stefano Off the North West Cape of Australia in 1875*. It was never produced.

this memoir that he had written as a 16-year-old with a ghost writer. I read it and kicked it around and didn't think much of it [and] didn't know how to make it into a movie. This is 1994-1995 now, and I already had a kid and was married, and Ridley Scott decides to do the movie and we go off to make it.

Along the way, we needed sea shanties, which were work songs. It was to get people in rhythm and pull lines together and raise sails together and be coordinated. We needed some of these songs, [...] so I called [Larson] up and said, "You want to make some money? Write me a couple sea shanties, and I'll play them for Ridley and try and get them in the movie." We needed to have something on set to play so everyone could work together.

I was going down to the Caribbean to shoot the movie, and I flew through JFK, and Jonathan came out to meet me and stayed overnight at the hotel. They had an electronic player piano, and I remember [him] staring at it with such a sense of hate. We spent that night talking about these sea shanties, and Jonathan said he was on it.

So I'm down there on this shoot, and it's a three-month shoot, and I'm in the British Virgin Islands, and he overnights me cassettes. And I'm like, "Cool," but I didn't have a tape player with me. I said to Ridley that I thought we had the shanties and asked if he wanted to hear them, but he didn't have anything to play them on either. So Ridley Scott and I went to a bar in the middle of

St. Vincent, and it was empty because it was lunch time, and played these sea shanties over their stereo system. It's me and Ridley Scott in the middle of the Caribbean, listening to Jonathan Larson singing, "Yo ho! Yo ho!" and it was absurd and so funny, and Ridley looked over at me like, "Who is this guy?" and I was just like, "He's cool, I swear to God!" but Ridley thought they were amazing. The only reason the song didn't get used in the movie was because I had to fly back to the States for my daughter's birth. We filmed on this giant square rig sailing ship called the Eye of the Wind, and those guys had their own sailing songs, and on the day, they started teaching their songs to the cast, and that's what ended up in the movie.

More about *RENT*

Time to be on your way, comrade
It's been 525,600 moments clad
We were nomads together in a no-man's land.

—RENT (cut lyric)

As discussed in chapter seven, writing *RENT* was not a case of just sitting down and plopping out a show along a neat and easy timeline. There are all sorts of interesting issues regarding *RENT*'s development, and I chose to separate the sections below from the prior chapter for the sake of narrative cohesion. This appendix is for the diehard Rentheads who have to know all the little details.

RENT Choreographer Marlies Yearby on the show's iconic moments

I had never intended, when I choreographed 'Contact,' for it to remain on a wall. It was just something where I used the wall in the room, because the wall was there. I had intended that I would evolve this language - which I did many years later by accident when there was a tour where the wall could not fit in several venues, so I was called out to choreograph a Contact B-Version which had no wall. And I remember hearing Jeffrey [Seller] state something like, "Oh my goodness, that's almost better than--," and he caught himself, and I laughed to myself. There was never time to do more than swipe. I would swipe, and everyone would say, "That's great!" and my mind would be going, "No! That's just an outline. I need to now choreograph it," but for them, that was the choreography. It was always like that. Done! Done! Done! So when we went to the Nederlander, sure enough, there was a wall there, and immediately they had lit everything around the wall and had decided that it was going to be on the wall, so there was no time to evolve it. When we were going to Broadway, I thought, "OK, the wall's going. Good, now I can play further." And sure enough, that was the one thing they fought for, was to have a raising wall. It was the one thing that I was ready to let go and the one thing that kept following me everywhere.

The concept of the tables was there in my mind. Once I started dancing on top of the tables, especially with things like Angel jumping on the tables, which came in rehearsal when I was watching Wilson, naturally in the rehearsal room. He always jumped up into a cross-legged position. So I would watch him, and I kept thinking, "Wow, it would be interesting if he jumped up on the table and would dance on the table, and I'm pretty sure he could clear the table" (once I found out he would have four-inch heels), I thought he could clear the table, because of how effortlessly he could jump on the table and sit in a cross-legged position. That whole dancing on the table, the tables then began to be in each world - whether in the lot or the loft or the restaurant - it just became an intricate part of how the dance would express itself, because it became like another level or another surface. Another playing field. I loved the simplicity of the table and how it kept shifting the environment by just its simple movement. That felt very familiar to me, coming from the world of installations.

I think that there are landmarks in the show that people expect to see there: Angel jumping on the table, jumping off the table is key. Mimi kicking down the stair[s] is key. 'La Vie Boheme' gestures at the top, they need to see those gestures. I can change whatever I want to change, but they need to see those little head bouncing hand gestures, that needs to happen, and that goes through the show that way - certain landmarks that people know and fans actually enact in their seats. In reality, every show that was re-mounted changed. There were certain landmarks that we made sure were hit, but other things about it change and in a good way. It's the thing that has kept it alive. I do believe that Jonathan would have absolutely rewritten and been inspired by some of the things he saw in the room with characters addressing the work."

La Vie (La Opera) Bohème

While *RENT*'s core is an adaptation of *La Bohème* by Giacomo Puccini (libretto by Giuseppe Giacosa and Luigi Illica and based on short stories by Henri Murger), Larson had no problem taking liberties to enhance the story or characters - as always, a good song or key emotion was more important than maintaining minutiae. Though Aronson's scripts remained close to Puccini's structure and events, it is Larson's deviations which brought *RENT* into its own and make it both a modern story and a more complex and layered one than *Bohème*'s.

Ever the diligent researcher, Larson made comparison charts to contrast his creations with their Puccinian parallels, and some characters have direct 1:1 mappings (Puccini's Rodolfo is Roger, the flirtatious Musetta became Larson's Maureen, and even Parpignol the toy dealer becomes the Pied-Piper-like The Man, albeit for drug addicts), while others are more complicated. Marcello, a painter in *La Bohème*, is split into Mark, the filmmaker and bohemian narrator, and Joanne, Maureen's love interest, in *RENT*.[1] Benny is a combination of Benoit, *La Bohème*'s landlord, and the Viscount Paolo, with whom Puccini's Mimi flirts in *Bohème*'s cut third act, but is referenced in Puccini's final third and fourth acts. The homeless, police, and other ensemble characters are all original to *RENT*.

Larson also tracked *La Bohème*'s story beats based on the libretto and recordings, but did not see the show properly in person until he was already working on *RENT* in depth.[2] As producer Kevin McCollum remembers, "After we committed to the project, Jeffrey [Seller, one of *RENT*'s other producers] and I took Jonathan to see *La Bohème* at the [Metropolitan Opera,] because he'd never seen

---

1. Early drafts would imply Joanne is also supposed to be Alcindoro, Musetta's wealthy admirer whom she sends off during the cafe scene to get with Marcello, then sticks with everyone's bill.

2. He had, however, seen a puppet show version as a child.

it. We got out, and he said, '[Rodolfo] meets Mimi in the first 10 minutes!' We said, 'Exactly!'"[3] Following all the updates, restructures, and cuts, the following events in *RENT* are straight out of *La Bohème:*[4]

RENT Song Name	Relevant Action in (*RENT*)	Song in *La Bohème**
Tune-Up	Mark/Roger are broke and attempting to create.	Questo Mar Rosso
Rent	Mark/Roger burn their work to stay warm	Questo Mar Rosso/ Già dell'Apocalisse
Light My Candle	Roger and Mimi meet. They employ different tricks to stay together.	Non sono in vena! through Sì. Mi chiamano Mimì
Today 4 U	Angel describes being hired to kill a wealthy person's pet in exchange for a large sum of money	Abasso, abbasso l'autor!
You'll See	Benny comes to demand the rent.	Si può" - "Chi è là?
Christmas Bells	The group go shopping at St. Mark's Bazaar on Christmas Eve.	Arranci, datteri! Questa è Mimi, gaia fioraia

3. Presumably, this would have been in late 1994 or early 1995: 'Light My Candle,' Mimi's introduction, is 21 minutes in on the October 1994 studio recording (and had been at 27 minutes in 1993). The October 1995 demo has 'Light My Candle' starting after 17 minutes, and Larson ultimately got it down to 15 minutes by his death.

4. *La Bohème*, like most operas, is only broken into acts, not individual songs and scenes like most musicals. For a libretto, I relied upon William Weaver's translation in the ENO's Overture Opera Guide from 2010.

RENT Song Name	Relevant Action in (*RENT*)	Song in *La Bohème**
La Vie Bohème	The group have dinner and celebrate at a popular cafe.	Remainder of Act Two
Take Me or Leave Me	Maureen and Joanne fight over Maureen's endless flirting with others[1]	Dunque è propio finita!
Goodbye Love	Roger tells Mark that Mimi is getting ill, and he can't handle watching her die. The pair break up, and Mimi goes off with Benny.	Mimì è una civetta through Dunque è propio finita!
Finale A	Roger realises his love for Mimi. Maureen and Joanne bring a deathly ill Mimi to the loft, and the pair reconcile while the others search for ways to comfort her physically and find a doctor.	Act Four, excepting Dorme? - Riposa

One could argue that Maureen's performance piece is a throwback to Musetta's party in *La Bohème*'s cut third act, and references came and went throughout the drafts (Roger's joke in early drafts of 'La Vie Bohème' called Mark's film *The Parting of the Red Sea* while Marcello's painting in *Bohème* is *The Crossing of the Red Sea*, Benny's scene in Act One was tonally closer to Puccini), but if *RENT*'s skeleton comes from Puccini, its muscle is the turbulence between its characters, and that is entirely Larson.

Not Dying from Disease

Despite regularly selling off his books for extra money, Larson held on to his copy of *Illness as Metaphor and AIDS and its Metaphors* by Susan Sontag.[5] The book meant enough to him that he listed it as a direct influence on *RENT,* and his admiration for Sontag was strong enough to name-check her in 'La Vie Boheme'. Sontag's book, combining two essays looking at how American society interacts with tuberculosis, cancer, and AIDS and their sufferers, set the tone for Larson's handling of people with AIDS in *RENT.* In Larson's rejected 1994 NEA grant application, he wrote that *RENT* was:

> Inspired, in part, by Susan Sontag's AIDS AND IT'S [sic] METAPHORS, One aim is to quash the already cliched 'AIDS victim' stereotypes and point out that People Living with AIDS can enjoy full lives. RENT also attempts to contrast relationships in today's and Puccini's worlds. (Puccini's Rodolpho and Mimi instantly fall in love-then she dies. In RENT 'Roger' and Mimi do everything in their power NOT to fall in love- until they realize that they are both HIV +.) RENT also exalts 'Otherness', glorifying artists and counterculture as necessary to a healthy civilization. As John F. Kennedy said, "When power corrupts, poetry cleanses."[6]

In *Illness as Metaphor*, Sontag analyses the historical romanticism surrounding tuberculosis. At the time Henry Murger wrote the original short stories compiled in *Scènes de la vie de Bohème,*

---

5. Larson's copy is held with his papers at the Library of Congress.

6. Jonathan Larson. 'Statement of Concept,' stored as "NEA Statement of Concept 94" (Microsoft Word File). Contained within disk144.img. Jonathan Larson Papers, Music Division, Library of Congress, Washington, D.C.

the book upon which Puccini's opera and *RENT* are based, "TB is celebrated as the disease of born victims, of sensitive, passionate people who are not quite life-loving enough to survive."[7] By the end of the Romantic Era, the tubercular look - gaunt, thin, and emaciated - became the look for aristocratic women to aspire to, one which holds out to this day, including the 'heroin chic' look in the 1990s, which Sontag points out "[is] the last stronghold of the metaphors associated with the romanticizing of TB in the late eighteenth and early nineteenth centuries."

Cancer, on the other hand, has no romance: "Ostensibly, the illness is the culprit. But it is also the cancer patient who is made culpable."[8] Unlike TB, cancer is an internalised disease - a physical rebellion - and is spoken about with militaristic language born out of germ theory.[9] "Indeed," Sontag writes in the introductory update from *AIDS and Its Metaphors*,

> the transformation of war-making into an occasion for mass ideological mobilization has made the notion of war useful as a metaphor for all sorts of ameliorative campaigns whose goals are cast as the defeat of an 'enemy.' [...] Abuse of the military metaphor may be inevitable in a capitalist society, a society that increasingly restricts the scope and credibility of appeals to ethical principle, in which

---

7. Susan Sontag. *Illness as Metaphor and AIDS and Its Metaphors*. (New York: Picador, 1990), 25.

8. Ibid., 57. Thankfully, scientific and cultural advancements have been made in treating cancer since Sontag first published *Illness as Metaphor* in January 1978, and though attitudes towards cancer are less paranoid, they remain just as distancing. Sontag's essay also serves as a temporal touchstone, allowing cultural historians to get a snapshot of society at the time of publication.

9. Ibid., 65-66.

it is thought foolish not to subject one's actions to the calculus of self-interest and profitability.[10]

And, as would resurface with the AIDS crisis:

> Any important disease whose causality is murky, and for which treatment is ineffectual, tends to be awash in significance. First, the subjects of deepest dread (corruption, decay, pollution, anomie, weakness) are identified with the disease. The disease itself becomes a metaphor.[11]

Sontag wrote *Illness as Metaphor* to cope with her own cancer diagnosis, forcing herself to face the disease in a rational manner, and to help other cancer patients engage with their illness and a judgmental society. 10 years later, as a new epidemic raged, she wrote the follow-up essay, *AIDS and its Metaphors,* arguing that the distancing, fear-driven language of cancer had largely shifted to HIV and AIDS. It still presided over cancer patients, but the new threat created its own difficulties: "What makes the viral assault so terrifying is that contamination, and therefore vulnerability, is understood as permanent."[12] And whereas TB is an airborne disease and cancer a genetic mutation, "[t]he sexual transmission of this illness, considered by most people as a calamity one brings on oneself, is judged more harshly than other means - especially since AIDS is understood as a disease not only of sexual excess but of perversity."[13]

It can be difficult to remember how extensive and rapid advances in LGBT visibility and equality have been over the last

---

10. Ibid., 58.

11. Ibid., 58.

12. Ibid. 108.

13. Ibid., 114. She follows with a parenthetical aside - "I am thinking, of course, of the United States, where people are currently being told that heterosexual transmission is extremely rare, and unlikely - as if Africa did not exist."

30 years - especially as a result of action by or on behalf of AIDS patients during the epidemic. These patients, often forced out of the closet through their diagnoses, joined a movement attempting to encourage research on new treatments to save the lives of themselves and their loved ones. However, the height of the Reagan era was not the best time for perceived deviants seeking sympathy:

> Like syphilis is a disease of, or contracted from, dangerous others, AIDS is perceived as afflicting, in greater proportions than syphilis ever did, the already stigmatized. But syphilis was not identified with certain death, death that follows a protracted agony, as cancer was once imagined and AIDS is now held to be.[14]

> In contrast to cancer, understood in a modern way as a disease incurred by (and revealing of) individuals, AIDS is understood in a premodern way, as a disease incurred by people both as individuals and as members of a "risk group" - that neutral-sounding, bureaucratic category which also revives the archaic idea of a tainted community that illness has judged.[15]

> Making AIDS everyone's problem and therefore a subject on which everyone needs to be educated, charge the antiliberal [sic] AIDS mythologists, subverts our understanding of the difference between "us" and "them"; indeed, exculpates or at least makes irrelevant moral judgements about "them." (In such rhetoric the disease continues to

---

14. Ibid., 116.
15. Ibid., 134.

be identified almost exclusively with homosexual-
ity, and specifically the practice of sodomy.)[16]

Sontag's words struck a chord for Larson, whose best friend
since childhood was gay. And living at the epidemic's ground
zero as it existed - at times invisibly, side-by-side with the 1980s'
financial upswing and the first round of New York's gentrification
- Sontag's words must have hit him square in the heart and mind.
One can easily imagine the sympathetic composer reading lines
like, "Not only does AIDS have the unhappy effect of reinforcing
American moralism about sex; it further strengthens the culture of
self-interest, which is much of what is usually praised as "individu-
alism." Self-interest now receives an added boost as simple medical
prudence," with "YES! EXACTLY!"[17]

The question was how to make it work on stage.

One of Larson's biggest challenges was working out the balance of HIV+ and negative characters in the show. In Aronson's
scripts, Mimi was the only sick character, but Larson expanded
this to almost all of his protagonists in 1992, with Roger, Mimi,
Maureen, Collins, and Angel being HIV+ alongside virtually the
entire ensemble (excluding Benny), and Mark having an indeter-
minate status. In these initial drafts, Mark's fear was about being
tested (though not enough to not try and hook up again - albeit
safely - with the positive Maureen) and being torn between the hell
his friends went through from the disease and his survivor's guilt
if he lived.

By the 1994 studio production, Larson had cut back the
explicit references to the volume of HIV+ characters, and Mark
was definitely HIV-negative, but a segment wherein the characters'
medicine beepers go off was still a parade of characters and pills,

16. Ibid., 153.

17. Ibid., 161.

and Maureen was still HIV+. Sondheim told Larson he should "abandon making the majority of the principles HIV+, as it numbs the audience when they should feel something."[18]

Larson ultimately relented, reducing the HIV+ cast to Roger, Mimi, Collins, and Angel, along with ensemble members at the support group. "The quality about Jonathan," remembers Kevin McCollum, "wasn't just curiosity, but this great empathy that justice had to be done. He couldn't understand - he'd say, 'I'm writing this about my friends. My friends are dying too young - some gay, some straight,' and he had to write about them. He had to tell this story."

Indeed, Larson wanted to memorialise and celebrate his friends as much as possible, especially a trio who died from AIDS during *RENT*'s development. Gordon Rodgers, the group's cynic, had been childhood friends with Victoria Leacock. Tall and lanky, it was Rodgers who told off Larson for making Mimi too touchy-feely in early drafts of *RENT*. Alison Gertz was a young activist, one who spoke to Larson's political side. Pam Shaw, mentioned previously, died during the summer of 1995, when Larson was rehearsing *J.P. Morgan*. Living through it all was Matt O'Grady:

> Jon was always there for me with my health issues.
> He came with me to Friends In Deed.[19] He held
> my hand. He even volunteered by going in and
> answering the phone there. He listened to all my

---

18. Jonathan Larson. Letter to Stephen Sondheim. Box 14, Folder 7, Jonathan Larson Papers, Music Division, Library of Congress, Washington, D.C., 90H.

19. Friends In Deed is a support organisation for patients of life-threatening diseases founded in 1991. The group's philosophy focuses on living to the fullest in the present, despite tragic circumstances, and to stay resilient and in charge of one's own path. Larson immortalised the group as 'Life Support' in *RENT*.

For more information, see: http://www.friendsindeed.org/overview/

fears, all my concerns, and he made me laugh through it all."[20]

You Were(n't) Right

While *RENT* is appropriately regarded as Larson's grand work, he also wrote a trio of truly terrible songs for *RENT* - a reminder that no author is infallible. As was pointed out in the *RENT* collector book by numerous sources, Larson had difficulties coming to terms with the Mark-Maureen-Joanne relationship, particularly regarding the latter, and two of these songs address those characters.[21]

The first of Larson's missteps, 'Because You Were Right,' is a reconciliation number between Mark and Maureen in the first act. In early editions of *RENT*, Maureen waits in the 11th Street lot before her performance, sending Joanne off for cables to connect her new, state of the art (and Joanne-funded) equipment. Mark stumbles upon her while going with Collins and Angel to the support group meeting, and they trade barbs before he storms off, returning shortly thereafter. Musically, the song is an adult contemporary pop-ballad, gentle and warm.

Where 'Right' suffers is from being too long, too repetitive, and too sentimental. Initially conceived as a song called 'You'll Never Change,' wherein Mark and Maureen realise what they hated in each other and their relationship before reconciling, 'Change' was loaded with 'technology as relationship' metaphors, suggesting Maureen need to pick one lover or another.[22] From here, Larson stuck with the sniping feud, writing the song as reminiscences

20. Jonathan Larson Memorial Service. Video. 3 Feb 1996. Privately held by Victoria Leacock Hoffman, Washington, D.C.

21. Kate Giel, ed., *RENT*. (New York: Rob Weisbach Books, 1997), 25, 32.

22. Jonathan Larson. Handwritten Notes. Box 11, Folder 2, Jonathan Larson Papers, Music Division, Library of Congress, Washington, D.C., 12-15H.

294 | J. Collis

- "Remember that June in Cape May?"[23] and from there to "You thought you could (do this or that)"[24] and "Because of you I (did this)"[25] before ultimately evolving it into 'Because You Were Right'.

Structurally, 'Right' is a list song, where Mark and Maureen tell each other, "You were right about (thing)," going back and forth and ending each stanza with a quip:

> MARK
>
> You were right about Puccini
>
> You were right about Flaubert
>
>
> MAUREEN
>
> You were right about bikinis-
>
>
> MARK
>
> Not fair[26]

repeating the setup twice, making a confession:

> MARK
>
> Honestly
>
> I now can see
>
> I thought screwing was making love

24. Ibid., 24-25H.

25. Ibid., 42-45H.

26. Jonathan Larson. 'You Were Right' (Draft). Box 11, Folder 2, Jonathan Larson Papers, Music Division, Library of Congress, Washington, D.C., 59H.

MAUREEN

Modesty

I now agree

I didn't know the meaning of[27]

with breaks for the chorus:

I tried to change you

you tried to change me

All we could do

was argue and disagree[28]

and a bridge where the two confess their ease in talking as friends, before going back for one last chorus, this time to confess what they did wrong, and leading into a new chorus, this time admitting first what they did wrong, then what the *other* person did wrong. Finally, Mark asks Maureen why she left, leading into the final chorus:

MAUREEN

You couldn't deal

when I revealed

I was HIV

---

27. Jonathan Larson. 'You Were Right'. Box 11, Folder 2, Jonathan Larson Papers, Music Division, Library of Congress, Washington, D.C., 78H.

28. Jonathan Larson. Handwritten Notes. Box 11, Folder 2, Jonathan Larson Papers, Music Division, Library of Congress, Washington, D.C., 47H.

First appearance of the chorus as recorded, written in Larson's hand.

MARK

You shut me out

You'd scream and shout

if I showed sympathy[29]

As performed in the 1993 reading and on demo tapes, 'You Were Right' has some genuine emotion and serves a valid theatrical function (introducing Maureen's softer side, handling some of Mark's angst, setting up the early editions' Mark-Maureen-Joanne love triangle), but the song went on too long, played as sappy, and Larson knew it needed to be shortened or dropped. The line which truly sunk the song, however, was the closer:

MARK

I do miss your libido

MAUREEN

I do miss your pink torpedo[30]

The 'pink torpedo' line sets the tone for 'Love of My Life,' a fight between Maureen and Joanne written for the September 1995 revisions. Larson knew the couple needed a big number in the second act, but had difficulty placing it. In 1994, the pair sang 'Without You' as a reconciliation after breaking up in dialogue under 'Out Tonight'. However, 'Without You' was repurposed as Mimi's number, and a race was on to find a replacement.

When writing his revisions in 1995, Larson intended to replace 'Contact' with a new song, 'Wear The Pants,' which is described in his outline as:

---

29. Jonathan Larson. 'You Were Right'. Box 11, Folder 2, Jonathan Larson Papers, Music Division, Library of Congress, Washington, D.C., 79H.

30. Ibid., 79H.

<u>July Fourth</u> - Mo and Jo continue to
fight in bed, over the content of
Mo's new piece about the homeless
alternating with great sex-
Collins & Angel have passionate sex
throughout- under the sheets in the
hospital bed.[31]

Instead, Larson broke 'Contact' into two halves, inserting 'Love of My Life' before Angel's death throes:

(The sheet covering all principles is arranged to
look like a vaudville (sic) curtain, which rises,
revealing MAUREEN & JOANNE in bed.- (sic)
having just had
an argument- backs to each other)[32]

Experienced storytellers will already see the problem: a comedic song just before a major death, combined with a jarring musical shift, rarely makes for a good outcome. And while 'Love' has the big blowup Maureen and Joanne needed, Larson's lyrics were not his best:

JOANNE
You're the cockroach in my jam
You're the hepatitis in my clam
You're the extra ten pounds on my scale
You're the letterbomb (sic) in my mail

31. Jonathan Larson. *RENT* Rough Outline, Aug 1995. Box 16, Folder 3, Jonathan Larson Papers, Music Division, Library of Congress, Washington, D.C., 9H.

32. Jonathan Larson. *RENT* (New Act One Rough, 12 Sep 1995). Box 15, Folder 5, Jonathan Larson Papers, Music Division, Library of Congress, Washington, D.C., 77.

You're the splinter on my pinkie

You're a diaper with a stinkie

[…]

BOTH

In bed we're a dance- We're a pure *pas-de-deux*

We're a cherry-pie butterfly day at the zoo

Out of bed- We just quibble and bicker and fight

Over nonsense like "Who wears the dildo tonight!"[33]

The song ends with Maureen and Joanne agreeing that the only way to stay together is to just stay in bed and keep having sex.

In the *RENT* souvenir programme, director Michael Greif described 'Love of My Life' as "one of the worst songs ever written. The song was a straight out cat fight."[34] However, time was ticking, and *RENT* actually entered rehearsals with the song intact. Still, it was understood by all that a new song would be written, leading to this note in a revision from late November:

Here is where a boffo musical number will go for Maureen and Joanne.

I promise.[35]

Virtually all the interview subjects contacted for this book

33. Ibid., 77-78.

34. David Lipsky. *The Creation of RENT*. (Utica: Brodock Press, 2008), 18.

35. Jonathan Larson. *RENT* (December 1995 Draft), stored as '***12/95 Text' (Microsoft Word File). Contained within disk56.dmg. Jonathan Larson Papers, Music Division, Library of Congress, Washington, D.C.

Though the file is named 12/95, its created date is 29 November 1995 and last modified is 1 December 1995. I've left the blank lines from the original in for emphasis - they say so much about Larson's personality as a writer.

about *RENT* remember 'Love of My Life' and how awful it was - and it is indeed a terrible song - but its badness is overemphasised for two reasons. First, 'Love' is so bad as to be hilarious. It is a true 'Springtime for Hitler' moment, where the listener (or reader) does a double take in disbelief that a song written for two grown women would be so childish, but the simple melody is catchy enough to keep listeners from hitting stop, particularly on the demo recording where Larson sings both roles. Second, the song is a misfire which came at a time when Larson wrote otherwise strong new material like 'Happy New Year' and 'What You Own'. The missing breakup song for Maureen and Joanne easily gave the team their biggest creative nightmares: "I remember the anxiety we were all feeling about, 'When is this song going to arrive?'" The answer, as the anxious James Nicola was to discover, was incredibly close to *RENT*'s opening.

However, to find the worst song Jonathan Larson ever wrote, one needs to look back to the initial 1993 reading for the eleven o'clock number, 'US of Ease.' A Brechtian protest song, 'Ease' would have been at home in an Adelphi cabaret, performed by musically untrained singers. In the song, disgraced congressman Otam A. Densofla is forced to live on the street after his electorate impeaches him.[36] Desnofla is then confronted by Mark and the show's three main homeless characters, who tell their stories and reveal various shortcomings in American society.

Boiling the song down to its essence makes it sound naive and misguided, but in line with Larson's political leanings and writings. The interminable runtime (over eight minutes, or slightly longer than 'La Vie Boheme A' in the final show) and lyrics make it painful. No laughter was heard on either the soundboard recording

---

36. Otam A. Desnofla is Alfonse D'amato backwards. D'amato was a Republican senator from New York who campaigned against LGBT rights and the NEA.

from the June 1993 reading or the video recording, which used the camera's onboard microphone. The actors were visibly uncomfortable, and the song tanked - the audience had to be prompted by the cast to politely applaud.[37] "I remember thinking [it] was corny," says Coco Peru, "and I remember not feeling comfortable to say that to Jon. It was too pointed, too right on, and trying to be clever but not working, and I was so happy when I heard that it didn't make it into the show."

Compounding the cringe-worthiness is not just the lyric's immaturity, but the condescension and stereotypical portrayals of the homeless. After ex-congressman DeSnofla decries his new-found poverty, Rudy Ramirez (aka Squeegieman in the final script) offers a counterpoint. He used to be a stock trader, but went to jail in a scandal. Now living on the street, he sings:

> Now my business isn't all that risky
> I drink my whisky- hold out my hand
> Still I will admit I do get misty
> When I imagine things had gone the way we planned[38]

The group is then interrupted by a passing Halloween parade as they dance to brand names and signs of middle-class banality. Mark sings about being poor and alone as a trade-off for artistic freedom and revels in the indulgence:

> I don't even know what I'm achieving

37. Video: *RENT* 1993 Reading Act 2. Video. February 1996. Privately held by Victoria Leacock Hoffman, Washington, D.C.

Audio: *RENT* 1993 Reading Act 2, 17 June 1993. MAVIS 187207-9-22. Jonathan Larson Recordings, Recorded Sound Division, Library of Congress, Washington, D.C.

38. Jonathan Larson. *RENT* (1993 'Board Op Book'). Box 12, Folder 6, Jonathan Larson Papers, Music Division, Library of Congress, Washington, D.C., 75.

by still believing poverty's my fate

[…] It's a tiny track from the purist to the hack
From the out on the fringe to the media binge
From the avant gard [sic] to the old vangard [sic]
From fortune and fame to "Hey it's what's his name"[39]

A second homeless person follows, and the words keep getting worse:

Once they called me clinically psychotic

Not just neurotic- Legally coo-coo
Now they call me "Hey you off the grating"
God-damned degrading - but what to do?

Costs were going up at the asylum
They had to file-um for Chapter Nine
Now I'm on a permanent vacation
No medication-Besides this wine[40]

A second round of abstract dance follows, before Mrs. Chance, the homeless gospel sage, tells of her father dying, her mother running off, and how her faith is the only thing keeping her going:

Po' Black female's bottom of the ladder
But it don't matter- in God's big eyes
She can hear the voice of the one without a choice
And I rejoice in life, cause life itself's the prize[41]

39. Ibid., 76.
40. Ibid., 76.
41. Ibid., 77.

Sentimentalising poverty in the name of art has existed since long before Murger's *Scenes de la vie de la Bohème*, but attempting to addressing homelessness in such a slipshod, denigrating manner was inexcusable. Dramatically, the song failed to advance the plot or tell something interesting about the characters, which was vital as the show came out of the breakups of 'Goodbye Love' and moved onto one of *RENT*'s best cut songs, 'Open Road'. Even 'Ease''s music was awful, as a chintzy organ grinder and synthesised brass made the song sound like a cut-rate circus act putting society's freaks on display.

It was obvious that 'US of Ease' failed on every level. Larson even went so far as to drop it by early 1994 without even having a replacement ready, something he always showed hesitation to do in *Superbia* or other instances of *RENT*.[42] While 'Because You Were Right' and 'Love of My Life' had merits, albeit minor and sometimes dubious, 'US of Ease' was irredeemably bad.

For each of these songs, Larson wrote or printed out page after page of notes, lyrics, and revisions, crossing out one lyric for another and trying endlessly to make it work. However, *RENT*'s magic came from the songs which appeared almost organically, where the first draft provided enough of a structure - or at the very least enough good lines - to revise and build from. The sole exception turned out to be second act ballad 'Without You,' which brings the characters through spring and a series of breakups and reconciliations. Larson brainstormed endless metaphors to work from, trying to build the song upon set after set of lyrics, and even then needing to reassign the song twice, from a different couple on each verse to primarily Maureen counterpointed by Joanne to finally Mimi counterpointed by Roger. It would prove to be the

---

42. The only other instance is, as mentioned above, when Larson cut 'Love of My Life' and used a placeholder for roughly six weeks until he wrote 'Take Me or Leave Me'.

only time in the show's development where such fidgeting turned out to be worth the effort. If other overhauls, such as the opening number and the transition from 'Right Brain' to 'One Song Glory' would feature one large rewrite and then be revised, like a carpenter lathing a table leg from a raw block of wood and sanding it smooth, 'Without You' was a toothpick fashioned from a log with just sandpaper.

Making the Cut

While Larson struggled to replace his musical problem children, some good songs had to go along with the bad - not because the song itself was deficient, but rather because the circumstances surrounding it had changed.

One of the earliest examples is 'Love the Pain,' Angel's funeral song from the 1993 reading. 'Pain' is a gloriously depressing gospel number sung by homeless character Mrs. Chance:

> Lift yourself up
> Never ever give up
> You've got nothing to lose
> And the whole wide world to gain
>
> You'll see the depths of your gloom
> Become like the heavens above[...]
>
> Let go and love
> The pain"[43]

43. Jonathan Larson. RENT (1993 Reading Script with Narration). Box 12, Folder 6, Jonathan Larson Papers, Music Division, Library of Congress, Washington, D.C., 70.

'Love the Pain' was cut after Larson wrote 'I'll Cover You' and struck upon the idea of reprising it at Angel's funeral.[44] Even if he had not reached that decision, it would have been difficult to keep the song after scaling back the homeless characters from being supporting cast members to the ensemble.

Larson was also not above attempting to work older songs into the show. In addition to 'Valentine's Day' (discussed in Chapter 1) and the aforementioned 'White Male World,' he also tried to use a pop song from 1991, 'Open Road'. Larson wrote 'Road' during a trip to Texarkana with Jonathan Burkhart. As the latter recalls:

> In January of 1991, two weeks before George Bush started dropping bombs on what would be labeled 'The Gulf War,' Jonathan and I got into my pickup truck and drove from NYC to Texas.
>
> There was a night somewhere two weeks into the trip that we entered Texarkana. It was late, and we were in search for a place to sleep. On a small deserted street entering town, we saw a cat laying in the middle of the road. It had just been hit by a car. So we thought. A few feet off to the side was another cat inching its way closer to the dead cat. We stopped the truck and watched as the cat approached what we decided was its lover, sniffing death and then crying.
>
> Later that night in our $15 motel room, Jonathan penned 'Open Road'. It was based on loneliness, traveling in unknown places, and an unsure future.

Larson positioned 'Open Road' late in *RENT*'s second act for

---

44. Both songs, however, feature the ensemble counterpointing the solo with 'Seasons of Love'.

Roger to sing following his breakup and departure in 'Goodbye Love'. Driving out of New York, the character mournfully sings:

> Open Road
>
> Why can't I crack love's code?
>
> Time to fly
>
> No time to say goodbye- Goodbye
>
>
> Just try to forget her face
>
> Get yourself in the race
>
> There's a place that you have to go- Have to go[45]

As the bridge approaches, Larson - whether through skill or coincidence - ties the song back to Mimi's prior metaphor (the feline of Avenue B who dances at the Cat Scratch Club), and Roger, the hip cat rocker:[46]

> There's a hit and run cat on the highway
>
> Another cat sits, saying a prayer
>
> I swear- as I pass -she is glaring your way
>
> "Where did my love go," cry her eyes,
>
> "Tell me- where did my love go?"[47]

As Larson introduced new themes, he also had to make stepping stones of new material. For example, Mark's first flirtation with selling out came not with Alexi Darling's debut in 1995, but

45. Jonathan Larson. RENT (25 October 1994 Draft). Box 14, Folder 5, Jonathan Larson Papers, Music Division, Library of Congress, Washington, D.C., 87.

46. The term 'cat' for a musician or cool person goes back to the Jazz Age and had a resurgence in the 1950s.

47. Jonathan Larson. RENT (25 October 1994 Draft). Box 14, Folder 5, Jonathan Larson Papers, Music Division, Library of Congress, Washington, D.C., 87.

from Benny in the 1994 studio production. In 'Real Estate,' the ex-roommate-turned-broker tries to recruit his friend to join him in the world of property and finance. Mark gives it serious consideration, as he wallows in loneliness and self-pity:

> I'm all alone - my film's no prize
> But "I've got the stuff"
> At least everybody says so
>
> My friends have flown - or are dropping like flies
> And if that's not enough
> I'm in love with a lesbo
>
> My rent is due - my family's nuts
> I haven't had sex in a millenium [sic]
> I'm left with you - I hate your guts
> And it's only Ten A.M.![48]

Benny and a video-chain representative suggest the answer lies in Mark cleaning up his act and going corporate.[49] Mark is tempted, wondering if they could build low-income housing (Benny pretends to like the idea), and mopes when the representative tells him there's no money in making documentaries, anyway - "they like things sunny not truthful, honey."[50] Ultimately, her

---

48. Jonathan Larson. *RENT* (25 October 1994 Draft). Box 14, Folder 5, Jonathan Larson Papers, Music Division, Library of Congress, Washington, D.C., 83.

49. Jonathan Larson. Handwritten Note. Box 14, Folder 4, Jonathan Larson Papers, Music Division, Library of Congress, Washington, D.C., 84H.

In early lyrics, Benny also points out that real estate will land Mark a cornucopia of women.

50. Jonathan Larson. *RENT* (25 October 1994 Draft). Box 14, Folder 5,

insensitivity to the plight of the nearby homeless and her love of promotional merchandise convince Mark he's better off poor. Benny makes a last attempt, saying Mark's parents will finally be proud of him, but Mark recommits to his film project and finally swears off Maureen in the hopes of pursuing a more agreeable (and straight) girlfriend. The song inspired Larson to briefly consider merging Mark and Benny into a single character, but not enough to write anything past the actual question.[51]

In terms of positioning, 'Real Estate' came between 'Goodbye Love' and 'Open Road,' replacing 'US of Ease' to provide some respite in the largely downbeat second act. Unlike 'Ease,' 'Real Estate' is actually funny, and audiences can be heard laughing on recordings from the 1994 production. Larson did his research going into the song, taking extensive notes on tenants' rights and how the New York property market functioned, though these notes would be more useful in the following year's revisions than anything he wrote in 1994.

However, Larson's subsequent edits ultimately made 'Real Estate' redundant: Benny's position and attempts to recruit his friends were moved to the top of the show, Mark finally stopped pining for Maureen, and Larson was able to condense Mark and Roger's realisations into a single song, initially entitled 'Too Dangerous to Feel' before being reworked as 'What You Own'.

Jonathan Larson Papers, Music Division, Library of Congress, Washington, D.C., 85.

51. Jonathan Larson. Handwritten Note. Box 16, Folder 3, Jonathan Larson Papers, Music Division, Library of Congress, Washington, D.C., 62H.

Entire Years Strewn

As mentioned in Chapter Seven, Larson was assigned the task of writing backgrounds and a first act perspective for each of *RENT*'s eight principal characters. It was believed that by doing so, "the rewriting of the play would come in a simple burst."[52] Larson went back and forth with his dramaturge over the details as she asked questions encouraging him to probe deeper or fill in logical gaps. While *RENT*'s backstory and character relationships remained complex, Larson's documentation clarified the characters' motivations in such a way that his Autumn 1995 overhaul effectively brought the second act together, as well as most of the first.

Based on Larson's backstories, Mark Cohen grew up in Scarsdale, NY, the son of an executive lawyer and a non-society mother.[53] His older sister is more successful, but Mark has always been creative, making films instead of doing book reports, and went to Brown University to study film.[54] While at university, Mark lived with Benny, a scholarship student in film production pulling himself out of the South Philly slums. Benny produced Mark's final student film on the Exxon Valdez oil spill, but despite it winning awards, Mark's parents were furious: they financed his work believing it would be about environmental renewal, but instead it condemned the corporation - which Mark's father represented.

After graduating, Mark and Benny moved into the loft in which the play is set and tried to start their careers. During this

---

52. Lipsky, 18.

53. Summaries are based on:

Jonathan Larson. *RENT* Character Backgrounds and Stories (No internal document title), stored as '***EVERYTHING' (Microsoft Word File). Contained within disk53.dmg. Jonathan Larson Papers, Music Division, Library of Congress, Washington, D.C.

54. The successful older sister and creative school projects are based on Larson's own experiences.

time, Mark - working as a waiter at trendy restaurant DOJO (his film career stalled without funding) - met Maureen Johnson, an up-and-coming performance artist from a scandalised family (her pastor father was a child molester).[55] Maureen moved from New Jersey to upstate New York to study theatre and, after graduating and failing to get into Yale Drama School, fell in love with Mark and the work of Laurie Anderson, becoming a performance artist. Her work received positive reviews but no breakthrough success, and she moved in with Mark and Benny at the 11th St. loft, cheating on Mark left and right before realising that she was attracted to women, landing Joanne on her first trip to a lesbian bar. The two have been inseparable ever since.

Meanwhile, Roger Davis moved from Arizona to New York to cut an album with his band. Gigging across the city's rock circuit, he met his first serious girlfriend, an older painter named April. Despite the band's drummer and songwriter overdosing, April got Roger hooked on heroin, and they answered Mark and Benny's ad for a roommate. Benny, sensing an opportunity to restart his producing career, focused on Roger's band instead of Mark's films, but it all came crashing to a halt when April's suicide sent Roger into social and physical withdrawal.

Benny, having worked for building owner Bill Grey as the maintenance man in exchange for a massive rent discount, found himself attracted to Bill's daughter and, after establishing himself as a production assistant (thereby giving up his maintenance job) and showing responsibility, obeyed Alison's ultimatum to move uptown and work full time for her father. However, Benny has never given up on his entertainment mogul dreams and misses his old friends.

Mimi is a downtown girl through and through. In denial over being raped by her father, she ran away as a teenager, moved in with extended family, and became an erotic dancer to pay the bills.

---

55. DOJO is a real restaurant in New York.

Despite a troubled relationship with her mother, Mimi brings her younger siblings extra money at school during recess and feels guilty when she sees her old teachers: she'd been a promising student. She fully believes in the true Hollywood romance, despite being HIV+. Even though she attends support groups and tries to clean herself up, she routinely falls off the wagon. Six months before *RENT* begins, Mimi met Benny at the Cat Scratch Club, and he took her back to the building on 11th Street, where they made out and he agreed to let her move in for free.

Joanne's family are high-end political players from the wealthier DC suburbs. She was endowed from a young age with a 'liberal political conscience,' and went to all the best schools before establishing a legal aid organisation for New York's poor and underserved communities.[56] After realising she was attracted to women, Joanne first attempted to seduce her swim coach in 7th grade and became a regular on New York's club scene where, despite her beauty, her outfits were clearly designer and not authentic, betraying her wealth and status.

Collins is an orphan and a genius, joining the army at 15 and running away to be a houseboy before starting to teach at 19 and working for the best of technology's best while managing to become a poet laureate at the same time. Angel is a master of the streets, having lived in every New York zip code and served as a rent boy to the top of society.

In addition to having the shortest biographies, Collins and Angel also have the shortest - and simplest story:

---

56. Jonathan Larson. *RENT* Character Backgrounds and Stories (No internal document title), stored as '***EVERYTHING' (Microsoft Word File). Contained within disk53.dmg. Jonathan Larson Papers, Music Division, Library of Congress, Washington, D.C.

Collins is mugged on the street. Angel pulls him out of the dark alleyway and brushes him off. They fall instantly in love.

They stay in love all year, while hanging out with their wacky bohemian friends.

Until Angel dies of AIDS in September.

Collins returns to his life as vagabond anarchist, dedicating his work to Angel.[57]

In terms of underlying real life influences, Angel is an amalgamation of Larson's fashionable and generous best friend Matt O'Grady (who would dress in drag for Halloween), along with drag queen Clinton Leupp (aka Miss Coco Peru), and now-leading trans-activist Justin Vivian Bond, who was (and remains) close friends with Victoria Leacock and did, in fact, live on the streets for a time. At a memorial night held by Leacock, Bond told the story of how an incident which happened to v in university became the source of Mimi's funeral speech:[58]

> When they were getting ready to do [the work-shop] of *RENT*, [Jonathan] asked me, "Justin, tell me some of the things that drag queens say. Tell me some stuff I can use for this drag queen in this show," and I was like, "Whatever. I dunno, Jonathan, I'm sure that you want some stupid bitchy comments, because everybody thinks that drag queens are really bitchy and catty. I don't know, they're just people." I was totally dismissive, because I thought, "Oh god, here goes another straight guy trying to write another great thing

---

57. Ibid.

58. Bond uses the gender-nonspecific pronoun "v" to refer to "vself."

with drag queens in it, and it's never gonna happen. I've seen like 16 people try." I just didn't know. I just thought Jonathan's heart was in the right place, but what the hell [did] he know?

And then we were at a party last summer, and I was telling him this story about when I was in college and we were talking out in front of this dorm. These frat boys are screaming out the window, "Hey, you fucking faggot!" and we couldn't see them, because this light was shining in front of their window.[59] Nancy was there, and we were all really stoned and everything. And she started screaming, "Who are you, you pussies? Let me tell you something: [v] is more of a man than you will ever be and more of a woman than you will ever have!" And I was telling Jonathan this story, and it was so beautiful, and he's like, "That's great! That's great!" and I'm like, "Well yeah, I thought so... It's true..."[60]

Maureen was heavily based on dancer/choreographer Brenda Daniels. Larson had dated Daniels, and their tempestuous on-again/off-again relationship ended for the last time when she left him for a woman.[61] While Joanne was mostly a fiction, she displayed traces of Larson's professional friends, and the name not-so-gently poked at a lesbian friend's unpleasant partner. Roger's personality and charm were based on Roger Bart, while his desire to write the great American rock song was Larson himself - as

59. Nancy is Nancy O'Conner, another Adelphi alumnus and friend of Bond and Larson's.

60. Vicky's Larson Evening, Tape #3. Video. February 1996. Privately held by Victoria Leacock Hoffman, Washington, D.C.

61. Larson also wrote music for a trio of Daniels' dance pieces. Their collaborative efforts are covered in Appendix A.

was Mark's geekishness and upbringing. Mark's filmmaking background came from Eddie Rosenstein, Victoria Leacock, Jonathan Burkhart, and Todd Robinson. At the time, Rosenstein and Leacock were working in documentary and *vérité* films, Burkhart was a cameraman for Spike Lee, and Robinson was making movies in Los Angeles.[1] While Mimi is mostly based on her *Bohéme* counterpart, her optimism and sense of heart were heavily influenced by Janet Charleston. Benny was not based on anybody in Larson's life, but rather a personification of what Larson hated about New York's ongoing gentrification.

Mark and Roger's loft was based on Larson's own run-down apartment, complete with makeshift electrical work, bathtub in the kitchen, and broken gas heaters violating every possible variation of housing code. Larson moved into the flat in 1984, when a high school ex-girlfriend told him of a couple wanting to rent out a spare room. One half of that couple was painter Anne Egan - who went on to build Newt the Newt for *Away We Go!* While Egan and her boyfriend moved out after a couple years, Larson stayed at 508 Greenwich Street for over a decade. The flat was insecure (Larson's computer and synthesiser were stolen during a break-in, despite the deterrence of living on the top floor), located across the street from a loud garbage truck depot, and had no heat, thanks to a landlord who turned off the gas versus fixing problematic pipes.[2] Egan and her boyfriend tried, with limited success, to fix that problem themselves:

---

1. Leacock's father, Richard Leacock, was a key figure in the *Cinéma vérité* movement, where the performances are semi- (or entirely) improvised and the camera is a passive participant, rather than interfering with events through cinematography.

2. Larson references this fact in the song 'No More' from *tick, tick… BOOM!* – along with a surfeit of other genuine gripes about his apartment.

My boyfriend's mother, who is real cool, suggested, "Why don't you put a wood burning stove in [the] apartment?" Which we did, to save some money on heat. It's like the first line of *RENT*, "We live in a loft with a wood burning stove," and it's true. We did. What we would do is come home and find skids, which they used in our area because it's industrial. We'd break them up and shove them into the wood burning stove to get a little warmth before we went to sleep. It sounds ridiculous, but it was not so far-fetched from *La Bohéme*.[3]

As Mark says in *RENT*, "real life's getting more like fiction each day."

---

3. Vicky's Larson Evening, Tape #2. Video. February 1996. Privately held by Victoria Leacock Hoffman, Washington, D.C.

Synopses

Superbia v1 (Late 1986/Early 1987)

ACT ONE:

THE YEAR IS 2064. In the Incity control room, the Master Babble Articulator teaches its Clone to speak. As the Clone's utterances turn to business phrases ("Ma-ma... Mar-ket share!"), the MBA deems it ready to learn about mankind, beginning with the present in *Tapecopy #001 (Superbia)*: The Prods are at the top, designing Shapes and writing programmes for the Ins, whose lives are broadcast on a never-ending stream of reality TV and infomercials from Incity. The Outs live on Earth (now a giant suburb called Outland) and retail and consume the Shapes, which are designed to break, thereby ensuring a stable economy. Out lives and purchasing habits are dictated by the Media Transmitter (MT). All parties are content, and humanity has lived in a state of peace for 65 years.

In Outland, Josh Out #177583962 has true emotions (unlike everyone else), making him an outcast. He spends his days experimenting with broken Shapes. When his newest invention ends in an explosion, Josh wishes he was *Too Cold To Care*. To his surprise, a small part of the invention - an old music box - falls to the ground and opens, playing a nostalgic tune. Josh attempts to show the box to his family and is promptly ignored, causing him to leave.

Meanwhile, Mr. and Mrs. Prod #27 are vacationing with their daughter, Elizabeth In #319, in Outland's Badlands (a nature reserve) but are distressed that Elizabeth is reading an old book of musical theatre lyrics - reading has been outlawed. Informed that she is programmed to fall in love with top celebrity Studd Starr, Elizabeth threatens to deviate from her programme and flees. Her parents decide to spy on her and Elizabeth turns to her book for guidance *(Eye On Her/Mr. Hammerstein II)*. In the woods, a distraught Elizabeth meets the frustrated Josh. Despite her initially stand-offish attitude, he breaks the ice by quoting the companion volume to her songbook and offers to cheer her up with the music box. Elizabeth is initially wary, but Josh promises that she can feel again if she'll just *Turn the Key*. Won over, she offers to put Josh's name on the Incity guest list so he can unleash the box on all Superbia via MT. Mrs. Prod reports back to Mr. Prod, who arranges for an agent to kill Josh on the Incity shuttle.

While in flight, Josh and Elizabeth meet in secret and go over the plan. They sing a song of the happy ending to come *(Ever After)*, but are interrupted by Mrs. Prod. Josh reflects on how he stands with Elizabeth *(She Hates Me)* and is held up by Hank In #1313, an ex-celebrity promised a comeback for killing Josh. Josh uses the box on Hank, who deviates from his programme. Upon landing, Mr. and Mrs. Prod tell Elizabeth that they know about Josh and that his box doesn't work: she's always had emotions. The pair escort Elizabeth through a special entrance, keeping her from Incity's bouncer. While initially refused entry, Josh is escorted in by the mysterious Roi, who seemingly mistakes him for Hank *(Face Value)*.

Back in the Control Room, the MBA is teaching the Clone about Superbia's origins, playing back video of Incity's first broadcast, a 'We Are The World'-esque pop song entitled *Let's All Sing*.

ACT TWO:

Josh and Roi join the party in *Incity*. As Roi gets Josh high on electricity, the pair run into Elizabeth, who denies knowing Josh and goes off with Studd. The real Hank enters, chased by security, but Josh refuses to help and Hank is forced to flee. Roi takes Josh back to her flat, and his family watch in awe as their son grabs Roi's laser and starts *Doin' it on the Air*. Concerned about Elizabeth, Mr. Prod asks the MBA to intervene and learns Roi is a spy.

The next morning, a series of announcements are made on MT: Josh and Studd are nominated for Face Awards, and Hank remains on the run. Roi has taken away the music box and forces Josh to keep plugging into the power line. While Studd does his hair and makeup, Elizabeth writes Josh a note warning him about Roi and reminding him that he came to Incity to get the box on the air. Hank swears revenge on Josh and the Ins *(Sextet)*.

At the Face Awards *(A Tribute to Plastic Surgery)*, Josh and Roi are joined by Studd, Elizabeth, and Studd's agent, Tim Pursent. Tim offers to get Josh a place as a Prod, and Roi intercepts Elizabeth's note. A presentation is given by William Marcel, an ageing actor brought from the Outer Obscurity prison satellite to lend integrity to events. Marcel speaks out against the MBA and is beaten for deviating. Josh is awarded Face of the Year, and is now completely converted to being an In, only for Hank to enter, denounce him, and blast a hole through the satellite's hull *(Limelight)*. Only 15 minutes of air remain, and the Ins are thrown into chaos.

Elizabeth knows that Josh is the only person able to save the Ins, but he refuses to believe her, trusting that the MBA will save them. When he falters in a moment of confusion, Elizabeth begs him to *Come To Your Senses*, and he recovers.

In the Control Room, the MBA is giving the Clone its final instructions: As humanity is no longer cost-effective to maintain, the MBA will use nuclear weapons to exterminate Outland while Incity's inhabitants will drown in the vacuum. Josh and Elizabeth enter, destroying the MBA and the Clone with the powers of song and emotion. Josh impersonates the MBA, ordering the Ins to evacuate and, as he affirms his love for Elizabeth, the pair open the music box and leave it running for the cameras.

Superbia v2 (September 1989)

ACT ONE:

As the *Fanfare for the Bottom Line* plays, the theatre's curtains are pulled away to reveal a glossy black stage and projections of stars and planets on a rear scrim.

In Outland, Josh Out #177583962's family are crowded around the Media Transmitter (MT). They are joined by Elizabeth Out #69001, emotional outcast Josh's MBA-assigned mate. The group plug in and watch a special announcement, starting with the first ever Incity broadcast: a global interruption by legendary rock star Mick Knife informing the people of Earth that everything is going to be fine, war is over, and all people need to do is plug into their power sockets or grab the wires in their MTs and get high *(Let's All Sing)*.

Josh enters from exploring a forbidden zone just as the MT announces that humanity is to enter its next stage, starring "the INS and OUTS as 'The Victims!'" Realising what's about to happen, Josh decides to abandon everything and spend his last 35 hours being *Too Cold To Care* and partying in Incity. Elizabeth chases him down but he rejects her, giving her a rose and a true, passionate kiss as a parting gift.

On the Incity shuttle, Josh meets Studd Starr and his droid, Chip, who feeds him a line about how to get past Incity's bouncer. While this happens, Elizabeth undergoes an emotional awakening on Earth and decides to follow after Josh *(Uncomfortable)*. As the shuttle prepares to land, Studd contacts the MBA, who is approving an advert for humanity's upcoming *Delimbination* and reports Josh's arrival. Despite being caught out by Chip's false advice, Josh is led into Incity by a mysterious In named Roi *(Face Value)*.

Elizabeth leaves Outland, torn between her life of safety and the world of emotions she previously overlooked in favour of the MT (*Pale Blue Square*).

Once in *Incity*, Roi forces Josh to plug in and they encounter Studd and Chip. The pair are shocked to see him when Elizabeth enters. The reunion is brief, however, as Josh asks Elizabeth to return later and Roi drags him away, leaving Elizabeth to Studd. Back in Outland, Josh's family watch events unfold on MT as Josh and Roi start *Doin' it on the Air*. After a wild night, Josh lies awake with guilt before choosing to stay the course to coldness, plugging in to numb himself (*LCD Readout*).

The next morning, the MT announces that Josh and Roi's love scene has earned him a Face Award nomination. Studd is also nominated and basks in his own ego, yet finds himself frustrated by Elizabeth, who locked herself in the bathroom and refuses to join in a threesome with him and Chip. Elizabeth writes Josh a note, asking that they forget the previous night and try again: she's realised he was right, and that love has no bottom line. As the MT continues its announcements, the MBA determines that Josh is an ideal spokesman and first victim for Delimbination. When the MT reaches the full list of Face Award nominees, Studd is outraged that Josh is on the list. All parties, however, are eager for the awards to begin (*Sextet*).

ACT TWO:

The Awards are joined at the end of a massive production number - *A Tribute to Plastic Surgery*. Josh, Roi, Studd, and Elizabeth watch alongside Studd's agent Tim Pursent. Elizabeth gives Josh her note, but Roi plugs him in before he can read it. Mick Knife is wheeled out to give a speech, but decries the world he has created and is boo'ed off stage. Josh wins the award, having been completely turned into an In. When Elizabeth tries to get through to him, Roi has her sent to the Outer Obscurity prison satellite *(Limelight)*.

On Outer Obscurity, Elizabeth falls asleep and has a nightmare while watching the MBA's Delimbination announcement *(Elizabeth's Nightmare)*. According to the MBA, humanity is no longer cost-effective in its current form, so all people are to have their limbs and torsos removed before being hooked up to life support, staring forever at their screens. As Elizabeth imagines this happening to her and Josh, she wakes up and smashes her cell's MT.

Back in Incity, Josh is being exploited by Tim Pursent, but his rising star is cut off when Studd denounces him on the air *(Gettim' While He's Hot)*. Josh is also sent to Outer Obscurity and Studd takes his place as Face of the Year and Delimbination's spokesman. Josh's family are shown, disappointed that they won't also be *Doin' it on the Air (Reprise)*.

Returned to Outer Obscurity, Mick Knife brings the comatose Josh to Elizabeth's cell. The latter stirs and professes her undying love to the broken MT *(I Won't Close My Eyes)*. Elizabeth attempts to plug in by grabbing the exposed wires, but electrocutes herself instead. Josh's emotions are restored in tragedy when he reads her note, repeating that *Love has no Bottom Line* as Delimbination begins.

tick, tick... BOOM! 1991 (One-Man) Edition[4]

Jonathan's 30th birthday is on Monday, but his friends are throwing him a surprise party on the Saturday before. People ask if he's surprised. He isn't, but lies and says yes. He's panicking and often hears a faint series of ticks and booms. Michael, Jonathan's best friend and roommate, is moving out on Monday and holding Jonathan to a promise: If his career as a composer hasn't taken off by his birthday, he'll try working a real job at Michael's advertising agency. Jonathan's girlfriend Susan is back from a week at the ashram. He's skeptical of the place, but she's thinking of taking a job there and leaving New York. Jonathan's gifts are all junk, including a cheesy CD from Andy Goldman, literary manager of a prestigious theatre company. Andy asks how Jonathan's agent, Rosa Stevens, is doing. Jonathan doesn't know - she won't return his calls. Andy reminds Jonathan that his next grant application is due by Monday night. Jonathan doesn't have an idea for a new show, but lies and says he does. He laments turning 30 and wishes he could stay young forever *(30/90)*.[5]

Jonathan slips out to the roof for a joint and some air. Michael tries to calm him down, but fails. Jonathan wonders if their generation is cynical because they haven't been challenged like those before, but Michael tells him their generation has a burden to bear, then goes back to the party. Susan takes his place and asks if she should take the ashram job. Jonathan sidesteps the issue, seducing her for a quickie on the roof while Michael keeps the guests at bay *(Green Green Dress)*.

The next morning, Jonathan lies awake, unable to sleep or

---

4. This synopsis is based on recordings of tick, tick... BOOM! at the Village Gate, New York City, in 1991. I chose this version as the majority of interviewees referred to it as the show's peak.

5. In Boho Days, Jonathan instead sings about life in his neighbourhood and grungy flat in the title song, with the party scene taking place between verses.

think of a show idea, and debates if he can settle for the suburban ideal - or will his sense of social justice keep him focused on sending a message to the world? Either way, *Johnny Can't Decide*. Needless to say, the alarm goes off just as he's falling asleep. Having snarfed his entire birthday cake while fretting overnight, he grabs a dollar and goes to buy Twinkies - only to run into hot party girl Karessa Johnson and her rich new boyfriend. Embarrassed when Karessa introduces him as a writer of musicals, Jonathan throws his snack away while Karessa flounces around and tells him her new boyfriend's first play is about to be produced - and Monday is his 19th birthday. A nearby homeless man returns the treat - "Shit man, you need this more than me." *(Sugar)*

Jonathan works his *Sunday* shift as a waiter. Afterwards, Michael picks him up in a new BMW and they check out his equally new condo. The building is stunning, a polar opposite to the squalor where they currently live *(No More)*.[6] Back at home, Jonathan plays with his cat as his parents make their weekly phone call. Michael is acting cagey about something, but Jonathan is distracted by news of his sister's large bonus at work and how his brother-in-law sold a screenplay - one which he slaved over for a whole month. Susan buzzes in and tries to persuade him to leave New York, but Jonathan waffles. After finishing with his parents, Jonathan tries to talk to Susan again, but she's already hung up. He thinks of the strangeness around him and asks "is this *Real Life*?"[7]

Unable to unwind, Jonathan thinks about turning his experience on *Superbia*, the futuristic rock musical he wrote, into a musical. He talks about getting high and being inspired, presenting the show to his heroes, and how Andy took control of his one shot at a

---

6. In 30/90 and Boho Days, Jonathan sings 'Swimming,' wherein he frets while working out at the pool.

7. In 30/90 and Boho Days, Jonathan sings 'Debtor Club,' a song about living the yuppie lifestyle by racking up massive credit card bills.

staged production, only to miscast it and not allow him any of the elements which made the show special, blaming it on the unions. Even Jonathan's hero, Robert Rhymer, was disappointed, and left at the interval. Michael interrupts, saying they need to talk, but Jonathan doesn't want to leave his mental zone. All that thinking back on the experience does is making him question the point of working in the theatre. He bemoans the current state of Broadway (*Play Game*), asking why he cares, but then thinks back on all the good times he's had, and how the theatre became a passion, finding his answer (*Why*).

It's late evening and Jonathan has another idea: a sitcom about how Generation X took baby boomer indulgences to the next level, set as a western called *The Pioneers of the Extreme*. It's awful, and he throws out his notes. He thinks of Susan, and how she says he doesn't share his feelings. He does, just as songs, which he performs publicly at popular prices (*Therapy*). Susan enters to find a moping Jonathan. He doesn't want to go to the office the next morning, but can't stay as he is. Susan berates him for being too obsessed with his writing, and as they fight, she announces she's leaving. Jonathan stays focused on himself before it sinks in. Susan tells him to to breathe, to learn from experience, and to act, then walks off. Left alone, Jonathan wonders why he can't *Find the Key*, either to his heart or his work, hoping to at least get a song out of how he feels.[8]

It's Monday morning, and Jonathan tries to be optimistic about going to Madison Avenue. He psychs himself up and tries to think positively, only to turn up late. He joins a brainstorming session seeking a name for a fat substitute, but finds it soul crushing and stifling instead of inspiring. The session leader - Jonathan's ideal type - ruins his image of the perfect woman forever by putting

---

8. In 30/90 and Boho Days, Jonathan reflected on his relationship in the song 'See Her Smile'.

down all his ideas. In a moment of rebellion, Jonathan throws out the worst name he can think of and flees the room. On his way out, one of the other brainstormers proclaims it might work. Michael is unsurprised that Jonathan has cracked under the pressure, but reminds him that everything comes down to love or fear. Michael tries to calm his aggravated friend, asking what he's so afraid of. Jonathan rattles off a list of things, including that he doesn't want to lose his values like his friend. Michael reveals that he's HIV+ and leaves to catch a flight, shocking the disheartened composer.

Jonathan staggers out of the office and runs over to Central Park as it begins raining, finding himself at the Sheep's Meadow. The tick-boom sounds he's been hearing are everywhere, echoing and building in intensity. Michael was right - fear has taken over, and as much as he tries to teach his girlfriends about love, he's forgotten what it means. Instead, he finds inspiration in a flock of seagulls. He screams to them, and they fly away. Jonathan admits to his fears, his impotence in the face of his friends' suffering, his guilt over not living up to his family's expectations, and rages at the state of the nation. The seagulls create a formation: ACTION SPEAKS LOUDER THAN WORDS. Jonathan runs through the park, finding himself at the Delacorte Theatre, where Shakespeare plays are performed in the summer. Jonathan hops over a fence, rips the tarp off a rehearsal piano, and has found his idea: *tick, tick... BOOM! A Rock Monologue.* He runs to a payphone to call Michael, expressing his sympathies and thanking him for all he's done. Jonathan hears one final tick-boom, but is unafraid: it's the seagulls flying off. Jonathan has made his decision, and commits to confronting his fears and coming out stronger *(Louder Than Words)*.

tick, tick... BOOM! 2001 (Three-Man) Edition

It's Saturday night, a week before Jonathan's 30th birthday. He's worried that he's been a promising composer for so long, he's broken the promise. An odd combination of ticks and booms echo in the back of his mind. He frets about what his upcoming birthday means while his best friend, Michael, compares everything to business travel and his girlfriend, Susan, has arranged a big party where he'll play "Happy Birthday" for everybody. Jonathan goes into meltdown *(30/90)*.

Jonathan goes up to the roof to get some air, and Michael follows, offering to set his friend up with a market research job. Jonathan is appreciative - but wary - of the favour and is more excited about the upcoming workshop of his musical, *Superbia*. Susan questions whether he can give up writing to work a day job, but Jonathan is bummed about how his career's been going nowhere. They go to bed together *(Green Green Dress)*.

The next morning, Jonathan lies awake. Susan suggests they leave New York and settle somewhere calmer. *Johnny Can't Decide*, but first he has to go to his waiter job, serving obnoxious customers at *Sunday* brunch. After his shift, Jonathan goes with Michael to see the latter's new condo and realises that selling out could mean leaving his current squalor *(No More)*. Back at the old flat, Michael and Jonathan discuss Susan's desire to leave, and Michael begs Jonathan to come to a brainstorming session at his office. Jonathan caves in to the request, and Michael prepares for yet another business trip while Jonathan is on his weekly call to his parents. As usual, his sister and her husband are doing fantastically, her a law executive and him a screenwriter making fast sales. Another call buzzes in, and to Jonathan's shock and awe, it's his agent, Rosa, calling for the first time in months. She promises a room full of exciting people at the reading. After wrapping up with Rosa and his parents, Jonathan takes a call from Susan who wants him to come over, but she lives all the way across town and he can't afford a taxi. They bicker, and when Susan pushes the issue of moving, Jonathan clams up. She accuses him of not being able to communicate. They fight *(Therapy)*.

It's Monday, and Jonathan walks through Times Square on the way to Michael's office, disappointed to see nothing but imported musicals for tourists. He's warmly welcomed at the office, but quickly finds himself out of sync with the other participants' mindset. Cynically seeking an escape, Jonathan offers a sarcastic answer and blows the job. Michael's furious, but his plane is waiting and he admits that at the end of the day, normalcy can be its own reward *(Real Life)*.

After spending hours driving Michael's BMW back into the city and finding parking, Jonathan needs a *Sugar* fix. He awkwardly buys a pack of Twinkies, only to be caught by Karessa Johnson, a bubbly actress in the show. He tries to dodge, only to discover she has a sweet tooth as well. The pair bond over the show and snack cakes, and walk home together after rehearsal. Susan sees Karessa kissing him from the window and is jealous, but it's insult to the injury of leaving. She's made her decision to teach dance, rather than perform, and is packing her things. Jonathan has been too wrapped up in the workshop and freaking out about his birthday to offer the support she needs, and is departing New York the day after his birthday. Jonathan wishes he could just *See Her Smile*.

Finally, it's the day of the workshop. At first, Jonathan is panicking amidst an empty venue, but as the audience begin to file in and the composer sees his idol (Stephen Sondheim), his dread turns to excitement. Karessa delivers a knockout solo *(Come To Your Senses)*, and the audience seems to love the show.

The next morning, however, Rosa delivers the bad news: *Superbia* is too out there to be considered seriously for production, and everyone says to get in touch about whatever he writes next. Years of work came to nothing, and Jonathan goes to Michael's office to announce he's quitting the theatre, but Michael encourages him to stay with it - everyone has their choices to make. Jonathan lashes out, accuses his friend of selling out, living the easy life, and having nothing to fear or worry about. Michael counters by announcing he's HIV+, but hasn't said anything out of deference to Jonathan's other issues. He leaves his friend behind and goes back to work.

In a daze, Jonathan thinks back on his years of friendship with Michael, and finds himself he wandering through Central Park before stumbling over to the Delacorte Theatre and sitting down at a rehearsal piano. He sings about the two most important things to him, Michael and the theatre, and devotes himself to his path *(Why)*.

It's Saturday night and Jonathan's 30th birthday. Jonathan's fears are going away when he sees all his friends, but the phone rings just as he's starting to relax. He lets the machine get it, only to hear Sondheim praising the show and asking for a meeting to discuss his future. The ticks and booms are fading away, and Jonathan seats himself at the piano. He sings of making a better world *(Louder Than Words)* before playing *Happy Birthday*.

J.P. Morgan Saves the Nation[9]

The show takes place on the steps of Federal Hall, at the intersection of Wall and Broad Streets. The New York Stock Exchange is visible just down the street to the left, and the original J.P. Morgan Bank building is directly behind the audience. A giant statue of George Washington is visible at the top of the steps, a part of the building and not the show.

Uncle Sam greets the audience and tells how J.P. Morgan saved the nation in October 1907 by personally bailing out the stock market. A group of *All-American Businessmen* enter to worship Morgan and the system accordingly.

George Washington tells of days gone by and lost heroes, and of his lost influence in the face of change. Lady Liberty tells him to look to Hartford, Connecticut, where America's saviour is newly born - and then drops the baby. She panics, and Washington tries to convince her that their son is well. Washington, a strict disciplinarian, sends the young J.P. Morgan off to boarding school to become a banker. Liberty pines for her child *(I Loved a Sailor)*. Morgan returns, but is in poor health. Washington refuses to coddle the boy, and he spars with Liberty as Morgan leaves for university in Switzerland. Having finished his education, Morgan returns again, to find the family now living in London. His father is in business with a sharp businessman, George Peabody, and his mother is mentally unwell. Morgan is shocked by the change, and takes his father to task for not telling him. Washington canes Morgan with a switch *(The Beating/I Loved a Sailor)*.

Morgan comes back to the United States just as the civil war is breaking out. Uncle Sam tries to recruit the young man, but Washington is having none of it. He pays to have a substitute

9. This synopsis is based on the final production script and therefore differs from the published edition. I will annotate major differences accordingly.

sent instead - Morgan has a higher calling. Morgan is amazed by Manhattan, where his father has set him up in business, and dreams of working for the greater good *(There's An Office Down There)*.[10] Washington offers one last piece of advice before leaving: not everybody is as honest as he is.

Almost immediately, the forces of 19th Century Market Capitalism (aka the Devil) appear to tempt the young man. He accepts her challenge, and the Devil floods the market with paper money, initiating quantitive easing for the first time in American history *(Greenback Dollars)*. Businessmen celebrate their windfalls as their poorer comrades die in the field. Uncle Sam is desperate for rifles, and Morgan works behind the scene, lending money for private companies to buy old guns only to sell them back to the army at a profit to repay the loans. Morgan stays clean of the actual dealing, but Liberty and Washington take him to task for profiteering. Rising in the world of business, the Devil suggests Morgan enjoy the finer things in life *(Get All You Want)*, but Morgan only has eyes for Amelia Sturges, a wealthy society lady with tuberculosis. However, despite all his power and financial prowess, Morgan is incapable of curing her disease and she succumbs *(The Woman Died)*. Morgan shuts off his emotion and dedicates himself to work.

Uncle Sam attempts (and fails) to explain basic economics, and talks about how at the end of the American Civil War, all the new paper money was effectively worthless. Morgan suggests the government remove the money from circulation and take the economic hit which would go with it, but the Devil has a better idea: use the worthless money to buy worthless stock. The market begins to rise, and the age of the railroad baron begins *(Run That Railroad)*.

A melodrama occurs, wherein Liberty plays the role of a small local railroad and the Devil a Wall Street Magnate. Morgan saves

---

10. This song was added late in the rehearsal process and is not in the published script.

Liberty with a loan, despite the Devil's attack on his position, and takes a seat on her company's board to keep an eye on things. Liberty takes on the role of Morgan's second wife *(Susquehanna War)*.

Morgan takes his first vacation to Egypt, where he has a religious awakening. His bank, meanwhile, is buying up failing railroads left and right. Morgan returns to find his investments on the verge of ruin and begins dispatching his agents to make things right - or at least profitable *(He Don't Know How)*. The other railroad barons, however, are all too happy to engage in whatever underhanded action they can to get one over on each other. Morgan and Washington call for a *Gentleman's Agreement,* wherein Morgan will oversee disputes, and the barons agree just long enough to start beating each other to a pulp.

Washington leaves the playing area, and Morgan receives a series of *Telegrams* in reverse from Liberty, informing him that his father died after being gravely injured in an accident.[11] Morgan snaps at her, saying he doesn't want her pity and that she should be as revolted by him as everybody else. She wishes to reconnect with him, but Morgan spurns her and returns to work *(Your Loving Wife)*. The Devil promises riches, seducing him back to the markets *(Little Jack O' Diamonds)*.[12]

Uncle Sam yells at the stagehands as they change the set and then tells the audience to leave if they don't like it.

Morgan holds a banquet in his father's honour and finds himself liberated to conquer all he sees, proving himself a glutton for food, wealth, fine art, and historical relics *(Appetite Annie)*. At the end of the banquet, Morgan reveals it's Christmas season. All of his staff are on Santa's nice list, but they're uneasy about squealing on who's been naughty: Uncle Sam. Morgan finds out that Uncle Sam

---

11. This is based in reality - Morgan's telegrams were held so as to delay the news, but he received them all at once and read the death notice first.

12. These two songs are performed in counterpoint.

has been spending directly from the federal gold reserve, and the United States are rapidly going bankrupt. Morgan and Sam each refuse to back down to the other's demands, but as the reserves dwindle, Sam agrees to let Morgan sell government bonds overseas to raise money *(The Bailout)*. Morgan is wealthy enough that he personally guarantees the bonds on the government's behalf.

The Devil, however, has other ideas, and appears as rival railroad baron Eddie Harriman. Morgan admits that he has his eye on one of the largest railroads in the nation, but the Devil says he must be crazy - she (actually being John D. Rockefeller) owns a majority. Morgan and the Devil go wild buying up stock to block each other, sending the rest of the market into a panic. Morgan wins the battle, but has left a mess behind in his wake. The Devil slinks off, mocking the victor as he deals with the chaos they invoked.

Liberty speaks as a preacher, comparing the US economy to the lost Israelites receiving manna from heaven in the desert - but the people were greedy and offended their financial Lord by placing their savings into speculations, leading to *The Panic*. Banks are failing left and right, but Morgan refuses to help - until the New York Stock Exchange is so cash-strapped that it is incapable of functioning. Morgan writes a personal cheque for US$25 Million and delivers it himself to keep the markets from collapsing *(Hold On To Your Money)*.

In celebration, Morgan opens a grand library to the public to display his art and historical artefacts, but his speech is interrupted by a woman (Liberty) begging for spare change. Morgan sends her off, but feels a moment of guilt. Liberty bemoans how her son has lost his spirit in a miserable world *(I See A Man)*. Photographers mob Morgan, and Liberty tries to hold them back to no avail.

Uncle Sam gleefully serves Morgan with a subpoena to testify before Congress as an example of the evils of over-concentrated wealth. Morgan claims not to know all the details of his business at this point, having entrusted it to his deputies, but believes he has acted entirely for the good of the nation and the companies he's acquired. Uncle Sam and George Washington are less than impressed. When Morgan says that the government is incapable of untangling his corporate web, Washington scorns Morgan for not doing it for them.[13] The committee adjourns, and the Devil explains the *Proceedings* - the whole thing is a show trial to make the common man feel better and to teach Morgan the impact of his actions.

An elderly Morgan is sitting alone, and tells Congress that he is still willing to do anything he can to assist the country in a moment of need. However, his status is ruined and he is seen as toxic. The Devil tries to convince Morgan to change his image, but the old man is aware that his time has come. He retires to Egypt to sail up the Nile - knowing that the Devil ultimately won - but hoping history will remember him for the good he did *(Sail On)*.

---

13. This scene is significantly longer and more technical in the published script.

RENT 1990 (Aronson) Edition

It's Christmas Eve, and painter Mark and playwright Ralph are freezing and failing to create. They rant about their choices in life, how Mark's girlfriend left him for a yuppie, how Ralph is too mired in writer's blocked to get laid, and annoying family members *(Rent)*. Cornell, a philosophy PhD candidate, comes in and half-heartedly hacks away at his thesis. He suggests the group pack up and start a restaurant in *Santa Fe*. Shaun, a musician and the last roommate, played a Wall Street party and got a nice payoff. The group have groceries, including *Meat and Vegetables* for once. The phone rings, and it's the landlord, asking where the rent is *(Wine's Whine)*. Nobody's paid his share.

The group go out except for Ralph, who has to meet a deadline. Mimi, their upstairs neighbour, knocks on the door and asks to borrow a light bulb. She drops her key and Ralph pretends not to find it. They get to know each other *(I Write Plays* for Ralph, *I Make Sculptures out of Found Objects* for Mimi). Ralph invites her to dinner, and they two fall in love *(I Should Tell You)*.

Shaun and Cornell are at a nearby cafe where two homeless people are loudly hitting up the patrons for cash *(Any Money?, Dollar)*. Shaun gives them each a buck. Mark shows up, and commiserates with Cornell and Shaun that he needs a *Warm Body* to keep him company. The three sigh over their lack of women. The street is suddenly full of life, with people telling each other to *Have a Happy* Christmas. One of the homeless people is selling stuff he's found or stolen, Ralph buys Mimi a paper flower, and the trio are impressed by Mimi's looks (and art degree from Kansas). Just as the mood is picking up, Mark's ex, Suzanne, enters with Martin, her new yuppie boyfriend. Mark tries to ignore her, but she demands to be the centre of attention and jumps on a table to sing her new political anthem, *When I Turn to Shit*. Everybody is embarrassed, especially Martin, who gladly runs off when Suzanne asks for some stomach medicine. Suzanne hits on Mark, and their rocky relationship begins again. Shaun finds out his wallet was stolen, but Suzanne has Martin's briefcase and pays the bills with his credit card.

It's February, and Suzanne and Mark are living at a local night club. She sings there at night, he paints murals. The cleaner hates cleaning up after the punters, but loathes the snow even more *(Shovel Shuffle)*. Mimi comes to visit, asking Mark why Ralph has become so withdrawn *(Why Does He?)*. She hides when Ralph appears, and Ralph feels the relationship is over *(It Just Isn't Working)*, but confesses his real problem is that Mimi is obviously sick *(Watching her Shrink)*. To make matters worse, one of Mimi's academic friends has been hitting on her. Ralph decides to let her go so she can live somewhere with heat and regular meals. When Mimi starts sobbing, Ralph realises she's heard him. The two break up *(My Velvet Case)*, as do Mark and Suzanne over his jealousy and her perceived infidelity *(So This is it Then)*.

It's now Spring, and Ralph and Mark are back in their old apartment, still unable to create out of pining for their lost loves *(Dry)*. Shaun and Cornell have bought a meagre dinner, and the group try to pretend it's a posh feast *(Swordfish Marinara)*. Suzanne rings the bell, along with an emaciated Mimi, who is clutching a cane. Mimi's professor boyfriend dumped her for speaking to community groups about women with AIDS, and she had to move out. The group awkwardly, silently watch over her *(Waiting for Death Ballet)*. Suzanne breaks the silence and demands they send for a doctor. Cornell decides to pawn his coat to buy Mimi a pair of gloves for her freezing hands, and drags Shaun along *(My Old Jacket)*. Mark and Suzanne go to another room, leaving Ralph and Mimi alone. Mimi hopes to be reincarnated into a simpler being *(I Believe)*. The two embrace and reprise the warnings they gave each other at the start of their relationship. Cornell and Shaun give Mimi the gloves, and tell her the weather is beautiful. She dies, leaving everybody crushed. A doctor enters and silently confirms the death.

RENT 1993 (First Public Reading) Edition

ACT ONE:

The show begins on Christmas Eve in a loft lit by candles and moonlight. Musician Roger Davis and videographer Mark Cohen are huddled under blankets trying to stay warm and failing to be artistic. Roger plucks out a solo on his guitar, but pops a string, causing all the electrical equipment to blow. The two jump around, sarcastically rant about killing themselves to spite exes and family, bust up the furniture, and burn the remains along with their old creations, trying to stay warm as they worry about an impending visit from the landlord: *Rent* is due.

In a nearby lot, Tom Collins is mugged for his coat and helped afterwards by homeless trio Rudy Ramirez, Mrs. Chance, and Dogman, plus street performer Angel. Collins and Angel fall in love at first sight, and the group huddles around a smudge pot while dreaming of warmer climes *(You Okay Honey/Santa Fe)*. On the other side of the lot, performance artist Maureen Johnson is fretting over the new equipment lover Joanne Strudwick has bought her: neither of them knows how to set it up, and they share a tense moment when Maureen reminisces how Mark could handle her gear. She then frets about her falling T-Cell count before sending Joanne home for cables *(Female to Female)*.

In the loft, Mark and Roger hide from a knock on the door, fearing the worst. It turns out to be Collins, loaded down with food, smokes, and booze *(Bustello Marlboro)*. He introduces the pair to Angel, who tells them how a rich woman hired him to kill a neighbour's yappy dog *(Today 4 U)*. Landlord Benjamin Coffin enters, talking on his hip new cellular phone and planning a trip to Aruba with his wife. He demands three months' owed rent (Mark and Roger haven't paid since first moving in) so he can complete a deal to open a discount franchise. The group gives Benny the run-around and learn whose dog just died before Angel points out that Benny's car is being towed away *(A Little Business)*.

Below the loft, Mimi Marquez dreams of dancers performing "skewed takes on 'normal' activities" and the music combines with "sampled 'hospital sounds,' soundbites from the 'Evening News,' and 'the wail of a screaming infant,'" before the Grim Reaper appears. Mimi wakes up in a panic and shoots up.[14] *On the Street,* Mrs. Chance is harassed by the police.

As Mark, Collins, and Angel prepare to head back out, Angel asks why Roger is staying behind and moping. Mark explains Roger's tendency to sulk and how the latter threatens to flee New York *(He Says)*. Roger attempts to get in touch with his *Right Brain,* thinking of driving along the seafront and a passionate encounter. He is interrupted by Mimi knocking on the door, asking "would you *Light My Candle?*" Mimi falls for him, but Roger tries not to fall in love with her as he tells of his dead ex and learns that she uses heroin - a habit he painfully kicked. Roger tries to hide Mimi's stash, but she recovers it.

Back in the lot, Mark and the new lovers pass Maureen. Mark goes over to her, and she awkwardly tries to kiss up to him to fix her equipment, but he, still angry about being dumped, walks off *(Female to Male)*. In the loft, Mimi has shot up and wants Roger to take her *Out Tonight.*

Mark, Collins, and Angel are at an HIV+ support group. Members of the group ask "*Will I* lose my dignity?" and at the end of the song, the Reaper reappears. After the meeting, Mark returns to fix Maureen's equipment, and they reconnect while admitting what they learned from each other *(You Were Right)*. Maureen

---

14. This segment was narrated at the reading, but Larson never scored music for the segment and it was ultimately never performed.

reveals that she felt Mark couldn't cope with her HIV status, Mark felt she was pushing him away when he tried to be there for her. Joanne returns to see them in an embrace.

Roger doesn't feel the love tonight. He rejects Mimi's advances, telling her to come back *Another Day*. She tries to centre herself with the message she learned at the same HIV+ support group the trio were at earlier. It's not enough, and Roger kicks her out.

It's St. Mark's Place, a busy park-turned-bazaar, where Angel buys Collins a coat, Mark and Roger discuss their dating issues, and Roger prevents Mimi from buying a new stash, inviting her to dinner *(Christmas Bells)*. The group convenes to see Maureen perform an avant garde piece about a blind cow in a desert punishing herself for getting cable TV. A bull spews a party line, saying an orchard will bloom there again, but the cow says it will only occur with action before jumping *Over The Moon*.

Following the performance, the bohemians and friends go to the nearby Life Cafe where congressman Otam A. DeSnofla - famous for hating the NEA - declares war on all liberal and fringe members of society. The principles celebrate *La Vie Boheme* as Collins and Angel grow closer, Mimi and Roger skirt the issues between them, and Mark and Maureen have a quickie in the bath-room, causing Joanne - sent to pack up after the show - to dump Maureen. DeSnofla is photographed with Angel and a riot breaks out when he orders the police to clear the area. Various beepers go off, reminding the cast to take their various AIDS medications. Roger and Mimi unpack their baggage, reveal their HIV+ status to each other, and fall in love *(I Should Tell You)*.

ACT TWO:

The stage has been reset with risers, and opens at a funeral *(Seasons of Love)* before going into flashback. Mimi is hitting the drugs as hard as ever, and she sings lead in Maureen's new piece, telling of her years on the street and passion for rough sex while Maureen has tried (and failed) to patch things up with Joanne, sending Mark into jealous fits. Collins and Angel remain blissfully happy. As *Valentine's Day* comes to an end, Roger has walked out on Mimi, and Mark, Maureen, and Joanne are all on the outs. We see the funeral choir again *(Seasons of Love B)*.

It's Easter, and the homeless are still suffering. The lovers make up, get sick, and part as Joanne decides that she needs Maureen *(Without You)*. For Collins and Angel, time is running out: Angel is sick, and Collins is by his side. On a stormy summer night, Angel has a fevered dream of sex and death, and everybody's relationship is back on the rocks *(Contact)*. At the end of the song, the Reaper appears for the last time and takes Angel's hand: it's his funeral, and the Bohemians deliver their eulogies before Mrs. Chance implores them to embrace life and *Love the Pain*.

After the funeral, the bohemians fight and Mimi is revealed to be dating Benny, the landlord. Roger would rather head out of town than confront Mimi's declining health, leaving her despondent in Benny's arms *(Goodbye Love)*. The pastor kicks the group out for being unable to pay the funeral bills, only to discover that DeSnofla has lost his congressional seat and wealth. He laments his exile from the *US of Ease*, joined by the homeless trio as they explain how they wound up on the streets. Mark concludes that his life may not be so bad. Roger faces the *Open Road* and bemoans his breakup with Mimi, returning to New York when he finds out her phone has been disconnected.

It's Christmas Eve again. The homeless are still broke and on the outs. Roger and Mark are single and bitter about the women in their lives, but Collins has hacked the local ATM and brought the proceeds, just as Benny busts in with an eviction notice. Roger threatens to reveal Benny's affair to his wife when Maureen shows up with a ravaged and feverish Mimi. Mark and Maureen offer things for Collins to sell so they can get Mimi a doctor, and Collins decides to sell the coat Angel bought him. Roger and Mimi reconcile before she passes out. Roger wails, but Mimi's fever begins to break and she lives another day. *(Finale)*

RENT 1994 (Studio Production) Edition

ACT ONE:

The phone rings in a dark apartment on Christmas Eve. An answering machine picks up: musician Roger Davis is being fired for no-showing at his bartending job. The lights fade up and we see a distraught loft full of old industrial equipment and jerry-rigged electronics. Roger, along with his videographer roommate Mark Cohen, are huddled under blankets, freezing. They let another call go to the machine. This time it's Mark's mother, wishing him a merry Christmas - but reminding him that they really won't pay any more of his bills. A third call, and one bringing doom: it's ex-roommate-turned-landlord Benny, saying he's on the way to collect the rent - he's got a big deal in the works *(Phone Message #1)*. Roger tries to pick out a melody on his guitar, but it's so cold, a string snaps and all the circuits in the loft blow.

The pair rage, jumping around to try and stay warm, and making sarcastic comments about killing themselves and cursing their ex-lovers. At the same time, philosopher Tom Collins is mugged for his coat in the lot next to the building, and he's helped afterwards by Angel. Across the lot, Maureen Johnson and Joanne Jefferson are trying to set up for Maureen's performance that night, both stressed beyond belief. Mark and Roger smash up some spare crates for firewood and light it with their own music and screenplays for kindling, panicking about how to pay the *Rent*.

For Mark, the answer's simple: run away. As he tries to leave, Roger mocks him for fleeing everything, not least his lesbian ex-girlfriend. Mark returns the favour by accusing Roger of hiding behind his HIV+ status rather than doing something with what's left of his life. The pair trade barbs, each wanting an aspect of the other's life (Mark wants Roger's charisma, Roger, Mark's work ethic) *(Cool/Fool)*. They're interrupted by a knock on the door and, fearing the worst, hide. However, it turns out to be Collins, loaded down with food, smokes, and booze *(Bustello Marlboro)*. He introduces the pair to Angel, who tells them how a rich woman hired him to kill a neighbour's yappy dog *(Today 4 U)*.

Benny arrives and can't believe how his former friends are still struggling when he's made it big - he just had to do *A Little Business*. Now, he needs to buy one more building before he can clear the block and rebuild, anchored by a video franchise. He tells the group that Maureen's show - a protest against him - needs to wrap early so they can fence off the lot, and tries to collect the rent. The group distract him, learning whose dog Angel killed as a result. Benny tries one last time to collect, but Angel points out Benny's car is being towed away, and the group are temporarily saved.

In the lot, Maureen is freaking out over getting her equipment set up, and fights with a frustrated and in-over-her-head Joanne before sending the latter home to fetch a missing cable *(Female to Female)*.

Mark and Collins tell Angel about how Benny used to live with them, and Angel invites the others to join him and Collins at an HIV+ support group before Maureen's show *(He Says)*. Roger rudely declines, and Mark tells him off for it. Mark touches a nerve when pointing out that as much as Roger says he loved his suicidal ex-girlfriend, he never drives the car she left him. When Mark tries to drag him to the support group one last time, Roger responds violently and sulks in a corner. Mark worries about Roger's withdrawal, but Roger knows Mark's benefitting professionally from his concern by shooting documentary footage. Mark, Collins, and Angel leave.

Roger attempts to get in touch with his *Right Brain*, thinking of driving along the seafront and a passionate encounter. He is interrupted by Mimi knocking on the door, asking "would you *Light My Candle?*" She falls for him, but he tries not to fall in love with her as he tells of his dead ex and learns that she uses heroin - a habit he painfully kicked. He tries to hide her stash, but she recovers it from him and shoots up.

As Joanne goes digging for cables, her parents leave a message on her answering machine: Joanne's mother is up for a prominent political position and they need her - alone - to come visit and help prepare *(Phone Message #2)*. Joanne, unable to find the cable, returns to Maureen, who wishes Mark was there instead - at least he knows how his way around the stage. Joanne fumes, and the two tentatively make up before Maureen remembers where the cable was, sending Joanne off again. What Maureen can't remember, though, is her lines *(Female to Female #2)*.

Confronted by everything he fears in a single person, Roger rejects Mimi's advances, telling her to come back *Another Day.* She tries to centre herself with the message she learned at the same HIV+ support group the trio were at earlier. It's not enough, and Roger kicks her out.

After the meeting, Mark films a homeless woman being harassed by the police, thereby driving away the cops, but when he keeps shooting, she tells him off *(X-Mo Bells #2/Bummer)*. Collins and Angel try to cheer him up, and the trio dream of a warmer, simpler life *(Santa Fe)*. Mark spots Maureen in the lot, and after a brief moment of panic, decides enough is enough and goes to confront her. Left alone, Collins and Angel declare their love for each other *(I'll Cover You)*. At a late HIV+ support group meeting, an attendee asks "*Will I* lose my dignity?" - a question the homeless population and main characters consider as well.

Maureen spots Mark and tries sucking up to him to get technical help. Mark takes advantage of the situation, asking Maureen about her new lesbian life before begging her to come back. Maureen tells him to find someone new - he'll get *Over It* - but gives him a kiss when he fixes her equipment. Joanne returns just in time to see the end of their exchange, and the trio split awkwardly.

Mark rejoins Collins and Angel, and they head to St. Mark's Place for some last-minute shopping and Christmas cheer before Maureen's show. Angel buys Collins a coat, and to Mark's surprise, Roger is there as well. Mark thinks Maureen is going to come back to him, but Roger ignores Mark's ramblings to fret about Mimi - who he sees about to buy another stash. The singer intervenes, apologising for his behaviour and inviting her to dinner. She agrees. Maureen has one final moment of stage fright *(Christmas Bells)*.

In the lot, Maureen performs an avant garde piece about a blind cow in a desert punishing herself for getting cable TV. A bull spews a party line, saying an orchard will bloom again in the desert, but the cow says it will only occur with action before jumping *Over The Moon*.

After the show, the group go to the nearby, trendy Life Cafe. Benny is there, along with a representative from Blockbuster Video, and the two are hammering out their deal. Benny tells Mark and Roger they're off the hook - for now - and asks Mimi why she'd hang out with such losers, implying they're close. He points out that gentrification will do the neighbourhood good, and declares their ideal Bohemia dead. Mark and the group reply by holding a mock funeral and celebrating *La Vie Boheme*. Joanne comes in and out, still stuck as Maureen's errand girl, and their physical affection gets some unwanted attention from the Blockbuster lady - which the others use to taunt the latter further. Mark attempts to proposition Maureen, but is shot down. Mimi is angry that Roger's been ignoring her, and he admits to being afraid and holding back. Mark gets a shot of the Blockbuster rep hugging Angel, and she runs off in embarrassment, chased by Benny. Beepers go off, telling various HIV+ characters to take their medication. Roger discovers Mimi's

HIV+ status as a result. Joanne returns to see Maureen giving Mark a hug after taking her medication and fumes, telling everybody that a riot broke out when Benny ordered the police to clear the lot. Roger and Mimi unpack their issues and fall in love *(I Should Tell You)*.

ACT TWO:

The following Halloween. An answering machine greeting informs callers of a funeral, and a doctor's secretary leaves Mimi a message that her blood work is in and she needs to see a doctor ASAP *(Phone Message #3)*. At the funeral, a choir sings a gospel song in honour of the deceased *(Seasons of Love)*.

Lights hit, and the show flashes back to Valentine's Day. The characters occupy various beds. Mimi begs a distant Roger to take her *Out Tonight*, Collins and Angel snuggle up, and Mark is still pestering Maureen. Joanne has taken her back, but they're already on the verge of another breakup. We see another flash forward to the funeral *(Seasons of Love B)*.

It's spring, and Mark is still hounding Maureen *(Phone Message #4)*. The characters change beds to reflect the passing of time, as Maureen and Joanne sing of missing each other and reconcile *(Without You)*.

Another call signifies the start of summer: one of Collins' students can't find "The Story of O" at her local bookstore and wonders if he's really gone off to steal an air conditioner *(Phone Message #5)*. A thunderstorm breaks out, and Angel has a fevered dream of sex and death. By the end, Mimi and Roger have broken up and Maureen and Joanne are again calling it quits. Things are over for Collins and Angel as well: the latter has succumbed to AIDS and died *(Contact)*. Mimi, Mark, and Maureen deliver eulogies at the funeral, and Collins sings of his lost love to the coat Angel bought him *(I'll Cover You: Reprise)*.

Civilities break down after the funeral. Roger's finally making good on his promise to leave New York, Mimi is going out with Benny, and Joanne is tired of Maureen walking all over her. Mark tries to be a peacemaker, and Collins begs them to remember how much Angel wanted everyone to be friends. Roger storms off when he sees Mimi close with Benny, and Mark tries to get his friend to reconcile his relationship, but to no avail. Roger is terrified to see Mimi die, and Mark, when asked for advice, confesses his own helplessness - he's buried himself so far under his work that he's forgotten how to live. Mimi overhears the entire conversation, and tearfully tells Roger *Goodbye, Love* before running off.

The pastor kicks the group out of the church for being unable to pay the funeral bill, but Benny offers to cover the costs. Mark groans about how nice it would be to have money and a sex life, and Benny admits that he's been wanting Mark to join him as a *Real Estate* mogul. The Blockbuster woman agrees, and Mark briefly considers the offer before deciding it's more important to finish his film. Meanwhile, Roger faces the *Open Road* and bemoans his breakup with Mimi, returning to New York when he finds out her phone has been disconnected.

It's the following Christmas, and nobody knows where Mark, Roger, and Mimi are *(Phone Message #6)*. The homeless are living in a new lot, and Mark and Roger are again forced to heat themselves up by bouncing around - but this time it's to pack. They joke about killing themselves again, and Collins shows up with a gift: he's hacked an ATM to give them free money. Benny appears on a motorcycle, presenting the boys with an eviction notice, but it's too late: they're already moving to Brooklyn. Benny reveals that his wife forced him to drop the Blockbuster arrangement and threatened to cut him off from her trust fund if he kept doing underhanded deals. He offers to let the group stay if they can pay the rent, but omits mentioning Mimi. Mark and Roger threaten to reveal Benny's affair, but Benny dumped Mimi when her HIV infection progressed and rescinds his offer. Roger throws Benny's phone out the window when Maureen and Joanne show up with an emaciated Mimi. The latter had been living in a nearby park, and the group give Collins things to sell to pay for a doctor. Collins says farewell to his coat. Mark has come to terms with Maureen's relationship, and tells her and Joanne that he's finished his film about the group. They pray for Mimi to live while she and Roger come clean. Exhaustion forces her to pass out and Roger wails, but Mimi's fever begins to break and she lives another day. *(Finale)*

RENT 1995 (Intermediate Overhaul) Edition

ACT ONE:

It's *Halloween (I)*, and a crew from TV show "Buzzline" is filming a funeral. Most of the crew are frustrated, as director/host Mark Cohen is clearly distracted and wondering what he did to end up in this situation.

It is now ten months earlier, on Christmas Eve. In an industrial loft, Mark is huddled up in a blanket, as is his roommate, Roger. Mark's mom leaves him a message, wishing him a merry Christmas and imploring him to make up with his father over the scandal his last film caused *(Voice Mail #1)*. As Roger attempts to *Tune Up* his guitar, Mark sets up a camera, and announces his grand vision to make a new film - both to spite his ex, Maureen, and to try breaking out of a slump. Mark shoots footage around the apartment, of Roger with the guitar his father left, and of the painting Roger's girlfriend April made before leaving a note that she and Roger were both HIV+ and slitting her wrists.

Benjamin Coffin III, the pair's ex-roommate, enters needing a favour: the city's rezoning their block, which means he can open his new high-end entertainment studio. However, Maureen's holding a performance in protest, and her new girlfriend Joanne has made sure the press know about it. Benny has pulled some strings, and the police will move in if needed, but he'd rather his friends solve things amongst themselves and get Maureen to cancel. Mark and Roger receive an ultimatum: stop the show, pay the rent he's not been charging them, or leave. They have until midnight to decide. Roger tries to pick out a melody on his guitar, but a string breaks in the cold and the power blows.

The pair thrash around the loft and rant - Mark about how

nothing he could make up for a film is more messed up than reality and Roger about his lost connection with music, as they worry about how to pay the *Rent*. On the upside, old buddy Collins is back in town. He demands Roger leave the house for the first time after six months, but is instead summoned to the loft. Before Collins can hang up the phone, two hoodlums mug him for his coat. In the lot, Joanne is trying to set up Maureen's equipment, calm the worried diva, and deal with a homeless man who just relieved himself on some sound gear, causing it to short out. Mark and Roger torch their old creations in an attempt to stay warm, and the nearby police precinct prepares for the worst. The homeless man from earlier overhears the call going out on a policeman's radio and spreads word of an impending riot. Maureen calls Mark in a panic, begging him to fix her equipment. He caves in and agrees to do it, and along with Roger, figures Benny won't follow through on his threat. The pair decide to stand against him.

On the street, Angel is playing drums when Collins crawls out of some bushes. The two fall in love at first sight and Angel offers moral and physical support *(You Okay Honey?)*

Mark has left to fix Maureen's equipment, and Roger asks how he can make it in his current state of mind. He fiddles with another guitar, hoping to write one last song before he dies *(One Song Glory)*. He's interrupted by a knock at the door: downstairs neighbour Mimi Marquez needs him to *Light My Candle*. The two hit it off, but Roger is on edge - especially when Mimi accidentally drops her heroin - Roger is a recovering addict. He finds her stash and tries to hide it from her, but to no avail.

While Joanne continues fumbling with Maureen's equipment, her parents leave a message on her answering machine, informing her of their posh plans for the holidays, reminding her that her real job is in legal aid for underprivileged families, and telling her to come home - alone - for her mother's upcoming high-powered confirmation hearing *(Voice Mail #2)*.

Collins has finally made it to the loft, and announces he's been fired from his position at MIT. He introduces Mark and Roger to Angel, who is loaded after a wealthy woman hired him to kill her neighbour's yappy dog. Angel tells them of the incident, of what happened to Collins, and how they connected *(Today 4 U)*.

Mark leaves with Collins and Angel and films a homeless woman being harassed by the police, causing the officer to back off. When he continues filming, the woman reveals how insulted she feels as a result *(X-Mo Bells #2/Bummer)*. Collins and Angel try to cheer Mark up, and the trio dream of a simpler life in warmer climes *(Santa Fe)*.

Back in the loft, Mimi is shooting up and trying to come onto Roger, who is instead trying his best to ignore her *(Out Tonight)*. In the lot, Mark makes plans to meet up with Collins and Angel at a nearby HIV+ support group meeting before he has an awkward encounter with Joanne. She says everything is great, but Mark warns her that she's dancing the *Tango: Maureen*. He fills Joanne in on their shared lover's past, complete with her routine infidelities. Mark fixes the equipment, but Joanne is depressed.

Mark then literally stumbles in late to the *Life Support* meeting, where regular attendee Gordon finds it hard to swallow the group's upbeat "live life as fully as you can" message - he finds fear in everything and his brain keeps telling him he should be long dead.

Mimi's finished shooting up, and Roger's had enough. He rails at her for being a user and for bothering him when he's trying to work. She tries to centre herself with the affirmation from Life Support and calm Roger down with it as well, but he's having none of it: if she cleans up, she can try again *Another Day*. Overcome by fear and rage, he throws her out of the loft.

It's *Halloween (II)* again, and the "Buzzline" crew are shocked that the mourners are attending in costume. Mark reflects on the prior Christmas and how it's burned itself into his mind. The segment producer is pissed off, but the cameraman reminds them that the funeral is for one of Mark's friends. Mark recalls the end of the Life Support meeting and a young man who asked "*Will I* lose my dignity?"

Christmas Eve, and Joanne is on the phone with Maureen. Her attempts to gather press and a huge audience have failed and everything Mark warned her about has turned out to be true *(We're Okay)*. Mark leaves Collins and Angel, and the pair declare their love for each other *(I'll Cover You)*.

At St. Mark's Place, the homeless are upset over the lack of donations. Angel buys Collins a coat, and to Mark's surprise, Roger is there as well. Mark talks about meeting Joanne, but Roger ignores him to fret about Mimi, who he sees about to buy another stash. The singer intervenes, apologising for his behaviour and inviting Mimi to dinner. She agrees to go. Benny calls the police to inform them the protest is still on *(Christmas Bells)*.

Maureen gives her performance, a piece about meeting Elsie, a cow who used to be an advertising mascot but now lives in a digital desert where new walls and buildings are cutting off all sense of community. Elsie wants to escape, feeling that her world is about to explode. The homeless man who peed on Maureen's equipment gets on stage, and Maureen subtly tries to get him to leave, but fails. She continues that a dog - Benny - gave up his poor, independent roots to be a rich woman's lapdog. Benny (the dog) says the cow is just having female issues, and wonders who'd want to leave: everything an artist needs to be huge is there in the digital desert.

Maureen finishes the piece by being granted a drink of Elsie's milk before the cow jumps *Over the Moon*.

After the show, the gang go to the trendy Life Cafe. Benny is there with a police sergeant, and gloats about how Maureen had no press, no audience, and the homeless man on stage. Roger asks why Benny's wife wasn't there, and the group find out whose dog Angel killed. Benny comes on to Mimi, asking why she'd hang out with such losers when he's trying to clean up the area, then says everyone's idealised Bohemia is only found in fiction - and the idea is dead. In rebellion, the others throw a mock funeral and celebrate *La Vie Boheme*. Joanne comes back and forth from the lot, stuck serving as Maureen's pack-mule. Mark and Maureen reconcile, and he blesses her relationship with Joanne. Mimi is frustrated at Roger's inattention, and he admits that he's got issues holding him back - but so does she. A pair of beepers go off, and they both reach for their HIV medication, revealing their status to each other.

Benny orders the police to clear the lot and board up Mark and Roger's building. Joanne returns and orders Maureen to pack her bags. She tells the group that the homeless are refusing to leave, staying put and mooing. A riot has broken out.

Halloween (III). It's started to rain, and Mark remembers new beginnings. Amidst the Christmas Eve chaos, Roger and Mimi confess their flaws and fall in love *(I Should Tell You)*.

ACT TWO:

The funeral. A costumed choir comes forward and sings a gospel tribute to a fallen friend *(Seasons of Love)*.

It's New Year's Eve. Mark, Roger, and Mimi are working out how to break back into their building *(Happy New Year A)*. Mimi announces that she's going clean and wants to get her GED. Roger can't believe he's actually happy, and Mark's the only one taking things seriously. Maureen enters, and we find out Mark sold his footage of the riots to the local news. Maureen and Joanne, though, are still on the outs. Maureen calls her ex-girlfriend, begging for forgiveness, but Joanne is already there and gives Maureen a second chance. Mark and Joanne, now buddies, concoct a scheme to break in. This time, Maureen has to do the leg work. Collins and Angel enter, dressed to the nines and as close as ever.

From inside the loft, Mark sees that power is restored. His mother has left him a congratulatory message on making the news - even his father's impressed. Mark's also received a message from Alexi Darling, executive producer of a hip news show, asking him for a meeting *(Voice Mail #3)*.

Mark announces he's taking whatever they offer, and Maureen decides to plan another protest. Angel blowtorches the locks, and the building is reopened. Benny enters, seeking forgiveness and good PR *(Happy New Year B)*. The group have him figured out and refuse his offer. Angry, Benny implies that it was only because Mimi came to seduce him and he had pity as her ex - she says she visited him on her way to her erotic dance job, but turned down his advances. Angel brokers a hasty and uneasy peace, and Mimi and Roger tentatively move on - though she gives into temptation and buys a new stash.

Another glimpse of the funeral… *(Seasons of Love B)*

It's Easter, and Mark is starting to question his new job, delivering cheesy segments around the city *(Buzzline I)*. Mimi is back on the drugs and hiding it from Roger, who thinks she's hiding an affair with Benny before he learns the truth. He leaves. Collins is in hospital but recovers, though Angel takes his place. Mimi sings of how she needs Roger in her life, and they make up *(Without You)*.

Mark delivers another cringe-worthy segment for *Buzzline (II)* on the 4th of July.

A feverish orgy breaks out on stage *(Contact A)*. Everybody is under a giant sheet, which splits like a vaudevillian curtain, to reveal Maureen and Joanne having a fight. Maureen got a grant off the back of "Over the Moon" and accuses Joanne (whose parents were on the committee) of jealousy, now that the latter's legal aid foundation isn't getting any attention. They kiss, but break down into a comedic fight before deciding the only way to stay together is to never stop screwing *(Love of My Life)*. The curtain closes, and Angel appears above the action in a feverish dream of sex and death. He disappears as the music cuts off, and everybody ended up having a bad time in the sack, the straw breaking the back of each relationship except one - Collins is alone because Angel has died *(Contact B)*.

Mimi, Mark, and Maureen eulogise Angel at the funeral, and Collins mourns his relationship and lost lover *(I'll Cover You: Reprise)*. Outside the church, Mark cracks. He can't turn his friend's death into a soundbite-friendly news story. Fights break out as the others leave the church: Roger's sold his guitar and is leaving New York, Mimi's hooking up with Benny, and Maureen and Joanne are barely talking to each other. Mark and Benny try to calm the other four down, but to no avail. Collins berates the group for not heeding Angel's wish that they all remain friends. Maureen and Joanne get back together - albeit tensely - and leave. Mark confronts Roger over abandoning Mimi, but Roger turns it back on Mark: who is he to pass judgement when he hides behind his camera? Mark points out that Mimi still loves Roger, but that she's with Benny because he can pay her medical bills. Roger can't cope and leaves, but Mimi has heard everything and just wants to say *Goodbye Love*. Scared, she begs Benny to pay for her to go to rehab. He agrees, but she finds no comfort in his arms.

Collins is kicked out of the church for not being able to pay the funeral bill. Benny offers to pay, and Collins apologises because Angel killed Benny's dog. Benny doesn't sweat it - he always hated the thing. Mark tries to film his segment again, but fails. He thinks of Angel, and Roger, from the road, thinks of Mimi. Finding their projects' souls in their missing friends, Mark quits his TV job, asking his father to hire a lawyer, and Roger returns to New York *(What You Own)*.

It's winter, and nobody knows where Mark, Roger, and Mimi are *(Voice Mail #4)*. The homeless are still down on their luck, and in the loft, Mark is showing Roger a rough cut of his film… only for the power to blow *(Finale A)*. The pair are living rent-free, with Benny's wife making him stay away after learning of his affair with Mimi. Collins shows up with some money, having hacked a nearby ATM, and while the group dream of leaving, they admit they'd never be able to live anywhere but New York. Maureen shows up along with Joanne and an emaciated Mimi, who's been living in a nearby park post-rehab. Deathly ill with a high fever, she asks to see Roger one last time. The pair apologise to each other and admit their love, but Mimi passes out from exhaustion. Roger sings her the song he's been working on all year *(Your Eyes)*, and Mimi appears to die, but ultimately stirs. She saw Angel in a heavenly light, and was sent back to Earth. Her fever starts to break, and she lives another day *(Finale B)*.

RENT 1996 (Broadway) Edition[15]

ACT ONE:

It's Christmas Eve in a freezing East Village loft which overlooks a tent city full of homeless people. Inside, filmmaker Mark Cohen and his musician roommate, Roger Davis, are attempting to start new projects: Mark a verité documentary, and Roger a new song. Mark describes their loft before pointing out that Roger has just emerged from six months of heroin withdrawal, and they playfully give each other a hard time until the phone rings *(Tune Up #1).*[16] They let the answering machine pick up, and it's Mark's mother, wishing him a Merry Christmas and offering her condolences that Maureen, Mark's recent ex, turned out to be a lesbian *(Voice Mail #1).* Mark resumes shooting, only to be interrupted again by the phone *(Tune Up #2).* Old friend Tom Collins is back in town and needs the key to get inside. Mark tosses it down, but before Collins can come in, he gets mugged for his coat. Confused, Mark instantly picks up when the phone rings again. This time it's ex-roommate-turned-landlord Benjamin Coffin III, who's on his way to collect the last year's rent despite previously promising that they could live there for free. Benny is curious about Maureen's performance that night, but new girlfriend Joanne has also shut Mark out of Maureen's professional life. Dejected, Roger tries to pluck out a melody on his guitar, but the fuse goes on his amp, taking their jerry-rigged power hookup down with it.

The pair jump and thrash around the loft and rant - Mark about how nothing he could make up for a film is more messed

---

15. Structural differences from Larson's final script are presented as footnotes to demonstrate posthumous revisions.

16. Mark's opening monologue, describing the loft, was constructed from stage descriptions following Larson's death. The idea most likely came from the 1994 studio reading, where the character narrated most of the show's settings.

up than reality and Roger about his lost connection with music, as they worry about how to pay the *Rent*. In the lot, Joanne is trying to set up Maureen's equipment and calm down the worried diva. Collis is worse for wear after being attacked, and Mark and Roger torch their old creations in an attempt to stay warm. Maureen calls Mark in a panic, begging him to fix her equipment. He caves in and agrees to do it, and along with Roger, figures Benny won't follow through on his threat. The pair decide to stand against him.

On the streets, Angel is playing drums when Collins crawls out of some bushes. The two fall in love at first sight and Angel offers moral and physical support *(You Okay Honey?)*

Mark heads out to fix Maureen's equipment and takes a shot of the reclusive Roger, informing the camera that the musician's girlfriend left a note saying they had AIDS before killing herself *(Tune Up #3)*.[17] Roger wishes he could write an amazing song before the disease takes him *(One Song Glory)*, but there's a knock on the door just as he gets into the zone. Thinking it's Mark come back to get something, Roger is surprised to see downstairs neighbour Mimi shivering and asking "Would you *Light My Candle?*" The pair hit it off, but Roger is wary when Mimi accidentally reveals herself to be a heroin user. Roger pretends not to find her dropped stash, but Mimi manages to get it from him and leaves.

As Joanne grows increasingly frustrated with Maureen's sound gear, her parents leave a message on her answering machine informing her of their posh plans for the holidays, reminding her that her real job is in legal aid for underprivileged families, and telling her to come home - alone - for her mother's upcoming high-powered confirmation hearing *(Voice Mail #2)*.

Mark's found Collins and Angel and brings them back to the

---

17. In Larson's final draft, 'Tune Up #3' is split to bookend 'You Okay Honey?'

loft, complete with a bucket of goodies courtesy of Angel, who was commissioned by a rich woman to kill her neighbour's annoying dog. He regales the crew with the story and how he found Collins injured on the street *(Today 4 U)*. Benny arrives and explains what's going on: the block with their building and the neighbouring lot have been rezoned, and Benny wants to tear down the building to create a high-end production studio subsidised by expensive condos. However, Maureen's show has the potential to create a lot of negative press, and if Mark and Roger can convince her to call it off, he'll give them a written contract guaranteeing them a free place to live. They refuse, wondering where their friend's sense of social justice has gone *(You'll See)*.[18]

In the lot, Mark has an awkward encounter with Joanne. She says everything is great, but Mark warns her that she's dancing the *Tango: Maureen*, and fills Joanne in on their shared lover's past, complete with her routine infidelities. Mark fixes the equipment, but Joanne is depressed.

After leaving Joanne, Mark literally stumbles in late to the *Life Support* meeting, where Gordon, one of the regular attendees, finds it hard to swallow the group's upbeat "live life as fully as you can" message - he finds fear in everything and his brain keeps telling him he should be long dead. Alone at home, Roger expresses the same regret.

In her apartment, Mimi is going through various outfits and trying to look her best: she has to go *Out Tonight* and begs Roger to go with her. Roger, however, is gripped with fear: Mimi represents everything he's had to kick since April's death, and he reacts poorly. Mimi tries to centre herself with a mantra from the Life Support group, but this just infuriates Roger more and in a moment of panic, he throws her out, telling her to try *Another Day*. Back at

---

18. In Larson's script, the running order goes 'Today 4 U' -> 'You'll See' -> 'Voice Mail #2.'

the meeting, someone asks "*Will I* lose my dignity?" The question resounds with all the characters. Roger regrets what he's done and leaves the house for the first time in six months to find Mimi.[19]

After the meeting, Mark films a homeless woman being harassed by the police on the street, causing the officer to back off. When he continues filming, the woman rebuffs him for insulting her by doing so *(X-Mo Bells #2/Bummer)*. Collins and Angel try to cheer Mark up, and the trio dream of a simpler life in warmer climes *(Santa Fe)*. Mark leaves Collins and Angel to try and persuade Roger to join them at Maureen's show. The new lovers declare their devotion for each other *(I'll Cover You)*.[20]

In the lot, Joanne is back in charge as she managing a work crisis over the phone, but also out of her depth as she quizzes Maureen about Mark's accusations. Her parents buzz in and they share a moment, but her joy is short-lived as it turns out Maureen has a neighbour over - one who happens to be a sexy Calvin Klein model. Joanne leaves to fetch Maureen on her motorcycle *(We're Okay)*.

In St. Mark's Place, the homeless are upset over the season's false generosity. Angel buys Collins a coat, and to Mark's surprise, Roger is there as well. Mark quizzes him about Mimi, who Roger sees about to buy another stash. He intervenes, apologising for his behaviour and inviting her to dinner. She agrees. Benny is on the phone with his wife, and finds out his chief backer (aka his father-in-law) is coming to Maureen's show *(Christmas Bells)*.

Maureen gives her performance, an avant-garde piece about a cow desperate to escape a digital desert where nothing is real.

---

19. In Larson's final draft, 'Another Day' is followed by 'Door/Wall,' a song cut following Larson's death. In the song, Roger tries to pick out a song but stares at the door. Mark is caught between his creative goal and knowing something is special about this night.

20. In Larson's script, 'Will I?' goes here.

A sellout bulldog named Benny enters and blames it on the cow being female. The cow lets Maureen drink her milk before jumping *Over the Moon*.[21]

After the show, the gang go to the trendy Life Cafe. Benny is there with his father-in-law, and gloats about how Maureen had no press and no audience. Roger asks why Benny's wife wasn't there, and the group find out whose dog Angel killed. Benny comes on to Mimi, asking why she'd hang out with such losers when he's trying to clean up the area, before saying everyone's idealised Bohemia is only found in fiction - and the idea is dead. In rebellion, the others throw a mock funeral and celebrate *La Vie Boheme*. Joanne comes back and forth from the lot, stuck serving as Maureen's pack-mule. Mimi is frustrated at Roger's inattention, and he admits that he's got issues holding him back - but so does she. A pair of beepers go off, and they both reach for their HIV medication, revealing their status to each other. They find a corner and lay their cards on the table, falling in love *(I Should Tell You)*.

Joanne returns, angry that Maureen was flirting with another woman, and tells the performer to pack. She also has news from the lot: Benny's locked up Mark and Roger's building and ordered the police to clear the lot, but the homeless are refusing to budge, and are sitting there mooing. The crew celebrate as a riot breaks out nearby. Roger and Mimi share a kiss. Mark films it all *(La Vie Boheme B)*.[22]

---

21. In Larson's script, the intruding homeless man from the November 1995 edition is still there.

22. In Larson's final script, Mark's speech is a single, simple line: "Focus on this moment."

ACT TWO:

The company form a line across the front of the stage and sing *Seasons of Love*, setting in motion the highlights of the following year.

It's New Year's Eve. Mark, Roger, and Mimi are working out how to break back into their building *(Happy New Year A)*. Mimi announces that she's going clean and wants to get her GED. Roger can't believe he's actually happy, and Mark's the only one taking things seriously. Maureen enters, and we find out Mark sold his footage of the riots to the local news. However, Maureen and Joanne are still on the outs. Maureen calls her ex-girlfriend, begging for forgiveness, but Joanne is already there. She gives Maureen a second chance, and reveals the group may also have a legal right to stay in the building. Mark and Joanne work out how to break in and make Maureen do the leg work. Collins and Angel enter, dressed to the nines and still like newlyweds.

Inside the loft, Mark finds out their power is restored. His mother has left him a message, wishing him a happy new year and congratulating him on making the news - even his father's impressed. He's also received a message from Alexi Darling, executive producer of a sleazy news show, who wants a meeting *(Voice Mail #3)*.

Mark considers taking the offer, and Maureen decides to hold another protest. Angel blowtorches the door, and the building is reopened. Benny enters, seeking forgiveness and good PR *(Happy New Year B)*. The group have him figured out, and refuse his offer. Angry, Benny implies that it was only because Mimi came to seduce him and he had pity as her ex. She counters that she visited him on her way to her erotic dance job, but turned down his advances. Angel brokers a hasty and uneasy peace, and Mimi and

Roger tentatively move on - though she gives in to temptation and buys a new stash.

On Valentine's Day, Mark is on his own. Roger's moved in with Mimi, though Benny succeeded in planting doubts in his head. Collins and Angel have vanished. Maureen and Joanne are rehearsing their new show, but keep fighting. Maureen is sick of giving in to Joanne's wishes, and Joanne wants Maureen to stop hitting on anything that moves. The two spat, hating the other's personality but loving the person before calling it quits *(Take Me or Leave Me)*.

Spring approaches, and the company reflect on the passage of time *(Seasons of Love B)*.

Mimi is late coming home one night, and Roger blows up at her, assuming she was with Benny. He won't listen to her and leaves. Mimi hasn't been seeing Benny, but is back on heroin. She and Roger long for each other as a source of stability in a world moving too quickly around them *(Without You)*. They make up, as do Maureen and Joanne.

It's the end of summer, and Alexi Darling is still trying to get Mark to work for her *(Voice Mail #4)*. He's equally enticed and repulsed.

Angel has a fevered dream of sex and death, the couples all entwining as he succumbs to AIDS *(Contact)*. Mimi, Mark, and Maureen deliver eulogies at his funeral, and Collins says goodbye to his lover, singing to the coat Angel bought him *(I'll Cover You: Reprise)*.

After the funeral, Mark calls Alexi's office to confirm he's taking the job. He wonders how his friends have all wound up like this, reflects upon the emotional toll it's taking on him, and the coincidences which brought them together *(Halloween)*.

Fights break out as the others leave the church: Roger's sold his guitar and is leaving New York, Mimi's hooking up with Benny, and Maureen and Joanne are barely talking to each other. Mark and Benny try to calm the four down, but to no avail. Collins berates the group for not being there for him in his moment of need, and reminds them that Angel wanted everybody to be friends. Maureen and Joanne get back together, albeit tensely, and leave. Mark confronts Roger over abandoning Mimi, but Roger turns it back on him: who is he to pass judgement when he hides behind his camera? Mark points out that Mimi still loves Roger, but that she's with Benny because he's in a better place to take care of her now that she's increasingly sick. Roger can't cope and leaves, but Mimi heard everything and just wants to say *Goodbye Love*. Scared, she begs Benny to pay for her to go to rehab. He agrees, but she finds no comfort in his arms.

Collins is kicked out of the church for not being able to pay the funeral bill. Benny offers to pay, and Collins apologies because Angel killed Benny's dog. Benny doesn't sweat it - he always hated the thing. He invites Mark and Collins for drinks, but Mark has to go to his meeting with Alexi. A few weeks into the job and he's already regretting it, seeing that Roger was right: he's been hiding in his work. He thinks of Angel, and Roger, from the road, thinks of Mimi. Finding the their projects' souls in their missing friends, Mark quits his job and Roger returns to the city *(What You Own)*.

It's winter, and nobody knows where Mark, Roger, and Mimi are *(Voice Mail #4)*. The homeless are still down on their luck, and in the loft, Mark is showing Roger a rough cut of his film... only for the power to blow *(Finale A)*. Benny's letting them stay for free, as someone tipped his wife off about Mimi. Collins shows up with some money, having hacked a nearby ATM. While the group dream of leaving, they know they'd never be able to live anywhere but New York. Maureen shows up at the loft along with Joanne and an emaciated Mimi, who's been living in a nearby park post-rehab. Deathly ill with a high fever, she asks to see Roger one last time. The pair apologise to each other and admit their love, but Mimi passes out from exhaustion. Roger sings her the song he's been working on all year *(Your Eyes)*, and Mimi appears to die, but ultimately stirs. She saw Angel in a heavenly light, and was sent back to Earth. Mimi's fever starts to break, and she lives another day *(Finale B)*.

Acknowledgements

As with any theatrical work, no one person is responsible for every single aspect of production, and this book is no exception to that rule.

First, I would like to thank the Larson family for approving this project.

Second, I cannot rave enough about the amazing teams at the Library of Congress who put up with my endless and often unreasonable requests. Special thanks are due to Mark Horowitz, head of the Music and Performing Arts division, who worked tirelessly to help acquire Larson's archives for the Library and subsequently process them, and Jan McKee, the poor soul in Recorded Sound who handled my obscenely long digitisation and replication requests, then listened to me natter endlessly about what I'd find on this or that tape on my visits. Likewise, the engineers at the Packard Campus for Audio-Visual Conservation deserve the sigh of relief they can now let out, and many thanks are due for the incredible work they do digitising and preserving the Library's collections.

A massive debt of gratitude is also due to Amy Asch, who initially catalogued Larson's papers and recordings for the family between 1996 and 2001, compiling them in a catalogue and then passing the material over to the Library of Congress.

Both Jonathan Burkhart and Victoria Leacock Hoffman took more than their fair share of calls and emails, providing endless information and support along the way, as well as the latter for providing access to her collection of video material.

Likewise, I cannot thank my editors enough. Helen McCarthy was a saint amongst saints, and her advice provided a level of clarity I could not have found on my own. Robert Berg provided additional editing services and listened to me fanboying and talking about this project for far, far too many years, also providing a theatre studies viewpoint in editorial. An additional copyedit was performed by M.M. Chabot.

I also received steady (and much needed) moral support from Eric Svejcar, who has the amazing ability to parse rambling, overcomplicated emails as I worked out how to intelligibly express ideas.

The most amazing thing is that almost all of the people listed above have managed to put up with me going back to my first work on *Static* in the summer of 2011.

John Calhoun at the New York Public Library also assisted in providing early access to the En Garde Arts collection. Doug Reside of NYPL also assisted with additional information regarding Larson's digital material.

A remarkable number of Larson's former associates, from the Adelphi years to his time on *RENT* were kind enough to answer questions and speak to me, either by email, telephone, or in person, over the years I've spent working on what you've just read. They are, in alphabetical order:

David G. Armstrong (who also provided copies of materials not held by the Library of Congress and answered his fair share of extra messages), David Auburn, Karen Azenberg, Carol Bixler, Gerry Brennan, Patrick Briggs, Jane Brucker, Scott Burkell, Jonathan Burkhart, Karen Butler, Jon Cavaluzzo (who sadly passed away as the project neared completion), Gilles Chiasson, Janet Charleston, Paul Clay, Brenda Daniels, Stephen DeRosa, Nancy Diekmann, Beth Emelson, Alison Frasier, Bob Golden, Seth Goldman, Paul Scott Goodman, Anne Hamburger, Rodney Hicks, Julianne Hoffenberg, Jeffrey M. Jones, Dan Kagan, Maggie Lally, Julie Larson McCollum, Julie Lawrence, Victoria Leacock Hoffman, Richard Levinson, Michael Lindsay, Jodie

Markell, Michael Mastro, Marin Mazzie, Kevin McCollum, Marisa Miller, Michael J. Murnin, Jim Nicola, Matt O'Grady, Karen Oberlin, Pippin Parker, Coco Peru, Dr. Nicholas Petron, Jean Randich, Amy Reusch, Jeremy Roberts, Todd Robinson, Traci Robinson, Eddie Rosenstein, Neil D. Seibel, Michael Simmons, Steve Skinner, Larry "Ratso" Sloman, Stephen Sondheim, Alicia Stone, Tim Weil, Andrea Wolper, George Xenos, and Marlies Yearby.

Bibliography

Books:

Asch, Amy. *Jonathan Larson: A Guide to His Songs, Shows & Scores.* New York: Finster & Lucy Music, Ltd. Co., 2001.

Asch, Amy, and Maggie Lally. "Jonathan Larson Rocks Broadway" and "Conversations with Jonathan Larson" in *The Playwright's Muse.* Edited by Joan Herrington. New York: Routledge, 2002.

Bordieu, Pierre. *On Television.* Translated by Priscilla Ferguson. New York: W. W. Norton and Co. Inc., 1998.

Brecht, Bertolt. *Brecht on Theatre: The Development of an Aesthete.* Translated by John Willett. London: Methuen, 1964.

Burdick, Jacques. *Theater.* New York: Newsweek Books, 1974.

Chernow, Ron. *The House of Morgan: An American Banking Dynasty and the Rise of Modern Finance.* New York: Grove Press, 2010.

Goode, Eric, and Jennifer Goode. *Area: 1983-1987.* New York: Harry N Abrams, 2013.

Jones, Jeffrey M., and Jonathan Larson. *J.P. Morgan Saves the Nation.* Los Angeles, CA: Sun & Moon Press, 1995.

Larson, Jonathan. *Rent.* Edited by Kate Giel. New York: Rob Weisbach Books, 1997.

Larson, Jonathan. *Rent: The Complete Book and Lyrics of the Broadway Musical.* New York, NY: Applause Theatre and Cinema Books, 2008.

Larson, Jonathan, and David Auburn (additional material). *Tick, Tick... Boom!: The Complete Book and Lyrics.* New York: Applause Theatre & Cinema Books, 2009.

Lipsky, David. *The Creation of RENT.* Utica: Brodock Press, 2008.

Miranda, Lin-Manuel, and Jeremy McCarter. *Hamilton: The Revolution.* New York, NY: Grand Central Publishing, 2016.

Mitchell, John Cameron (Text), and Stephen Trask (Music). *Hedwig and the Angry Inch.* Woodstock, NY: Overlook Press, 2000.

Pavis, Patrice. *Dictionary of the Theatre: Terms, Concepts, and Analysis.* Translated by Christine Shantz. Toronto: University of Toronto Press, 1998.

Prebble, Lucy. *Enron.* London: Methuen Drama, 2009.

Puccini, Giacomo, Gary Kahn, and Philip Reed. *La Bohème.* Richmond: Oneworld Classics, 2010.

Rapp, Anthony. *Without You: A Memoir of Love, Loss, and the Musical Rent.* New York: Simon & Schuster, 2006.

Schulman, Sarah. *People in Trouble.* New York: Dutton, 1990.

Schulman, Sarah. *Stagestruck: Theater, AIDS, and the Marketing of Gay America.* Durham: Duke University Press, 1998.

Singer, Barry. *Ever After: The Last Years of Musical Theater and Beyond.* New York: Applause Theatre & Cinema Books, 2004.

Sondheim, Stephen. *Finishing the Hat: Collected Lyrics*

(1954-1981) with Attendant Comments, Principles, Heresies, Grudges, Whines and Anecdotes. New York: Alfred A. Knopf, 2010.

Sontag, Susan. *Illness as Metaphor ; And, AIDS and Its Metaphors.* New York: Picador USA, 2001.

Sternfeld, Jessica. *The Megamusical.* Bloomington: Indiana University Press, 2006.

Wollman, Elizabeth L. *The Theater Will Rock: A History of the Rock Musical: From Hair to Hedwig.* Ann Arbor: University of Michigan Press, 2006.

Articles & Theses[23]

"About - Friends In Deed," *Friends In Deed.* Accessed 29 Jan. 2016. Available http://www.friendsindeed.org/overview/.

Anderson, Jack. "Aggression and Passion in Many Guises," *New York Times* 08 Jan 1990. Accessed 26 Jan. 2016. Available http://www.nytimes.com/1990/01/08/arts/reviews-dance-aggression-and-passion-in-many-guises.html.

Applestone, Jessica. "Break a Leg: The Theater Project at Housing Works," *The Body*, September 1998. Accessed 29 Jan. 2016. Available http://www.thebody.com/content/art30410.html.

Ballmer, Randy. "The Real Origins of the Religious Right," *Politico*, 27 May 2014. Accessed 29 Jan. 2016. Available http://www.politico.com/magazine/story/2014/05/religious-right-real-origins-107133.

---

23. Newspaper and magazine which were held in Larson's archives are cited directly in the footnotes, but in the interest of brevity, are not broken out and listed here. Larson often kept inspirational and relevant clippings with his notes, mostly editorials from the New York Times.

Barnes, Clive. "Larson Tops at Tuning Into Musicals," *New York Post*, 22 July 2001, accessed 25 January 2016, http://nypost.com/2001/07/22/larson-tops-at-tuning-in-to-musicals/.

Hahn, Tommy. "Billy Aronson: The Inspiration for *RENT*," *Skylight Opera Theatre*. Accessed 29 Jan. 2016. Available http://www.billyaronson.com/musicals_rent_skylight.php.

Horowitz, Mark E. "The Craft of Making Art: the Creative Processes of Eight Musical Theatre Songwriters," *Studies in Musical Theatre* 7, no. 2 (2013): 261-283.

Istel, John. "Did the Author's Hyper-Romantic Vision Get Lost in the Media Uproar?" *American Theatre*, Jul/Aug 1996. 13-17.

Istel, John. "'I Have Something to Say' An Interview with Jonathan Larson." *American Theatre*, Jul/Aug 1996. 13-17.

Kornbluth, Jesse. "Inside Area: The Wizardry of New York's Hottest Club," *New York*, 11 Mar 1985, 32-41. Accessed 27 Jan. 2016. Available https://books.google.de/books?id=JrwBAAAAMBAJ&printsec=frontcover&redir_esc=y#v=onepage&q&f=false.

Lefowitz, David. "Off-B'way *Promise* Uses Larson Songs, Sept. 10-27," Playbill, 10 Sep 1997. Accessed 29 Jan. 2016. Available http://www.playbill.com/news/article/off-bway-promise-uses-larson-songs-sept.-10-27-71433.

"Limón Technique," José Limón Dance Foundation. Accessed 29 Jan. 2016. Available http://limon.org/training/limon-technique/.

Nelson, Steve. Sleeve Notes for *Jonathan Sings Larson*. New York: PS Classics, 2007.

Nemy, Enid. "Lampoon is Back," *Chicago Tribune*, 09 Feb. 1989. Accessed 29 Jan. 2016. Available http://articles.chicagotribune.com/1989-02-09/features/8903040110_1_matty-simmons-jujamcyn-theaters-ritz-theater.

O'Brien, Glenn. "Culture Club," *New York Times T Style Magazine*, 27 Aug. 2006. Accessed 27 Jan. 2016. Available http://www.nytimes.com/2006/08/27/style/tmagazine/t_w_1576_1577_well_area_.html.

Reside, Doug. ""Last Modified January 1996": The Digital History of *RENT*," *Theatre Survey* 52, no. 2 (Nov. 2011): 225-340.

Rosenberg, Gabriel. "*Rent* 20 Years Later: Co-Creator Billy Aronson Looks Back," *Mediander Blog*, 20 June 2014. Accessed 29 Jan. 2016. Available http://blog.mediander.com/rent-20-years-later-co-creator-billy-aronson-looks-back/.

Schlatter, James F. "En Garde Arts: New York's New Public Theatre," *PAJ: A Journal of Performance and Art* 21, no. 2 (May, 1999): 1-10.

Thomson v. Larson [1998]147 F.3d 195 (United States Court of Appeals, Second Circuit.). Accessed 29 Jan. 2016. Available http://caselaw.findlaw.com/us-2nd-circuit/1392355.html.

Tommasini, Antony. "A Composer's Death Echoes in His Musical," *New York Times,* 11 Feb. 1996. Accessed 29 Jan. 2016. Available http://www.nytimes.com/1996/02/11/theater/theater-a-composer-s-death-echoes-in-his-musical.html?pagewanted=all.

Tommasini, Antony. "The Seven-Year Odyssey That Led to
Rent," *New York Times*, 17 Mar. 1996. Accessed 29 Jan.
2016. Available http://www.nytimes.com/1996/03/17/
theater/theather-the-seven-year-odyssey-that-led-to-rent.
html?pagewanted=all.

Tommasini, Antony. "Some Advice for *Rent* From a Friend,"
New York Times, 28 July 2002. Accessed 29 Jan. 2016.
Available http://www.nytimes.com/2002/07/28/theater/
some-advice-for-rent-from-a-friend.html.

Titrington, Elizabeth. ""Over the Moon": The Creation and
Development of *RENT* by Jonathan Larson." MFA
diss., University of Maryland, 2007. Accessed 28
Jan. 2016. Available http://drum.lib.umd.edu/bit-
stream/1903/6943/1/umi-umd-4445.pdf.

Wundram, Bill. "A Broken Heart on Broadway," *Quad-City
Times*, 12 Mar. 2003. Accessed 29 Jan. 2016. Available
http://qctimes.com/news/opinion/editorial/columnists/
bill-wundram/a-broken-heart-on-broadway/article_250d-
4bc4-5a35-509a-a8ff-5d82af8164b8.html.

Non-Print Material (Non-Archival)

Barrie, Michael & Jim Mulholland, writers. *Amazon Women on the
Moon*. DVD. Directed by Joe Dante, Carl Gottlieb, Peter
Horton, John Landis, & Robert K. Weiss. Los Angeles:
Universal, 1987.

Golden, Bob & Jonathan Larson, writers. *Away We Go!* DVD.
Directed by Jonathan Larson. New York: Unky's Music,
LLC, 2004.

Golden, Bob, Paul Scott Goodman, Jonathan Larson, Rusty
Magee, & Jeremy Roberts (as "Sacred Cows"). *A New*

Beginning (The Story of Adame and Yves). New York: Sacred Cows, 2013.

Larson, Jonathan, writer. *Jonathan Sings Larson*. CD. Compiled & Produced by Steve Nelson. New York: PS Classics, 2007.

Larson, Jonathan, writer. *RENT* (Original Broadway Cast Recording). CD. Dreamworks, 1996.

Larson, Jonathan, writer. *tick, tick... BOOM!* (Original Off-Broadway Cast Recording). CD. RCA Victor, 2001.

Mitchell, John Cameron (Text) & Stephen Trask (Music), writers. *Hedwig and the Angry Inch* (Original Off-Broadway Cast Recording). CD. Atlantic, 1999.

Mitchell, John Cameron (Text) & Stephen Trask (Music). *Hedwig and the Angry Inch*. DVD. Directed by John Cameron Mitchell. Los Angeles: Fine Line Features, 2001.

National Lampoon, writers. *Lemmings* (1973 Off-Broadway Cast Recording). CD. London: Decca, 2001.

O'Brien, Richard. *Shock Treatment*. DVD. Directed by Jim Sharman. Los Angeles: Twentieth Century Fox, 1981.

Puccini, Giacomo (Composer). *La Bohème* (Performed 16 Jan. 1982). DVD. Conducted by James Levine. Produced by Franco Zeffirelli for The Metropolitan Opera. Hamburg: Deutsche Grammophon, 2009.

Schwarz, Jeffrey. *No Day But Today: The Story of* Rent. DVD. Los Angeles: Automat Pictures, 2006.

Stanton, Andrew & Pete Docter. *Wall-E*. DVD. Directed by Andrew Stanton. Los Angeles: Pixar, 2008.

Wentzy, James. *Fight Back, Fight AIDS: 15 Years of ACT UP*. Streaming Video. New York: ACT UP New York. Accessed 29 Jan. 2016. Available http://www.actupny.org/video/.

Public Archives

En Garde Arts Ephemera, Billy Rose Theatre Division, New York Public Library, New York, NY.

En Garde Arts Records, Billy Rose Theatre Division, New York Public Library, New York, NY.

Jonathan Larson Papers, Music Division, Library of Congress, Washington, D.C.

Jonathan Larson Recordings, Recorded Sound Division, Library of Congress, Washington, D.C.

Private Archive Material

1/2 MT House (Rehearsals and Runthrough). Video. Privately held by Victoria Leacock Hoffman, Washington, D.C.

1/2 MT House. Script & Papers. Privately held by David G. Armstrong, New York, NY.

Garden Party. Video. Privately held by Brenda Daniels, Winston-Salem, NC.

I Make Me A Promise. Video. Privately held by Victoria Leacock Hoffman, Washington, D.C.

Jann Wenner Home Movies (Scored by Larson). Videos. Privately held by Victoria Leacock Hoffman, Washington, D.C.

Jonathan Larson Personal & Memorial Recordings. Multiple Videos. Privately held by Victoria Leacock Hoffman, Washington, D.C.

The Naked Truth. Perf. 5 Nov. 1990. Video. Privately held by Victoria Leacock Hoffman, Washington, D.C.

Pageantry. Script & Papers. Privately held by David G. Armstrong, New York, NY.

Sacrimmoralinority. Multiple Videos. Privately held by Victoria Leacock Hoffman, Washington, D.C.

Sacrimmoralinority. Papers. Privately held by David G. Armstrong, New York, NY.

Saved! Papers. Privately held by David G. Armstrong, New York, NY.

Superbia. Perf. 11 Sep. 1989. Video. Privately held by Victoria Leacock Hoffman, Washington, D.C.

RENT (1993 Production). Video. Privately held by Victoria Leacock Hoffman, Washington, D.C.

RENT (Off-Broadway Backstage Footage, Broadway Rehearsal Footage). Multiple Videos. Privately held by Victoria Leacock Hoffman, Washington, D.C.

RENT (1998 Cast Montages). Video. Privately held by Victoria Leacock Hoffman, Washington, D.C.

RENT (Italian Cast Footage). Multiple Videos. Privately held by Victoria Leacock Hoffman, Washington, D.C.

tick, tick... BOOM! (One-Man Edition). Multiple Videos. Privately held by Victoria Leacock Hoffman, Washington, D.C.

tick, tick... BOOM! (Korean Productions). Multiple Videos. Privately held by Victoria Leacock Hoffman, Washington, D.C.

About the Author

J. Collis earned his Master of Arts in Theatre Studies from the Royal Central School of Speech & Drama before working as a part-time freelance theatre and media critic. Following a path into production, he has since moved into content localisation and streaming media. He currently resides in Berlin, Germany.

Permissions Acknowledgments

Emotional Fallout

Words and Music by Jonathan Larson and Michael Lindsay

Falling Apart

Words and Music by Jonathan Larson and Michael Lindsay

Female 2 Female

Words and Music by Jonathan Larson

Finale (Coda) - Presidential Politics

Words and Music by Jonathan Larson

Gentleman's Agreement

Words and Music by Jonathan Larson and Jeffrey M. Jones

Happy New Year

Words and Music by Jonathan Larson

Herstory

Words and Music by Jonathan Larson and Nicholas Petron

Hosing The Furniture

Words and Music by Jonathan Larson

I Won't Close My Eyes

Words and Music by Jonathan Larson and Michael Lindsay

Likability/La Di Da
Words and Music by Jonathan Larson
Copyright (c) FINSTER & LUCY MUSIC LTD. CO.
All Rights Controlled and Administered by UNIVERSAL MUSIC CORP.
All Rights Reserved Used by Permission
Reprinted by Permission of Hal Leonard LLC

Louder Than Words
Words and Music by Jonathan Larson
Copyright (c) FINSTER & LUCY MUSIC LTD. CO.
All Rights Controlled and Administered by UNIVERSAL MUSIC CORP.
All Rights Reserved Used by Permission
Reprinted by Permission of Hal Leonard LLC

Love Of My Life
Words and Music by Jonathan Larson
Copyright (c) FINSTER & LUCY MUSIC LTD. CO.
All Rights Controlled and Administered by UNIVERSAL MUSIC CORP.
All Rights Reserved Used by Permission
Reprinted by Permission of Hal Leonard LLC

Love The Pain
Words and Music by Jonathan Larson
Copyright (c) FINSTER & LUCY MUSIC LTD. CO.
All Rights Controlled and Administered by UNIVERSAL MUSIC CORP.
All Rights Reserved Used by Permission
Reprinted by Permission of Hal Leonard LLC

Money Is Power (The Lesson)
Words and Music by Jonathan Larson and Nicholas Petron
Copyright (c) FINSTER & LUCY MUSIC LTD. CO.
All Rights Controlled and Administered by UNIVERSAL MUSIC CORP.
All Rights Reserved Used by Permission

Now We've Got You Thinking (Words)
Words and Music by Jonathan Larson and Michael Lindsay

1/2 M.T. House
Words and Music by Jonathan Larson

One Song Glory
Words and Music by Jonathan Larson

Open Road
Words and Music by Jonathan Larson

Out Of My Dreams
Words and Music by Jonathan Larson

Proceedings

Pura Vida

Real Estate

Rent

U.S. Of Ease
Words and Music by Jonathan Larson
Copyright (c) FINSTER & LUCY MUSIC LTD. CO.
All Rights Controlled and Administered by UNIVERSAL MUSIC CORP.
All Rights Reserved Used by Permission
Reprinted by Permission of Hal Leonard LLC

Valentine's Day
Words and Music by Jonathan Larson and Michael Lindsay
Copyright (c) FINSTER & LUCY MUSIC LTD. CO.
All Rights Controlled and Administered by UNIVERSAL MUSIC CORP.
All Rights Reserved Used by Permission
Reprinted by Permission of Hal Leonard LLC

The Vision Thing
Words and Music by Jonathan Larson
Copyright (c) FINSTER & LUCY MUSIC LTD. CO.
All Rights Controlled and Administered by UNIVERSAL MUSIC CORP.
All Rights Reserved Used by Permission
Reprinted by Permission of Hal Leonard LLC

When I Grow Up
Words and Music by Jonathan Larson and David Armstrong
Copyright (c) FINSTER & LUCY MUSIC LTD. CO.
All Rights Controlled and Administered by UNIVERSAL MUSIC CORP.
All Rights Reserved Used by Permission
Reprinted by Permission of Hal Leonard LLC

Where Is The Dream?
Words and Music by Jonathan Larson and Maggie Lally
Copyright (c) FINSTER & LUCY MUSIC LTD. CO.

While Male World
Words and Music by Jonathan Larson
Copyright (c) FINSTER & LUCY MUSIC LTD. CO.

Who Am I?
Words and Music by Jonathan Larson and Hal Hackady
Copyright (c) FINSTER & LUCY MUSIC LTD. CO.

With Open Eyes
Words by Nan Knighton, Music by Jonathan Larson
Lyrics Copyright (c) 1998 KNIGHT ERRAND MUSIC

You Were Right
Words and Music by Jonathan Larson
Copyright (c) FINSTER & LUCY MUSIC LTD. CO.

Printed in Australia
AUHW021827221121
355783AU00014B/17